Audacity Personified

Audacity Personified

THE GENERALSHIP OF ROBERT E. LEE

Edited by Peter S. Carmichael

LOUISIANA STATE UNIVERSITY PRESS

BATON ROUGE

Published by Louisiana State University Press
Copyright © 2004 by Louisiana State University Press
All rights reserved
Manufactured in the United States of America
LOUISIANA PAPERBACK EDITION, 2015

DESIGNER: Andrew Shurtz
TYPEFACE: Whitman
TYPESETTER: Coghill Composition Co., Inc.

LIBRARY OF CONGRESS CATALOGING-IN-PUBLICATION DATA

Audacity personified : the generalship of Robert E. Lee / edited by Peter S. Carmichael.
p.   cm.
Includes index.
ISBN 978-0-8071-2929-6 (cloth : alk. paper) — ISBN 978-0-8071-6232-3 (pbk. : alk. paper) —
ISBN 978-0-8071-6233-0 (pdf) — ISBN 978-0-8071-6234-7 (epub) — ISBN 978-0-8071-6235-4 (mobi)
1. Lee, Robert E. (Robert Edward), 1807–1870—Military leadership.
2. Generals—Confederate States of America—Biography.
3. United States—History—Civil War, 1861–1865—Campaigns.
4. Confederate States of America. Army—Biography.
I. Carmichael, Peter S.
e467.1.l4a93 2004
973.7′3′092—dc22

2003021936

The paper in this book meets the guidelines for permanence and
durability of the Committee on Production Guidelines
for Book Longevity of the Council
on Library Resources.
∞

FOR ROBERT K. KRICK

Who made the summers from 1986 to 1991 at
Fredericksburg and Spotsylvania National Military
Park an invaluable experience for a young historian
and who has done more to save the battlefields of
Robert E. Lee's army than anyone else.

CONTENTS

ILLUSTRATIONS

PREFACE

NOBODY WOULD DENY the importance of Robert E. Lee to Confederate military history, but many sensible people have wondered if the world needs another book on the South's greatest commander. Can anything new and original possibly be said about the general? Can historians justify more poking and prodding into Lee's personal life or military career? It would seem that the burning embers of Lee history have all but died out and that no amount of stoking could spark new debate. Looking at Lee-related publications over the last ten years—a time of remarkable and unprecedented productivity—seems to confirm that nothing more could be said about the Virginian. Most of the recent literature, whether favorable or critical, retells the same old anecdotes, repeats the same laudatory myths, and relies on the same secondary sources to understand Lee's thinking without ever delving into manuscript and primary materials related to the general. Even today many pro-Lee scholars make arguments that differ little from Lee's Lost Cause defenders like Jubal Early. It is tempting to believe that the well has dried up, that Lee scholarship has reached its apogee, and that any future endeavors about the Virginian will simply result in the casting of old wine in new bottles.[1]

---

1. Early's prominent role in the Lee cult and the Lost Cause in general has been examined by a number of scholars, including Thomas L. Connelly, *The Marble Man: Robert E. Lee and His Image in American Society* (New York: Alfred A. Knopf, 1977); Gaines M. Foster, *Ghosts of the Confederacy: Defeat, the Lost Cause, and the Emergence of the New South* (New York: Oxford University Press, 1987); William Garrett Piston, *Lee's Tarnished Lieutenant: James Longstreet and His Place in Southern History* (Athens: University of Georgia Press, 1987); and Gary W. Gallagher, "Jubal A. Early, the Lost Cause, and Civil War History: A Persistent Legacy," in *Lee and His Generals in War and Memory* (Baton Rouge: Louisiana State University Press, 1998), 199–226.

Excessively laudatory treatments of Lee published in the last fifteen years and containing al-

The staleness that pervades Lee scholarship partially stems from the fact that historians have been mired in the same old questions. Did Lee, despite his army's repeated bloodlettings, further Southern war aims while sustaining the Confederate people in their struggle for independence? Was Lee, at the same time, too addicted to the offensive, too bloodthirsty, and too eager to abandon the defense when he should have been concerned about preserving his army? No one would dispute the importance of this line of inquiry (in fact a number of essays in this volume address the issue), and the scholarly response has been diverse, broadly ranging from those who have ranked Lee as the South's foremost military leader, the Confederacy's best chance for ultimate success, to those who have come down hard on the general by arguing that his strategic beliefs were woefully disconnected from the logistical realities facing the Confederacy. Although his individual campaigns might have been brilliantly conceived and executed, revisionists have argued that Lee's constant attacking and reliance on frontal assaults actually dried up Southern manpower.[2]

The revisionists, it appears, are riding the crest of a powerful historiographical counterattack. Their numbers continue to grow, adding to their ranks those who want to redeem the reputation of Lt. Gen. James Longstreet

---

most no original research include Paul D. Casdorph, *Lee and Jackson: Confederate Chieftains* (New York: Paragon House, 1992); Charles P. Roland, *Reflections on Lee: A Historian's Assessment* (Mechanicsburg, Pa.: Stackpole, 1995); William Franklin Chaney, *Duty Most Sublime: The Life of Robert E. Lee as Told through the "Carter Letters"* (Baltimore: Gateway, 1996); John M. Taylor, *Duty Faithfully Performed: Robert E. Lee and His Critics* (Dulles, Va.: Brassey's, 1999); and Al Kaltman, *The Genius of Robert E. Lee: Leadership Lessons for the Outgunned, Outnumbered, and Underfinanced* (Paramus, N.J.: Prentice Hall, 2000).

2. An assessment of Lee historiography can be found in Archer Jones, "What Should We Think about Lee's Thinking," *Columbiad* 1 (summer 1997): 73–85. For a superb compilation of critical and positive evaluations of Lee's military career, see Gary W. Gallagher, ed., *Lee the Soldier* (Lincoln: University of Nebraska Press, 1996). For the best of Lee's critics, see J. F. C. Fuller, *The Generalship of Ulysses S. Grant* (1929; reprint, Bloomington: Indiana University Press, 1958); Russell F. Weigley, *The American Way of War: A History of United States Military Strategy and Policy* (New York: Macmillan, 1973); Thomas L. Connelly and Archer Jones, *The Politics of Command: Factions and Ideas in Confederate Strategy* (Baton Rouge: Louisiana State University Press, 1973), esp. chap. 3; and Alan T. Nolan, *Lee Considered: General Robert E. Lee and Civil War History* (Chapel Hill: University of North Carolina Press, 1991). A response to Lee critics that also summarizes the arguments of both sides can be found in Gallagher, *Lee the Soldier*, 275–90.

and other "misunderstood" Confederates, often at the expense of Lee. "Old Pete's" amazing resurgence has resulted in an equestrian monument of the general at Gettysburg and a national organization that conducts a scholarly seminar on the First Corps commander each year. In a recent *New York Times* article, the author noted that the reputation of Lee was sagging, while popular enthusiasm for Ulysses S. Grant was surging upward. Michael Shaara's Pulitzer Prize–winning novel *The Killer Angels* (1975), the basis of Ted Turner's 1993 film *Gettysburg*, underscores the shift in popular thinking about Lee during the 1990s. Audiences felt a deep sympathy for the misunderstood Longstreet, while Lee came across as the primary culprit for Confederate defeat—a shocking reversal of the traditional explanation for Southern defeat in Pennsylvania. Martin Sheen portrayed Lee as a reserved Virginia aristocrat whose hard exterior could not be penetrated, even by close associates like Longstreet. After watching the movie, many lamented that they had not connected with the "real" Lee. In a recent publication Richard McCaslin explores how the general tried to play the part of George Washington his entire life.[3] McCaslin makes valuable connections between Lee and his idol, revealing the general's quest for Victorian perfection, that radical innocence that conflicted with the more emotional side of his personality. Many scholars still believe that the inner Lee eludes them, that he was a mythical, distant figure whose human side was obscured by the Christlike depictions of the Lost Cause.

Both Emory Thomas and Michael Fellman, in separate biographies, responded to this call by bringing together the public and private side of Lee. They have consequently shattered the Victorian façade of the heroic Virginian, revealing the human Lee who wanted to liberate himself from a self-imposed sense of duty that called for rigid piety, self-control, and a general perfectionist version of manhood. Fellman and Thomas, despite an annoying tendency to engage in armchair psychiatry, have offered some of the most innovative work on Lee in the last decade. Their interpretations fall between the hero worship of Douglas Southall Freeman and the aggressive personal attacks of one of the first Lee critics, Thomas L. Connelly.[4]

3. Richard B. McCaslin, *Lee in the Shadow of Washington* (Baton Rouge: Louisiana State University Press, 2001).

4. See Emory M. Thomas, *Robert E. Lee: A Biography* (New York: W. W. Norton, 1995); and Michael Fellman, *The Making of Robert E. Lee* (New York: Random House, 2000).

For the most part, the revisionist critique of Lee's generalship lacks the originality found in the less-military-oriented work of Thomas and Fellman. With the exception of Alan Nolan, the revisionists advertise "new" arguments, but they tend to support such claims with little original research.[5] Most begin with Douglas Southall Freeman's work as a point of departure, using the assumptions of Lee's most influential biographer to launch their own criticisms. In the end they basically turn Freeman's ideas inside out. In a backhanded way, it is a tribute to the Richmonder that his interpretations have had such a profound and enduring influence.[6] While Freeman's work, like any scholar's, should come under scrutiny, the revisionist swipe at him reveals a troubling tendency to work from the assumptions of other historians without a thorough reading of the primary sources. The consequences have been lethal to the Lee debate. Sweeping generalizations about the general's strategic thinking, his battlefield performance, his relations with civil authorities, his use of staff officers, his estimation of the western theater, and his fighting nature have been boldly made from the revisionist pulpit. But most of these arguments are static, timeless interpretations that would have been more persuasive if they were sufficiently grounded in the specific political and military situations that Lee confronted.[7]

5. Among critical Lee books that stand out as particularly unpersuasive and unimaginative, and in the end only fuel the skepticism that Lee's generalship does not need further evaluation, see John D. McKenzie, *Uncertain Glory: Lee's Generalship Re-Examined* (New York: Hippocrene, 1997); Edward H. Bonekemper III, *How Robert E. Lee Lost the Civil War* (Fredericksburg, Va.: Sergeant Kirkland's, 1998); and Michael A. Palmer, *Lee Moves North: Robert E. Lee on the Offensive* (New York: John Wiley & Sons, 1998). Somewhat less critical but in keeping with armchair generalship of the revisionist school is Bevin Alexander's *Robert E. Lee's Civil War* (Holbrook, Mass.: Adams Media, 1998).

6. Few historians have done more to define the intellectual contours of a single field than Douglas Southall Freeman has with his scholarship on Robert E. Lee and the Army of Northern Virginia. His work was meticulously researched and beautifully written. While I acknowledge the tremendous influence and importance of Freeman's scholarship, I believe that too many historians use him as a starting point rather than the pertinent primary sources. See Freeman, *R. E. Lee: A Biography*, 4 vols. (New York: Charles Scribner's Sons, 1934–35); and *Lee's Lieutenants: A Study in Command*, 3 vols. (New York: Charles Scribner's Sons, 1942–44).

7. My criticisms of the revisionist literature should not obscure the many fine Lee-related publications that have incorporated manuscript research, offered new conceptual frameworks, and shied away from the dangers of armchair generalship. Joseph L. Harsh has provided us with model military studies that offer powerful interpretations of Lee. His work on Lee's army in

Revisionists would have been able to pay closer attention to change over time if they had made better use of Lee-related manuscript sources. Such material should have been the foundation of their inquiries. Instead, they tend to begin with a premise, usually one that counters a Freeman contention, and then selectively use evidence that supports their preconceived conclusions. While one may question the methods of the revisionists, it would be unfair to challenge the sincerity of their effort. They should be commended for raising tough questions about Lee that historians had shied away

---

1862 breaks new ground. See Harsh, *Confederate Tide Rising: Robert E. Lee and the Making of Southern Strategy, 1861–1862* (Kent, Ohio: Kent State University Press, 1998); and *Taken at the Flood: Robert E. Lee & Confederate Strategy in the Maryland Campaign of 1862* (Kent, Ohio: Kent State University Press, 1998). Other scholars who have offered well-researched and useful scholarship on Lee include George C. Rable, *The Confederate Republic: A Revolution against Politics* (Chapel Hill: University of North Carolina Press, 1994); Steven E. Woodworth, *Davis & Lee at War* (Lawrence: University Press of Kansas, 1995); Gary W. Gallagher, *The Confederate War: How Popular Will, Nationalism, and Military Strategy Could Not Stave Off Defeat* (Cambridge: Harvard University Press, 1997); and J. Tracy Power, *Lee's Miserables: Life in the Army of Northern Virginia from the Wilderness to Appomattox* (Chapel Hill: University of North Carolina Press, 1998). There are also a number of valuable Lee-related essays in Gary W. Gallagher's Military Campaigns of the Civil War Series. See Gallagher, ed., *The First Day at Gettysburg: Essays on Confederate and Union Leadership* (Kent: Kent State University Press, 1992); *The Second Day at Gettysburg: Essays on Confederate and Union Leadership* (Kent, Ohio: Kent State University Press, 1993); *The Third Day at Gettysburg and Beyond* (Chapel Hill: University of North Carolina Press, 1994); *The Fredericksburg Campaign: Decision on the Rappahannock* (Chapel Hill: University of North Carolina Press, 1995); *Chancellorsville: The Battle and Its Aftermath* (Chapel Hill: University of North Carolina Press, 1996); *The Wilderness Campaign* (Chapel Hill: University of North Carolina Press, 1997); *The Spotsylvania Campaign* (Chapel Hill: University of North Carolina Press, 1998); *The Antietam Campaign* (Chapel Hill: University of North Carolina Press, 1999); and *The Richmond Campaign of 1862: The Peninsula & the Seven Days* (Chapel Hill: University of North Carolina Press, 2000) Other recent campaign studies that offer challenging interpretations of Lee include John J. Hennessy, *Return to Bull Run: The Campaign and Battle of Second Manassas* (New York: Simon & Schuster, 1993); Harry W. Pfanz, *Gettysburg: The Second Day* (Chapel Hill: University of North Carolina Press, 1987); Pfanz, *Gettysburg: Culp's Hill and Cemetery Hill* (Chapel Hill: University of North Carolina Press, 1993); and Pfanz, *Gettysburg: The First Day* (Chapel Hill: University of North Carolina Press, 2001). On the Overland Campaign, see Gordon C. Rhea's trilogy, *The Battle of the Wilderness, May 5–6, 1864* (Baton Rouge: Louisiana State University Press, 1994); *The Battles for Spotsylvania Court House and the Road to Yellow Tavern, May 7–12, 1864* (Baton Rouge: Louisiana State University Press, 1997); and *To the North Anna River: Grant and Lee, May 13–25, 1864* (Baton Rouge: Louisiana State University Press, 2000).

from until the 1977 publication of Connelly's *The Marble Man: Robert E. Lee and His Image in American Society.*[8]

The recent deluge of Lee publications reveals the necessity of moving beyond timeless generalizations about his Confederate experience. A more focused analysis of Lee's generalship is needed, one that explores specific issues or moments in his career in relationship to time, place, and, above all, the general's own words. It is time to break down the interpretive edifices that have been constructed around Robert E. Lee and rediscover the building blocks that earlier scholars have assembled. The big questions about if Lee bled the Confederacy to death, if he possessed a modern view of war, or if he understood popular will cannot be answered until historians break away from the prevailing assumptions in the existing secondary literature. This requires historians to go back to the archival trenches and dig and sift through the raw manuscript material, to discover the true nature of Lee's ideas and how they might have changed over time.

This collection of essays responds to that challenge by reexamining the Confederate chieftain through his own reports, papers, and private letters. No single question or conceptual framework unites these essays. The authors offer widely different assessments of Lee the soldier. Some are critical and some are positive. Even though a lack of harmony exists over key aspects of Lee's generalship, the authors come together by offering new perspectives on the general's military career, many of which call into question longstanding beliefs that have been accepted as dogma since the publication of Freeman's remarkably influential and detailed *R. E. Lee: A Biography.* The essays in this book draw their interpretive edge from primary sources, the words of Robert E. Lee and his contemporaries.

The opening essay addresses one of the most hotly contested questions of Lee scholarship—why did the general remain devoted to the offensive even though such aggressive tactics drained precious manpower? Too many scholars have attributed Lee's audacity to his combative instincts. This is a timeless argument that does not take into account the general's rationale for attacking

8. Reviewer Albert Castel recognized the important historiographic shift that was taking place with the publication of *Marble Man* and the furor that it would generate among the general's supporters. See his review of *The Marble Man* in *Civil War Times Illustrated* 17 (June 1978): 50.

and how it changed over time. While many factors motivated Lee to assume the offensive at different stages of the war (some more important than others, depending on the situation), it is clear that he searched for a decisive battle of annihilation. This was not a constant goal, but it inspired many of his operations, even after Gettysburg. Lee wanted to deliver the coup de grâce to the Army of the Potomac because he correctly believed that the Confederacy could not win a protracted conflict. This was a realistic goal when his army had the necessary manpower and logistical resources before the fall of 1863. The horrendous losses at Chancellorsville and Gettysburg, which effectively destroyed Lee's offensive capacity, did not deter him from trying to achieve a climactic victory in the Overland Campaign. Although most Civil War officers recognized that the battlefield only brought Pyrrhic victories at best, Lee never readjusted his thinking during the last year of the war. The Virginian's expectations of Lt. Gen. Richard S. Ewell at the battle of the Wilderness reflect a jarring gap between the commanding general's expectations and what could realistically be achieved by his army.

In trying to secure a Waterloo-like victory, Lee also attacked because he believed that the Southern people craved aggressive action from their generals. While this was certainly the popular mood in 1862, when most Confederates interpreted defensive tactics as passivity, civilian expectations had changed by the start of the Overland Campaign. During Ulysses S. Grant's spring and summer offensive in 1864, the Southern people not only preferred conservative tactics as a way to preserve the lives of loved ones in the army but also praised Lee for his mastery of the defense. In the end Lee's use of the offensive after Gettysburg was based on at least two false assumptions: first, that he could destroy at least a portion of the Federal army in a pitched battle, and second, that the Southern people continued to demand hard fighting from their generals.

William J. Miller shifts from Lee's grand strategy to the general's operational thinking by focusing on the Seven Days fighting of 1862. He has discovered that most historians of the campaign have operated from Freeman's assumption that Lee sought to engage George B. McClellan and destroy his army in one grand battle, beginning with the engagement at Mechanicsville on June 26 and continuing to Malvern Hill on July 1. David J. Eicher, in the most recent military history of the Civil War, contends that Lee wanted to pitch into the Federals outside the Confederate capital.[9] Miller offers an alternative thesis. He believes that Lee, at least at the start of the campaign, wanted to maneuver McClellan away from Richmond and avoid deadly frontal assaults. Miller also reconstructs how Lee's ideas evolved during the course of the campaign, but always notes the limits of our knowledge because Lee said so little about his operations. What is clear, according to Miller, is that the general attempted to destroy a portion of the Union army at Gaines's Mill, and on three consecutive days—June 29, June 30, and July 1—he wanted to annihilate the retreating Federals south of the Chickahominy River. But Miller warns that too much has been read into Lee's summation of the campaign when the commanding general lamented that "under ordinary circumstances the Federal Army should have been destroyed." This statement has led historians to assume that Lee's intention, beginning with General Orders No. 75 and continuing with every engagement from Mechanicsville to the James River, was to obliterate the Army of the Potomac. Miller disagrees that destruction of the Union army was Lee's fixed goal from the start of the campaign. By reexamining key primary sources, Miller shows how Lee's purposes and motivations were fluid, constantly changing in relation to the ebb and flow of the campaign.

Likewise Gordon Rhea challenges the Freeman school by overturning the notion that Lee anticipated his adversary's movements with uncanny precision. A closer inspection of the Overland Campaign reveals a Lee puzzled by Grant's strategic designs, so much so that he miscalculated the enemy's intentions on six different occasions from May 4 to May 25, 1864. In some of these instances, Lee endangered his own army. This was especially true on the eve of the May 12 attacks at Spotsylvania, when he thought Grant was retreating to Fredericksburg instead of massing for a major attack. Fortunately for Lee, as Rhea points out, fumbling by Union officers often saved the Confederate chieftain from his own mistakes. In the end Rhea concludes that Lee's greatest strength, one overlooked by most of his biographers, was his ability to recover from his own errors by turning perilous situations into moments of opportunity. Lee might have lacked prescience, but the general displayed remarkable resourcefulness in confronting an army nearly double

9. David J. Eicher, *The Longest Night: A Military History of the Civil War* (New York: Simon & Schuster, 2001), 280.

the size of his own by exploiting the mistakes of his adversary and quickly rebounding from his own.

Even Lee's most strident defenders have long questioned the efficiency of the Army of Northern Virginia's staff system. Many have claimed that the general was not attuned to the demands of modern war because he did not surround himself with enough men to ensure the smooth operation of the army's bureaucratic machinery. While Robert E. L. Krick acknowledges that Lee needed more support personnel at headquarters, he believes that too many historians have overemphasized the scarcity of the general's staff numbers. Many of these critics have overlooked the fact that Lee did indeed have a numerous staff, though most of its members were part of a general staff that did not see him on a daily basis. Lee, as Krick observes, had good reason to limit his personal entourage. More than anything else, Confederate armies needed able-bodied men in the ranks to shoulder muskets, not bureaucratic dead weight. Lee wanted to set the right example for his subordinate officers. By turning to the general's own words, Krick has also uncovered that Lee constantly reworked and improved the army's staff system from almost the moment he assumed command in June 1862. In fact Lee recognized fundamental deficiencies in the staff system and strove to eliminate them until the end of the war. Many of these problems, however, stemmed from the youthfulness of the Confederate nation and could not be solved by one man. While the Confederate commander was not an innovator, he managed to implement key reforms that met the changing demands of war. The final test of any staff system, Krick asserts, is the efficiency of the army in the field. And in every campaign, except for the Seven Days Battles, the Army of Northern Virginia far exceeded this yardstick.

In the fifth essay Max R. Williams continues the evaluation of Lee away from the battlefield with a revealing examination of the general's relationship with North Carolina governor Zebulon B. Vance. In an attempt to shore up political support at home while boosting the spirits of Tar Heel soldiers in the ranks, the governor visited the Army of Northern Virginia in March 1864. A dramatic and powerful speaker, Vance inspired his fellow North Carolinians with a series of rousing addresses. During the course of the tour, he met privately with Lee, forging a partnership that continued after the governor returned home. Lee advised Vance on the defense of Wilmington, desertion in western North Carolina, and the need to promote the accomplishments of

North Carolina regiments. The general communicated with Vance by circumventing Pres. Jefferson Davis and the Confederate War Department. The governor, in turn, showed himself an energetic Confederate, always trying to meet the requests of Lee even if it meant stripping troops from his home state. The wartime correspondence of both men, Williams argues, is at variance with the tradition that Lee always submitted to civilian authority and that Vance was an unwavering champion of states' rights who obstructed the Confederate war effort. Williams also calls into question the popular assumptions that Lee was blind to events outside the Army of Northern Virginia and that his influence on the general affairs of the Confederacy was negative.

In the final essay Mark Bradley examines Lee as general in chief of the Confederacy during the final months of the war, focusing on his interconnected relationships with Jefferson Davis and Gen. Joseph E. Johnston. Bradley believes that Lee should have been more forceful with the Confederate president, that he should have bluntly told Davis that final victory was an impossibility, and that he should have pushed for seeking terms with the North as the proper and best course for the Confederacy. Unlike Johnston, who was brutally honest with Davis about the hopelessness of the military situation, Lee held back and refused to admit defeat when virtually everyone else had recognized that the end had finally come. Bradley also questions why Lee did not evacuate Petersburg sooner once the general had privately determined that his army could only be preserved by pursuing such a strategy. His desperate and costly attack against Fort Stedman on March 25, 1865, is puzzling when so little could have been gained and manpower was so scarce. Despite these failings, Bradley commends Lee for giving Johnston the necessary encouragement and flexibility to run his operations in North Carolina. Within this positive environment, Johnston waged an offensive campaign that kept William T. Sherman's juggernaut off-balance during the winter and early spring of 1865. While Johnston never achieved a decisive victory, he always looked for an opportunity to strike, revealing an aggressive side of the general that he had rarely displayed in previous campaigns. In the end Bradley credits Lee for creating a command situation in which Johnston blossomed, suggesting that he might have become one of Lee's most successful lieutenants if only time had been on the side of the Confederacy.

The essays in *Audacity Personified* demonstrate that it is impossible to write about Confederate history without confronting the influential work of

Douglas Southall Freeman. In breaking down his interpretations, however, the contributors remind us that scholarly assumptions sometime masquerade as standard "truths" in need of scrutiny. This book does not dismiss Freeman as a Lost Cause disciple who simply propagated feel-good myths about Lee. His writings were far more complex and critical than what many have given Freeman credit for. In a curious way this volume pays tribute to the Richmonder. One of the highest honors a historian can receive is when his work stands as the point of departure for a scholarly debate. Freeman's masterful writings will forever provoke Americans to consider Robert E. Lee in new and challenging ways.

The contributors to this volume made my job very easy. Mark Bradley, Robert E. L. Krick, Bill Miller, Gordon Rhea, and Max Williams accommodated my numerous requests in a timely manner and submitted essays that required little editing. Julie Krick did an impressive job of transforming rough sketches into final maps. Keith Poulter of *North & South* magazine graciously allowed portions of Gordon Rhea's article and my piece to be republished in this volume. I finished this book just as I was beginning my life with Elizabeth A. Carmichael. Her superb editorial suggestions greatly improved this manuscript, and her wonderful sense of humor and constant encouragement made the entire process a more enjoyable one.

PETER S. CARMICHAEL
University of North Carolina at Greensboro

Audacity Personified

Lee's Search for the Battle of Annihilation

PETER S. CARMICHAEL

To a packed audience at the Old Army War College in 1936, Douglas Southall Freeman explained that a great general must differentiate "what was practicable from what was desirable." "A soldier who cannot make that distinction," he declared, "will never get anywhere."[1] Freeman was referring to Gen. Pierre Gustave Toutant Beauregard, whose grandiose schemes of Northern invasion sometimes bordered on drug-induced hallucinations. If the historian had applied this same standard to Robert E. Lee, he probably would have reached a more incisive and critical interpretation of the Confederacy's greatest commander. By the fall of 1863, Lee's expectations far exceeded what his army could reasonably have accomplished. Two years of heavy battlefield losses had exhausted his army's offensive capacity. Yet the general remained devoted to the offense, always searching for that elusive battlefield opportunity to destroy the enemy. At various times during the Overland and Petersburg Campaigns, Lee drove his troops into battle with the same aggressive purposes that had defined his campaigns in 1862 and 1863. A victory of annihilation was not only an impossible goal but also often placed Lee's army on the operational and tactical offensive, a posture that clashed with the Confederacy's urgent need to conserve manpower.

Unlike many Union officers, such as Lt. Gen. Ulysses S. Grant, Maj. Gen. William T. Sherman, and Maj. Gen. George Gordon Meade, the commander of the Army of Northern Virginia never recognized that Civil War armies were virtually indestructible.[2] Lee's failure to grasp this crucial point, coupled

---

1. Douglas Southall Freeman, "Morale in the Army of Northern Virginia," in *Douglas Southall Freeman on Leadership*, ed. Stuart W. Smith (Shippensburg, Pa.: White Mane, 1993), 98.

2. On the indestructibility of Civil War armies, see Herman Hattaway and Archer Jones, *How the North Won: A Military History of the Civil War* (Urbana: University of Illinois Press, 1983), 46–47.

with his belief that attacking satisfied popular will, translated into costly strikes. In the final analysis Lee violated Freeman's maxim that all generals must understand what is practical. Early in the war, when his army possessed sufficient numbers, excessive aggressiveness mattered little against second-rate Union generals. Lee in fact emerged as the innovative tactician who could seemingly accomplish the impossible. Once his ranks had been depleted and his logistical base nearly exhausted, however, the Virginian needed to reevaluate his fundamental strategic assumptions. Instead he continued the elusive search for the battle of annihilation, which forced him to take chances, seize the initiative, and when possible, pursue the offensive.

Maintaining the initiative was difficult after Gettysburg, but Lee still looked for opportunities to strike the enemy and encouraged his subordinates to think offensively. He should have maintained a holding action in Virginia during the summer of 1864. This course would have strengthened the anti-war effort in the North while ruining Republican chances in the coming fall elections. Offensive battles, while capable of achieving such goals, posed too many risks. While it is true that he basically assumed a defensive stance against Grant, occasionally delivering a glancing counterblow, Lee revealed his overriding offensive commitment by sending Lt. Gen. Jubal A. Early into the Shenandoah Valley, with the purpose of achieving decisive battlefield victories. This mission precipitated large and costly battlefield failures for the South that ultimately revived the political life of Abraham Lincoln and the Republican Party.

Lee responded to the voice of public opinion throughout the war. While the Southern people had demanded offensively driven victories before 1864, the mood of civilians gradually softened after Gettysburg. Most Confederates recognized the value of the defense and the necessity of conserving manpower. Even those who did not understand the interplay between tactics and grand strategy acknowledged that the defensive would likely spare family members in the army. Lee, unlike most Civil War officers, recognized the war as a conflict between democracies, that the general population would play a crucial role in determining military success. Despite this sophisticated view of war, Lee failed to appreciate that defensive victories could sustain Southern morale in 1864 while serving to dishearten the North.

This argument follows the lead of scholars who believe that Lee's constant attacking undermined Confederate war aims, but it does not support many

ong Lee schol-
el Fellman sug-
et for pent-up
moment when
up through his
motional prec-
that had peri-
rior the young
ung women."⁵
t the general's
rge that ruled
ore than it re-
that Lee had a
ly attacked. In
historical mo-

e of his warlike
re, a man gov-
argument does
cultural value
on to society's
s defined man-
no Southerner
onal level, Lee
and governed

ularly his own
ffensive action
ned during his
homas has ob-
inst the poorly
." Lee admired

an irrepressible warlike spirit con-
aries, including highly respected ar-
ced the idea that passion for battle
ing on Lee's career, Alexander be-
n. Lee as decidedly the most auda-
apoleon, & I am not at all sure that
be held to have overmatched some
ee committed himself." In the final
ative instinct" in Lee "as strongly
n that Lee was naturally aggressive
ge A. Bruce suggested that the "im-
cribed by General Alexander, his 'up
eet, would not let him rest." Bruce
ongenial to his [Lee's] impulsive na-
artially blamed Lee's fighting blood

ation of *The Marble Man: Robert E.*
st scholars followed the tradition of
s aggressive impulses. In a startling
ine rush of battle created a blinding
r him to see how his losses wreaked
gunpowder turned Lee into a primal
ting his foe. "It may appear heretical
nbat," Connelly writes. Battle trans-
he insists, who "bled the Confeder-
piling up fifty thousand Confederate
n command. Frank Vandiver agrees
elly), noting that Lee was "addicted
th dearly.⁴

ederacy: The Personal Recollections of General
apel Hill: University of North Carolina Press,
Strategy of the Civil War," in *Lee the Soldier*,
aska Press, 1996), 117; Douglas Southall Free-
arles Scribner's Sons, 1934–35), 4:74.
. *Lee and His Image in American Society* (New
ndiver, "Lee during the War," in *Confederate*
lege Press, 1984), 19–21, 23–25.

e, 2000), 114–15.
ram Wyatt-Brown,
sity Press, 1982).

This psychological interpretation continues to resonate a▮ ars. In *The Making of Robert E. Lee,* published in 2000, Mich▮ gests that Lee's aggressive style of warfare provided an ou▮ sexual energy suppressed throughout his adult life. "At the▮ it was most needed," Fellman writes, "aggressiveness thrust▮ passivity and deep reserve. In a sense, the most approximate▮ edent for such an outburst was the considerable erotic ener▮ odically forced its way up through the carefully controlled ex▮ Lee had normally shown the world in his relationships with ▮

All of these scholars either explicitly state or suggest th▮ aggressiveness was a biological function, an uncontrollable▮ the inner man. This psychological interpretation obscures ▮ veals. No amount of historical evidence can prove the thesi▮ peculiar lust for combat, and, when aroused, he automatica▮ the end this interpretation blocks the search into legitimat▮ tives that influenced Lee's thinking.

Those who see Lee's offensive proclivities as a consequen▮ spirit unwittingly turn the general into an unthinking creat▮ erned by animalistic impulses. Upon closer inspection this ▮ not hold up. Aggressiveness is not a biological trait. It is ▮ whose meaning and importance continually change in rela▮ expectations. Lee came of age when courage and aggressiven▮ hood at the most fundamental level. Without these qualities ▮ could ever gain community acceptance as a man. On a per▮ probably believed that aggressiveness, if properly channele▮ responsibly, was the defining characteristic of manhood.[6]

The Virginian's academic courses at West Point, parti▮ studies of Napoleon's campaigns, made him an advocate of ▮ in the abstract. The practicality of this doctrine was confi▮ Mexican War service with Maj. Gen. Winfield Scott. Emory ▮ served that Lee, after witnessing Scott's successful assaults a▮ armed Mexicans, was convinced of "the efficacy of the offens▮

5. Michael Fellman, *The Making of Robert E. Lee* (New York: Random Ho▮
6. The best treatment of masculinity in the Old South can be found in Be▮ *Southern Honor: Ethics & Behavior in the Old South* (New York: Oxford Unive▮

"Scott's bold strategy and probably developed a confidence in attacking that made him miscalculate against an enemy well led and armed with rifles instead of much shorter-range muskets." By 1861 Lee firmly believed in the offense, not because it suited his aggressive impulses but because it offered the best chance for military success. He applied this philosophy after careful thought and deliberation, not as a natural reflex of his personality or an outlet for a repressed Freudian desire. He did not fight the war based on instinct. As Richard McCaslin cogently argues, Lee upheld the advice of contemporary military experts by fiercely guarding the initiative, concentrating his forces whenever possible, and attacking relentlessly, even if that brought heavy losses. "Nothing was more decisive" in the Civil War than offensive operations, writes McCaslin.[7]

Unfortunately, the decision to launch Maj. Gens. George Pickett and James Pettigrew's charge at Gettysburg is often seen as the fatal consequence of Lee's fighting blood. In fact this Confederate assault was a sound, though hardly brilliant, decision in light of everything that Lee knew up to the moment of the charge. Chancellorsville had instilled Lee with absolute confidence in his men, and he did not see any deficiencies in the army's offensive arsenal. July 1 at Gettysburg, which ranks as one of the most impressive victories in the history of the Army of Northern Virginia, confirmed Lee's belief that nothing could stand in the way of his charging legions. Routing the Federals through the Pennsylvania town also demonstrated the need to keep the tactical initiative. The second day of the battle, though ultimately unsuccessful, witnessed an incredible assault by Lt. Gen. James Longstreet. Despite the treacherous terrain and formidable odds, Longstreet's men came dangerously close to capturing Little Round Top, proving for a second time in two days that Lee's soldiers could deliver an attack with amazing striking power.[8]

7. Emory M. Thomas, *Robert E. Lee: A Biography* (New York: W. W. Norton, 1995), 140–41, 226; Richard B. McCaslin, *Lee in the Shadow of Washington* (Baton Rouge: Louisiana State University Press, 2001), 10.

8. Critical appraisals of Lee for pursuing the offense at Gettysburg include Edward A. Pollard, *Lee and His Lieutenants, Comprising the Early Life, Public Services, and Campaigns of General Robert E. Lee and His Companions in Arms, with a Record of Their Campaigns and Heroic Deeds* (New York: E. B. Treat, 1867); William Swinton, *Campaigns of the Army of the Potomac: A Critical History of Operations in Virginia, Maryland, and Pennsylvania, from the Commencement to the Close of the War, 1861–1865* (1866; rev. ed., New York: Charles Scribner's Sons, 1882), 340–41; James

The temporary successes gained during the first two days of fighting, the confidence engendered by the Army of Northern Virginia's short but storied history, and the great advantage in maintaining the tactical initiative made Lee's plan to attack the Union center on the final day of the battle a reasonable one. It was not the desperate gesture or foggy decision of a sick man who decided to roll the dice one last time.[9] Only with the advantages of hindsight, when the broken remnants of Pickett's and Pettigrew's divisions streamed back to Seminary Ridge, did the charge look like a horrendous mistake. On the afternoon of July 3, few in the army would have agreed with Longstreet that Lee was throwing away his troops in a needless attack. Everything up to that moment indicated the likelihood of success. Defeat brought out the armchair generals. An irritated Lee responded to his critics, who as the general pointed out, enjoyed all the advantages of hindsight: "I still think if all things could have worked together it would have been accomplished," Lee wrote to Jefferson Davis a few weeks after the battle. "But with the knowledge I then had, & in the circumstances I was then placed, I do not know what better course I could have pursued. . . . With my present knowledge, & could I have foreseen that the attack on the last day would have failed

---

D. McCabe Jr., *Life and Campaigns of General Robert E. Lee* (St. Louis: National Publishing, 1866), 393–95; H. J. Eckenrode and Bryan Conrad, *James Longstreet: Lee's War Horse* (1936; reprint, Chapel Hill: University of North Carolina Press, 1986), 213; and Alan T. Nolan, *Lee Considered: General Robert E. Lee and Civil War History* (Chapel Hill: University of North Carolina Press, 1991), 98.

For a favorable assessment of Lee at Gettysburg in general agreement with my conclusions, see J. F. C. Fuller, *Grant and Lee: A Study in Personality and Generalship* (1933; reprint, Bloomington: Indiana University Press, 1957), 197. Fuller understood why Lee remained on the offensive at Gettysburg but found fault with the general's tactical plan, which he considered unimaginative. Like Fuller, Freeman basically accepts Lee's reasoning for remaining on the offense, including the final attack on July 3. See Freeman, *Lee's Lieutenants: A Study in Command*, 3 vols. (New York: Charles Scribner's Sons, 1942–44), 3:178. Generally positive appraisals can also be found in Edwin B. Coddington, *The Gettysburg Campaign: A Study in Command* (New York: Charles Scribner's Sons, 1968), 362; and Harry W. Pfanz, *Gettysburg: The Second Day* (Chapel Hill: University of North Carolina Press, 1987), 26–27.

9. Vandiver, "Lee during the War," 17. Although the evidence is dangerously thin, Vandiver speculates that a number of physical factors adversely affected Lee's judgment: "Lee at Gettysburg was infirm, had been thrown from his horse a couple of weeks before, and had sprained his hands; he may have been suffering from infectious myocarditis, did have diarrhea, and stayed mainly in his tent."

to drive the enemy from his position," he concluded, "I should certainly have tried some other course."[10]

Although mistaken about the origins of Lee's aggressiveness and why he persisted in attacking at places like Gettysburg, the early critics asked the right questions about the general's advocacy of the offense. Was the Confederacy able to afford his daring offensive maneuvers and the brutal losses that attended his operations? In 1991 Alan Nolan refined the debate by focusing on Lee's contribution to the success or failure of Confederate grand strategy in his provocative *Lee Considered: General Robert E. Lee and Civil War History*. Following the tradition of George Bruce and J. F. C. Fuller, Nolan charged that scholars have focused too narrowly on the brilliance or boldness of Lee's individual battles without looking at the broader consequences of those engagements. "His campaigns and battles," Nolan writes, "are typically considered almost as disembodied, abstract events, unrelated to the necessities and objectives of the war." While admitting that Lee was a brilliant field commander, Nolan does not think Lee understood grand strategy as it applied to the Southern nation. He never worked within the Confederacy's limited manpower and manufacturing resources. Nolan came down hard on the general, arguing that Lee's combativeness contradicted the Confederacy's need for conservative military policy. According to Nolan, Lee should have pursued a defensive strategy similar to George Washington's in the Revolution. The Americans could not defeat the British in pure military terms, but within a flexible defensive strategy, they preserved their own forces while wearing down the enemy until it gave up. If Lee had emulated his hero, he might have exhausted the North's endurance by protecting his manpower through conservative maneuvers and defensive victories. Nolan argues that Lee actually precipitated Confederate defeat through his offensive-oriented strategy.[11]

Although Nolan's criticisms of Lee are excessive in places, he deserves credit for making the connection between Lee's tactical and operational maneuvers and its effect on national, or grand, strategy. This issue continues to

10. Robert E. Lee to Jefferson Davis, July 31, 1863, in *The Wartime Papers of Robert E. Lee*, ed. Clifford Dowdey and Louis H. Manarin (Boston: Little, Brown, 1961), 565.

11. Nolan, *Lee Considered*, 62. An excellent summation of his argument can be found in Nolan, "Did Robert E. Lee's Generalship Help or Hurt the Confederacy's Chances for Victory," in *The Color Bearer: The Journal of the American Blue & Gray Association* 1 (July 1992): 8, 10.

be the point of departure when evaluating Lee's generalship. In the fury over *Lee Considered*, many critics wasted so much energy attacking the author that they tended to ignore his arguments. In many circles any criticism of Lee the general constitutes the greatest heresy imaginable. No historical figure is beyond reproach, and Lee's record should be subjected to the same tough questions as that of Grant, Sherman, Longstreet, and other Civil War figures. Those who continue to defend Lee with the passion of a Jubal Early or William N. Pendleton do grave injustice to the historical memory of the general.[12] A critical, rigorous approach leads to a more sophisticated and complex portrait of the man rather than the simplistic, one-dimensional ideal that is fostered by Lost Cause disciples. Criticism of the general should not be interpreted as a personal attack against the man. Nolan's inquiry is an honest and sincere historical exploration to find the "real Lee." He should be recognized for his important contributions and insights as well as taken to task for the limitations of his arguments.

In the final analysis Nolan's interpretation suffers from a timeless approach that does not account for the Confederacy's changing military and political needs. Nolan insists that a defensive posture suited the Confederacy throughout the war. If Jefferson Davis and Lee had adhered to such a conservative policy in 1862 and 1863, they would have squandered amazing opportunities to strike a blow for independence. Furthermore, the Southern people demanded bold action from their armies, as Gary W. Gallagher conclusively demonstrates in *The Confederate War: How Popular Will, Nationalism, and Military Strategy Could Not Stave Off Defeat*. They denounced passive generals like

12. Some of the most influential Lost Cause writings on Lee include Jubal A. Early, *The Campaigns of Gen. Robert E. Lee: An Address by Lieut. General Jubal A. Early, before Washington and Lee University, January 19th, 1872* (Baltimore: John Murphy, 1872); John Warwick Daniel, *Ceremonies Connected with the Inauguration of the Mausoleum and the Unveiling of the Recumbent Figure of General Robert Edward Lee, at Washington and Lee University, Lexington, Va., June 28, 1883: Oration of John W. Daniel, LL.D. Historical Sketch of the Lee Memorial Association* (Richmond: West, Johnson, 1883); and Archer Anderson, *Robert Edward Lee: An Address Delivered at the Dedication of the Monument to General Robert Edward Lee at Richmond, Virginia, May 28, 1890* (Richmond: William Ellis Jones, Printer, 1890). For a modern critique of the Lost Cause school and its destructive influence on Confederate scholarship, see Gary W. Gallagher, "Jubal A. Early, the Lost Cause, and Civil War History: A Persistent Legacy," in *The Myth of the Lost Cause and Civil War History*, ed. Alan T. Nolan and Gary W. Gallagher (Bloomington: Indiana University Press, 2000), 35–59.

Joseph E. Johnston, whose constant retreating during the 1862 Peninsula Campaign unleashed a storm of public criticism. Lee himself came under fire early in the war when Southerners perceived him as passive and weak. North Carolinian Catherine Edmondston worried when she heard reports that Lee had assumed command of the Army of Northern Virginia after Johnston's wounding at Seven Pines. Earlier she had condemned Lee as an officer who was "too timid, believes too much in masterly inactivity, finds 'his strength' too much in 'sitting still.' "[13]

Even if one agrees with Nolan's rebuttal to Gallagher that Lee should not have satisfied the Southern populace's bloodthirsty cries, his condemnation of the Virginian's aggressive generalship does not make sense when looking at the Confederacy's specific strategic and political needs between 1861 and mid-1863. Offensive campaigns as implemented by Lee offered the South its best chance for success during this period. Beginning with the Seven Days and culminating with his tactical masterpiece at Chancellorsville, Lee emerged as the South's premier general by relying on offensive action. During the Pennsylvania and Maryland raids, Lee took calculated risks, both strategically and tactically, but these actions had a reasonable chance of securing either a peace settlement with the North or European recognition. A defensive posture would not have achieved these war aims, a crucial point that Nolan tends to diminish. At that stage of the conflict, when the South's manpower and resources were relatively plentiful and civilian morale was intact, Lee's aggressiveness complimented Confederate grand strategy. Gallagher and Joseph L. Harsh have assumed this position in their counterattack against Nolan and the "too much offense" school. Both historians stress the need to look beyond Lee's high casualties by focusing on the political effect of his victories. Lee's exploits damaged Northern morale while creating a Lee mystique that sustained Southern morale to Appomattox.

In *Confederate Tide Rising: Robert E. Lee and the Making of Southern Strategy, 1861–1862*, Harsh advances the pro-offensive argument by focusing on

13. Gary W. Gallagher, *The Confederate War: How Popular Will, Nationalism, and Military Strategy Could Not Stave Off Defeat* (Cambridge: Harvard University Press, 1997), 127, 132–33, 134, 135; Catherine Ann Devereux Edmondston, May 6, 1862, *"Journal of a Secesh Lady": The Diary of Catherine Ann Devereux Edmondston, 1860–1866*, ed. Beth Gilbert Crabtree and James W. Patton (Raleigh: North Carolina Division of Archives and History, 1979), 169.

what Lee understood as the keys to Confederate success. He grounds his interpretation in the realities of the struggle by paying close attention to how events unfolded in the minds of the participants. Many Lee critics, however, begin by looking back from Appomattox. From that perspective they often resort to monocausation, arguing that the depletion of Southern manpower was responsible for the Confederacy's demise. These writers impose a defensive grand strategy on the Confederacy as the only route to independence, then criticize Lee for failing to fight a kind of war that he rejected as hopelessly disconnected from the South's logistical capacity. According to Harsh, Lee realized that time was not on the Confederacy's side. With its relatively limited resources, the South could not simply outlast the North through a defensive strategy that might also encourage Federal armies to concentrate and overwhelm Rebel armies. "The same raw mathematics meant the South itself could not wage an overly protracted contest," Harsh writes. "Once the war had started, a logistical hourglass had been set on end, and its sands ran relentlessly against the Confederacy." He concludes, "Eventually, Confederate resources in men and materiel would diminish to the point they could not carry on the war while waiting for the North to tire of the struggle."[14]

Lee understood the stark truth of the numbers game, Harsh believes, and consequently did not think the South could win a protracted, defensive-oriented war. Harsh makes a valuable contribution by taking Lee on his own terms, by viewing the war from the general's perspective and not from the advantages of hindsight, one of the great weaknesses of the Nolan school. He convincingly argues that the Confederacy's limited resources actually compelled Lee to strike, that time was against him, and that Confederate armies could not remain inactive but would have to rely on the offense. In the end Lee adopted an offensive-defensive strategy that supported existing Confederate war aims and had already yielded important successes during the early months of the conflict. This strategy kept the enemy off balance, making it impossible for Northern armies to coordinate and concentrate against his smaller Army of Northern Virginia.[15]

14. Joseph L. Harsh, *Confederate Tide Rising: Robert E. Lee and the Making of Southern Strategy, 1861–1862* (Kent, Ohio: Kent State University Press, 1998), 59. Russell F. Weigley agrees with Harsh regarding the origins of Lee's offensive thinking. See Weigley, *A Great Civil War: A Military and Political History, 1861–1865* (Bloomington: Indiana University Press, 2000), 126–27.

15. Harsh, *Confederate Tide Rising,* 60–61.

Harsh and Gallagher have done much to rehabilitate Lee's contributions as an offensive-minded general. Ironically their interpretation, like Nolan's, suffers from a timeless quality. Neither historian fully appreciates the war's changing political and military situation. In fairness to Harsh, his scholarship focuses on the first two years of the war, but his defense of Lee's strategic vision applies to the post-1864 Virginia campaigns. Both Gallagher and Harsh also overlook how Northern and Southern expectations changed in 1864. Offensive victories were no longer necessary to bolster the South and depress the North. Moreover the Army of Northern Virginia lost the capacity to achieve a victory of annihilation after the crushing losses at Chancellorsville and Gettysburg. By the spring of 1864, the time had come for the Confederacy to try to outlast the North through a defensive strategy geared toward stirring political turmoil before the pivotal presidential election. Defensive victories not only preserved precious Southern manpower but also intensified Northern war weariness and dissent at a time when Lincoln desperately needed good military news. Offensive failures, particularly Early's Valley Campaign, had a devastating effect on the South while reviving Northern hopes that the end was near.

After Gettysburg, Davis and Lee needed to take fewer risks by assuming a more defensive-oriented strategy. The brutal losses of his earlier campaigns had destroyed the Army of Northern Virginia's offensive capability and decimated the ranks of midlevel officers as Lee's logistical base was shrinking. Even Freeman recognized the cumulative effect of Lee's repeated offensives, writing that "the army's hard-won battles left its ranks depleted, its command shattered by death or wounds, its personnel exhausted, its horses scarcely able to walk, its transportation broken down, [and] its ammunition and its commissary low."[16] In the context of the specific military and political situation prior to Gettysburg, Lee did not squander his resources in pointless attacks. The offensive presented the best chance for ultimate success at that stage of the war, and the commanding general took appropriate risks that resulted in unavoidable losses.

16. Freeman, *R. E. Lee,* 4:178. Steven H. Newton challenges conventional wisdom on this point, arguing that Confederate armies mobilized more men in the spring of 1864 than in the previous year. See Newton, *Lost for the Cause: The Confederate Army in 1864* (Mason City, Iowa: Savas, 2000).

Lee, it appears, never rethought his strategic assumptions after his failed Pennsylvania campaign.[17] He still preferred the tactical and operational offensive in order to achieve that complete and decisive victory. On August 31, 1863, in a letter to Longstreet, Lee wrote: "I hope you will use every exertion to prepare the army for offensive operations. . . . I can see nothing better to be done than to endeavor to bring General Meade out and use our efforts to crush his army while in its present condition." On October 11 he wrote Secretary of War James A. Seddon from Madison County, "I moved the army into this position with the hope of getting an opportunity to strike a blow at the enemy." During the Mine Run Campaign, when Meade's Army of the Potomac slipped away from the Confederate's formidable position, Lee was distressed by having lost an opportunity to pitch into the enemy. To his wife he lamented on December 4, 1863: "I thought he [Meade] had changed his mind, and that night made preparations to move around his left next morning and attack him. But when day dawned he was nowhere to be seen. . . . I am greatly disappointed at his getting off with so little damage."[18]

Lee's search for a climactic battle continued during the Overland Campaign but probably came to an end once Grant invested Petersburg in June 1864. His burning desire for a decisive victory was spelled out in a February 1864 letter to Davis. This document, in setting out his strategic plan, shows how little Lee's thinking had changed since Gettysburg. "If we could take the initiative & fall upon them unexpectedly," he wrote, "we might derange their plans & embarrass them the whole summer." Ultimately Lee hoped that he could secretly transfer Longstreet from Tennessee and launch a surprise raid across the Potomac. Even with his diminished numbers, the Virginian would not be satisfied with strictly defensive victories or partial triumphs. Instead he wanted his army to accomplish those powerful, all-encompassing victories that he had envisioned in 1862 and 1863, even if that meant invading the

17. Gary W. Gallagher believes that "offensive thoughts" continued to dominate Lee's thinking prior to the Overland Campaign. See Gallagher, "Our Hearts Are Full of Hope: The Army of Northern Virginia in the Spring of 1864," in *The Wilderness Campaign*, ed. Gary W. Gallagher (Chapel Hill: University of North Carolina Press, 1997), 58.

18. Robert E. Lee to James Longstreet, Aug. 31, 1863, in *Wartime Papers of R. E. Lee*, 594; Robert E. Lee to James A. Seddon, Oct. 11, 1863, in ibid., 607; Robert E. Lee to his wife, Dec. 4, 1863, in *Recollections and Letters of General Robert E. Lee*, ed. Robert E. Lee Jr. (1904; reprint, Wilmington, N.C.: Broadfoot, 1988), 116.

North again. Lee wanted to strike the first blow. Although he could never achieve those grand purposes, except for Early's brief raid into Maryland, his orders throughout the 1864 campaign bristle with fiery language imploring his army to win the great battle that would destroy the adversary. He instructed subordinates to "destroy," "wipe out," "crush," and "ruin" the enemy.[19]

While every Civil War officer hoped for a complete victory, most realized by 1863 that armies were virtually indestructible. Maybe a regiment, a brigade, or even a corps could be routed, but Civil War armies were able to respond effectively to such a breakthrough and prevent a disaster. The rifled weapon, the belief in entrenching, the maneuverability of Civil War units, and the natural advantage of the defense rendered the battle of annihilation a thing of the past. Examples of one side destroying an enemy army are rare. The Union victory at Nashville in December 1864 is perhaps the best example of such a victory, but the conditions of that engagement were unique—the Confederate army bordered on demoralization and was vastly outnumbered.[20]

Many Civil War officers understood that pitched battles could only achieve limited strategic consequences. This point should not have been lost on Lee, for on a number of battlefields he witnessed the resilience of Civil War armies. At Gaines's Mill, Second Manassas, and Chancellorsville, portions of the Federal army left the field in wild disorder. Even with the Northerners in this vulnerable, confused state, Lee could not deliver the killing blow; he could not achieve a complete battlefield triumph that permanently crippled the enemy. In striking contrast to Lee, the impossibility of achieving a cataclysmic victory struck George Gordon Meade after Gettysburg, his first battle as army commander. His army's quick recovery on the first day, after the rout of the Eleventh Corps, and his failure to crush Lee's retreating force against the Potomac gave him a realistic view of how to deal with the Army of Northern Virginia. "The Government insists on my pursuing and destroying Lee," Meade explained. "The former I can do, but the latter will depend on him as much as on me, for if he keeps away I can't destroy." He thought

19. Robert E. Lee to Jefferson Davis, Feb. 3, 1864, in *Wartime Papers of Robert E. Lee*, 666–67; Nolan, *Lee Considered*, 76–77.

20. Hattaway and Jones, *How the North Won*, 46–47.

it impossible to "pursue and destroy an army nearly equal to my own, falling back on its resources and reinforcements and increasing its *morale* daily."[21]

Lee, it appears, never had a similar revelation. His correspondence is sprinkled with complaints about his failure to crush the Army of the Potomac, and his frustration mounted as the war progressed. Even impressive battlefield triumphs did not leave him satisfied, including his lopsided defensive victory at Fredericksburg—he knew the Federals would draw fresh recruits and resume the offensive in the coming spring. Driving Maj. Gen. Joseph Hooker across the Rappahannock River during the Chancellorsville fighting did not ease his disappointment. "At Chancellorsville," he explained, "we gained another victory [and] our people were wild with delight—I, on the contrary, was more depressed than after Fredericksburg; our loss was severe, and again we had gained not an inch of ground and the enemy could not be pursued." As late as July 6, 1864, Lee still desired complete victories that swept the enemy from the field. He wrote to Davis: "If we can defeat or drive the armies of the enemy from the field, we shall have peace. All our efforts & energies," he added, "should be devoted to that object."[22]

During that pivotal spring of 1864, Lee still entertained the notion that he could destroy at least a portion of Grant's army, when in reality he could only hope to slow down or injure Grant's overwhelming force. Decimating the Army of the Potomac was out of the question. A close examination of the Wilderness reveals Lee's unreasonable expectations. His false hope of complete victory rested on an army that lacked the reserves to exploit the enemy's mistakes. Lee, however, wanted his subordinates to execute offensive maneuvers that the Army of Northern Virginia could only have achieved at the pinnacle of its strength and morale. Lee pinned his grand scheme, in part, on two mediocre corps commanders, Lt. Gens. Richard S. Ewell and A. P. Hill.

There is no question that Lee entertained doubts about Ewell and Hill at

21. Quote from ibid., 466.

22. Gary W. Gallagher, "The Yanks Have Had a Terrible Whipping: Confederates Evaluate the Battle of Fredericksburg," in *The Fredericksburg Campaign: Decision on the Rappahannock*, ed. Gary W. Gallagher (Chapel Hill: University of North Carolina Press, 1995), 129–34; Gallagher, *"Duty Faithfully Performed": Gen. Robert E. Lee, CSA* (Gettysburg: Farnsworth Military Impressions, 1997), 43; Robert E. Lee to Jefferson Davis, July 6, 1864, in *Wartime Papers of R. E. Lee*, 816.

the beginning of the spring offensive of 1864. Neither officer had demonstrated since Gettysburg that they would excel at corps command. Action at Bristoe Station sent Hill's stock on the decline at army headquarters. Ewell's poor health also troubled Lee, who hinted in the fall of 1863 that the Second Corps commander should consider a leave of absence. Although Lee expressed doubts about both men, he did not alter his supervisory style with either officer in the battles against Grant. Both men needed close guidance, but Lee, as he had always done, gave his subordinates ample latitude.[23]

Lee's style of leadership had worked well with "Stonewall" Jackson and Longstreet, but not with Ewell, as Lee himself admitted after the war. He told William Allan that he "had long known his [Ewell's] faults as a military leader—his quick alternations from elation to despondency[,] his want of decision &c." In the second battle of Winchester, Lee had sent Ewell ahead and instructed him that "he must be guided by his own judgment in any unforeseen emergency." Ewell was initially confident, encouraged about entrapping the Federals. Suddenly his optimism turned to caution when he located the enemy's works. Instead of showing initiative, as Lee had instructed, Ewell asked for directions from headquarters. At Gettysburg Lee also expressed dissatisfaction with the "*imperfect, halting way,*" in which Ewell fought the battle.[24] If Lee fully appreciated his subordinate's need for close guidance and explicit orders, then he should have been more forceful with Ewell.

At the Wilderness Lee issued unclear orders to Ewell, whose Second Corps occupied the Confederate left flank. On May 6, the second day of fighting, the commanding general wanted Ewell to cut the Federals off from Germanna Ford if it could "be done without too great a sacrifice." Lee's language was too ambiguous, giving the naturally cautious Ewell just cause to maintain a defensive position. When reflecting on Ewell's Wilderness record, his staff officer and stepson, Campbell Brown, complained about the vagueness of Lee's orders. "I have frequently noticed before & have also since this occasion," he wrote, "that Gen. Lee's instructions to his Corps Comrs are of

23. Freeman, *Lee's Lieutenants*, 3:330. For the finest biography of Richard Ewell, see Donald C. Pfanz, *Richard S. Ewell: A Soldier's Life* (Chapel Hill: University of North Carolina Press, 1998). On A. P. Hill, see James I. Robertson Jr., *General A. P. Hill: The Story of a Confederate Warrior* (New York: Random House, 1987).

24. William Allan, "Memoranda of Conversations with General Robert E. Lee," in *Lee the Soldier*, 11, 14.

a very comprehensive & general description & frequently admit of several interpretations—in fact will allow them to do almost anything, provided only it be a *success*. They caution them particularly against failure & very frequently wind up with the injunction to 'attack whenever or wherever it can be done to advantage.' "[25]

Lee's discretionary orders for May 6, moreover, reveal his vain hope that he could demolish at least a portion of the Army of the Potomac. An attack across Ewell's front would have sent his men across rugged terrain in the face of entrenched Federals. To make matters more problematic, frequent Union demonstrations had pinned down the Second Corps so that Ewell could not shift units from his front to his far left flank. Lee seemed oblivious to these limitations. In an 1868 conversation with William Preston Johnston at Washington College, the general reminisced about the Wilderness, complaining that "Ewell showed vacillation that prevented him from getting all out of his troops he might." He believed, "If Jackson had been alive and there, he [Jackson] would have crushed the enemy." Lee also confided to William Allen after the war that he wanted Ewell's movement to be "a full attack in flank & intended to support it with all [of] Ewell's corps and others if necessary, and to rout the enemy."[26]

Lee's invented schemes for Ewell bordered on fantasy. Ewell lacked any reserve troops, which were critical to a successful offensive. Not until Robert D. Johnston's brigade arrived at 1:00 P.M. did the corps commander have any men for such a maneuver, and even then his force was too small to achieve decisive results. Lee must have known this, even though he spent much of the battle on the Confederate right. His high hopes might have been realized in 1862, when his army had plenty of reserves for slashing attacks, but such an offensive stroke was not realistic in May 1864. After considerable delay Ewell finally launched a limited attack against the Federal right flank, captur-

25. Campbell Brown Memoir, Ewell Letterbook, folder 2, box 2, Tennessee State Library, Nashville. Studies of the Wilderness include Edward Steere, *The Wilderness Campaign* (New York: Bonanza, 1960); Robert Garth Scott, *Into the Wilderness with the Army of the Potomac* (Bloomington: Indiana University Press, 1985); Noah Andre Trudeau, *Bloody Roads South: The Wilderness to Cold Harbor, May–June 1864* (Boston: Little, Brown, 1989); and Gordon C. Rhea, *The Battle of the Wilderness, May 5–6, 1864* (Baton Rouge: Louisiana State University Press, 1994).

26. William Preston Johnston, "Memoranda of Conversations with General R. E. Lee," in *Lee the Soldier*, 29; Allan, "Memoranda of Conversations with Robert E. Lee," 11.

ing a few hundred prisoners and two Union generals but failing to inflict permanent damage against the enemy.[27]

The same desire to destroy Grant's army at the Wilderness continued to motivate Lee throughout the spring and early summer of 1864. When he mistakenly believed the Federals were retreating toward Fredericksburg during Spotsylvania, Lee wanted his army to catch the Army of the Potomac on the move, to regain the offensive and strike a decisive blow. He was determined, as he said along the North Anna, that "we must strike them a blow—we must never let them pass us again—we must strike them a blow!" Two days earlier, on May 23, Lee had promised Jefferson Davis that wherever Grant moves, "I am in a position to move against him, and shall endeavor to engage him while in motion." He added, "It seems to me [that] our best policy [is] to unite upon it [the Army of the Potomac] and endeavor to crush it." Speaking to Jubal Early after the battle of Cold Harbor, Lee stated, "We must destroy this army of Grant's before he gets to [the] James River."[28]

From the beginning of the conflict, the Virginian considered Northern demoralization essential to Southern victory. Nothing could stop the Union war machine, Lee wrote on February 28, 1863, "except a revolution among their people." He added, "Nothing can produce a revolution except systematic success on our part." Gary W. Gallagher has persuasively argued that Lee was well attuned to the political situation, a general who understood the modern demands of a mid-nineteenth-century war. Lee showed a remarkable understanding of the relationship between politics and the military as it related to national strategy. On April 19, 1864, he made this crucial point to Davis: "I think it important to unite as closely as possible the interests of the army with the interests of the citizens. They are one in reality & all for the

27. An elaboration of this argument can be found in Peter S. Carmichael, "Escaping the Shadow of Gettysburg: Richard S. Ewell and Ambrose Powell Hill at the Wilderness," in Gallagher, *The Wilderness Campaign*, 136–56.

28. Charles S. Venable, "The Campaign from the Wilderness to Petersburg," in *Southern Historical Society Papers*, ed. J. William Jones et al., 52 vols. (Richmond, 1876–1959; reprint, with 3-vol. index, Wilmington, N.C.: Broadfoot, 1990–92), 14:535; Robert E. Lee to Jefferson Davis, May 23, 1864, in *Lee's Dispatches: Unpublished Letters of General Robert E. Lee, C.S.A., to Jefferson Davis and the War Department of the Confederate States of America, 1862–1865*, rev. ed., ed. Douglas Southall Freeman and Grady McWhiney (New York: G. P. Putnam's Sons, 1957), 195; Early, *Campaigns of Gen. Robert E. Lee*, 37.

Country." During the war, he also paid close attention to Northern morale, always reading enemy papers to gauge the strength of the peace movement or chart other political developments. On a number of occasions, he suggested to Davis possible ways the Confederate government might fuel antiwar sentiment in the North. Up to 1863, Lee's offensive victories had a damaging, almost crippling, effect on the North, just as the general had desired. But after Gettysburg, when Northerners were becoming desperate for final victory, Lee did not need offensively gained victories to break the enemy's will. Any Union setback, no matter how it came, hurt the Republican administration and enhanced the chances of a Peace Democrat entering the White House.[29]

Such defensive victories as Cold Harbor on June 3 and the initial assaults against Petersburg June 15–18 sent Northern morale crashing downward. War weariness turned into open, violent dissent against the Republican administration during the summer of 1864. Lee, who had been brilliant in reading Northern tea leaves up to Gettysburg, suddenly lost his touch as a prognosticator of enemy morale. He consequently placed his army on the operational and tactical offensive for the wrong political reasons, for he could still land devastating body blows to Northern confidence through defensive measures. Although it is unreasonable to believe that Lee could have simply sat back and waited for Grant to throw away his legions in repeated frontal attacks, the Confederate commander needed to eliminate unnecessary offensive strikes during the summer and fall of 1864. In fairness to Lee it should be noted that he imagined Northern forces having their way with the Army of Northern Virginia if he simply conceded the offensive to his adversaries.[30]

Surprisingly Lee seems to have lost touch with his own words at this critical juncture of the war. In many of his earlier dispatches, he frequently stated that he must "embarrass," "baffle," and "frustrate" his adversary's offensive

29. Robert E. Lee to G. W. C. Lee, Feb. 28, 1863, in *Wartime Papers of R. E. Lee*, 411; Gary W. Gallagher, "An Old-Fashioned Soldier in a Modern War? Lee's Confederate Generalship," in *Lee & His Army in Confederate History*, ed. Gary W. Gallagher (Chapel Hill: University of North Carolina Press, 2001), 172–77; Robert E. Lee to Jefferson Davis, Apr. 19, 1864, in *Lee's Dispatches*, 161. For a discussion of Lee's understanding of politics, morale, and military strategy, see Harsh, *Confederate Tide Rising*, 58–59.

30. Phillip Shaw Paludan, *"A People's Contest": The Union and Civil War, 1861–1865* (New York: Harper & Row, 1988), 311–12; Gallagher, "Old-Fashioned Soldier in a Modern War," 177–78.

schemes. To this end the general did not have to press the offensive, particularly at a time when Northern determination was on the verge of cracking. Instead of building upon the defensive victories gained during the Overland Campaign, Early's aggressive action in the Shenandoah Valley negated these achievements. Early buckled under his commander's lofty expectations as he sought to demolish an enemy far superior in numbers and supplies. Anything less than bold battlefield triumphs, Early believed, fell short of Lee's goal. Pressure from headquarters ultimately led to offensive action at Cedar Creek on October 18, an unmitigated catastrophe for the Confederacy. This disaster, coupled with the loss of Atlanta and Mobile, secured Lincoln's reelection. The leading historian of the 1864 Valley Campaign has criticized Lee for pushing "Early into action, burdening him with an audacious, risky strategy against a formidable enemy. At no other time in the war had the brilliant Lee so miscalculated the strength of any enemy force." Lee could have depressed Northern morale by cautioning Early to preserve his force in the Valley while achieving the military goal of diverting Federal troops from Richmond and Petersburg.[31]

Southern demands for decisive battlefield victories, as Gary Gallagher has argued, encouraged Lee to attack, resulting in offensive actions like Early's Valley Campaign. "As citizens in a democratic republic," Gallagher writes, "Confederates consistently made known their opinions about how the war was being conducted. Newspapers, diaries, and letters facilitate the reconstruction of those opinions, revealing a public overwhelmingly devoted to the idea of carrying the war to the enemy, holding on to or recapturing Confederate territory, and otherwise taking an offensive approach."[32] While Gallagher is correct that Lee's aggressive victories gave the Southern people its best hope for nationhood in 1862–63, carrying them past the point when most would have deserted the cause, his interpretation breaks down when applied

31. Harsh, *Confederate Tide Rising,* 59–60; Jeffry D. Wert, "Jubal A. Early and Confederate Leadership," in *Struggle for the Shenandoah: Essays on the 1864 Valley Campaign,* ed. Gary W. Gallagher (Kent, Ohio: Kent State University Press, 1991), 34. For a superb account of the 1864 Valley Campaign, see Wert, *From Winchester to Cedar Creek: The Shenandoah Campaign of 1864* (Carlisle, Pa.: South Mountain, 1987).

32. Gallagher, *The Confederate War,* 127. For a more recent restatement of his argument, see Gallagher, "Old-Fashioned Soldier in a Modern War," 177.

to the spring of 1864, a time when Confederate expectations became more conservative and realistic.

A canvass of Confederate newspapers on the eve of the Overland Campaign indicates that the Southern people did not expect a grand battle of annihilation, nor did they envision Grant succumbing to one of Lee's dazzling offensives.[33] The days of slashing flank assaults were gone, most Confederate papers concluded, and any talk of invading the North was simply ludicrous. In fact Southern expectations were so modest that many predicted that military setbacks were inevitable once Grant crossed the Rapidan River. Most Confederate papers were in general agreement that all Lee needed to do was resist. A stalemate was perfectly acceptable.[34]

For many Confederates the most pressing question was if Lee could maintain his hold on Virginia. They did not concern themselves with grandiose offensive schemes.[35] A grinding, defensive warfare, most newspapers predicted, would thankfully preserve Virginia for the Confederacy. Most welcomed a less aggressive strategy as an appropriate course of action. In fact many newspapers warned of an inevitable Confederate retreat to Richmond because of Grant's overwhelming numbers. This, however, did not mean that all was lost. In a typical pronouncement before the Overland Campaign, the *Richmond Dispatch* expected that Grant "may win the day on the Rappahannock, and Richmond still not fall. He cannot so damage Gen. Lee, as to disable him from retiring to Richmond, and if forced to that extremity, the General can defend this place against all odds." Southerners accepted the

33. Although he detects a deep reservoir of optimism among Confederate papers and Southern civilians, Gary W. Gallagher notes that Southerners had tempered their expectations on the eve of the Wilderness. "Our Hearts Are Full of Hope," 39–41.

34. "A March into Pennsylvania," *Charleston Mercury,* Mar. 12, 1864. Many Southern papers tried to steel civilians for military defeats in the coming campaign, warning that any one battlefield disaster did not mean the end of the Confederacy. See, for example, "The Present Situation of Affairs," *(Wilmington, N.C.) Daily Journal,* Apr. 21, 1864; "The Spring and Summer Campaigns," *Richmond Daily Whig,* Apr. 30, 1864; "Are We Prepared," *New Orleans Daily Picayune,* May 22, 1864; "Something Decisive," *Richmond Daily Whig,* May 5, 1864; and "Look to the Other Side," *Richmond Daily Whig,* May 6, 1864.

35. For those Confederate papers that warned of Lee's withdrawal from Virginia, see "Will Virginia Be Abandoned," *New Orleans Daily Picayune,* Apr. 3, 1864; and "Southern View of the Situation," Apr. 8, 1864, *Mobile Advertiser and Register,* reprinted in *New Orleans Daily Picayune,* Apr. 30, 1864.

possibility of a retrograde movement because they believed that defensive victories could still be achieved, even if Lee abandoned the Rappahannock line. An editor for the *Memphis Daily Appeal* speculated on April 9, 1864, that if Lee's army retreated to Richmond and became a shield around the capital, that he could shatter Northern morale by simply deflecting Union attacks. Repulsing Grant's legions would "dishearten the North, confuse the succession to the presidency, and do much to engender an unruly strife between the factions at the North, and place ourselves upon the certain road to peace."[36]

Once the Overland Campaign began on May 5 at the Wilderness, Confederate papers applauded the defensive nature of Lee's actions as the public learned of the Army of the Potomac's horrendous losses. While it is true that the Southern papers always tried to put the best possible spin on military matters, there is little evidence to suggest that the commanding general was under significant public pressure to strike a counterblow against Grant. Most Confederates, it appears, were content to let Grant hammer away, to deplete his forces in futile frontal assaults while Lee preserved his army. The *Richmond Daily Whig* welcomed Grant's aggressiveness at the start of the campaign, writing on May 9, "a bully who rushes on an antagonist—is met, checked, forced back, thrown on the defensive, driven under cover, and who then skulks away in search of greater safety—is whipped. . . . It is a most gratifying reflection that this renewed triumph of our arms has been achieved at comparatively small sacrifice thus far of life." Two days later a North Carolina paper echoed the same sentiments: "General Lee would appear to act as though he thought that Grant's object was to weary our men out, and so he lets Grant weary himself and his men by making all the attacks." From the confines of Richmond's ordnance department, Josiah Gorgas drew comfort

---

36. "Richmond Not Taken," *Richmond Dispatch*, May 13, 1864; "Unity of Action," *Memphis Daily Appeal* (published in Atlanta), Apr. 9, 1864. For other Confederate papers that emphasized the political fallout that defensive victories would have on the North, see "The Path to Peace," *Memphis Daily Appeal* (published in Atlanta), Mar. 11, 1864; "The Last Hope," *Columbus (Ga.) Daily Enquirer*, Apr. 27, 1864; and "Their Failing Hopes," *Memphis Daily Appeal* (published in Atlanta), Apr. 30, 1864. Once the Overland Campaign began, a number of Southern papers noted the political chaos in the North that resulted from the Wilderness and Spotsylvania battles. See "Yankee News," *Richmond Whig*, May 28, 1864; and "How Things Look at Present," *Memphis Daily Appeal* (published in Atlanta), May 12, 1864.

from the fact that Lee's veterans could always seek battle behind trenches as the two armies battled across central Virginia. Although a series of flanking maneuvers had pushed the Army of the Potomac below the North Anna River, Gorgas considered Grant beaten. "A General who makes an unsuccessful attack & recoils from his adversary," he wrote in his diary on May 26, "can be said to be defeated."[37]

The common soldiers also responded favorably to defensive warfare. From the onset of the campaign, they had hoped that Lee would avoid the terrible losses that they could no longer afford. At the same time, the men also redefined victory, emphasizing Grant's inability to break their lines and drive them from a strong defensive position as the hallmark of success. A day after the failed Union attacks at Cold Harbor, a Richmond civilian was amazed to see Lee's veterans behind "triple lines of breastworks." "They have acquired quite a respect for this sort of intrenchement," he observed, "& work like beavers when they take up a new position. They began the war with a contempt for the Spade, but now thoroughly believe in it." A Columbus, Georgia, paper reported that Richmond was filled with wounded soldiers from the Spotsylvania fighting, who crowed with delight about the "advantages of firing into the enemy with grape and rifle balls from the lines of substantial breastworks." One injured Confederate boasted, "We just *mowed* them every time." Behind earthworks, the rank and file of the Army of Northern Virginia thought they were invincible.[38]

37. "Lee and Grant," *Richmond Daily Whig*, May 9, 1864; "The Situation," *(Wilmington, N.C.) Daily Journal*, May 11, 1864; Josiah Gorgas, May 26, 1864, *The Journals of Josiah Gorgas, 1857–1878*, ed. Sarah Woolfolk Wiggins (Tuscaloosa: University of Alabama Press, 1995), 111. For other Confederate papers that welcomed a more defensive posture in Virginia and considered the Overland Campaign a Southern success, see "Affairs on the Rappahannock," *Richmond Daily Whig*, May 16, 1864; "Richmond Not Taken," *Richmond Dispatch*, May 18, 1864; "Grant's Progress," *Richmond Daily Whig*, May 21, 1864; [?], *Columbus (Ga.) Daily Enquirer*, May 25, 1864; "The Vicksburg Game," *Richmond Whig*, May 31, 1864; "Federal Accounts from Virginia," *Memphis Daily Appeal* (published in Atlanta), June 3, 1864; "The War," *Richmond Sentinel*, June 8, 1864; and "The Present Aspect," *Memphis Daily Appeal* (published in Atlanta), June 11, 1864.

38. Carol Reardon, "A Hard Road to Travel: The Impact of Continuous Operations on the Army of the Potomac and the Army of Northern Virginia in May 1864," in *The Spotsylvania Campaign*, ed. by Gary W. Gallagher (Chapel Hill: University of North Carolina Press, 1998), 173; J. Tracy Power, *Lee's Miserables: Life in the Army of Northern Virginia from the Wilderness to Appomattox* (Chapel Hill: University of North Carolina Press, 1998), 22; Gorgas, June 4, 1864, *Journals*, 114; [?], *Columbus (Ga.) Daily Enquirer*, May 25, 1864.

Lopsided defensive victories, such as May 8, 10, and 18 at Spotsylvania and June 3 at Cold Harbor, nourished the hope in the Army of Northern Virginia that independence was not far off. Even Lee acknowledged that his retreat to the James and the persistent fighting behind earthworks had not damaged morale. Writing on May 23, he informed Davis that "the courage of this army was never better, and I fear no injury to it from any retrograde movement that may be dictated by sound military policy." By the end of the Overland Campaign, some were concerned that the Army of Northern Virginia had given up too much ground, but most praised Lee for his masterful retreat. Southern editors pointed to Grant's terrible casualties as proof that a defensive approach furthered Confederate war aims while stirring political dissent in the North. "We doubt whether in the whole history of war," wrote the *Memphis Daily Appeal*, "there was ever a more brilliant series of maneuvers than that by which Gen. Lee baffled and almost annihilated the army of Grant in Spottsylvania." The paper concluded: "His first campaign was most brilliant campaign. But we doubt whether even he, in 1862, was equal to the grand conceptions which are so peculiarly characteristic of this short campaign."[39]

The most telling sign that the Southern public did not seek unrestrained aggressiveness from their generals was their simultaneous condemnation of Grant's unrelenting attacks and praise of Lee's defensive tactics. To be sure, the press and the public would have found fault with Grant no matter what. But it is significant that many contemporary writers in 1864 began to emphasize Lee's defensive skills, not his audacity, as his greatest attribute. By the end of the Overland Campaign, many Southerners began to equate aggressiveness with discontentment, despondency, and foolhardiness, while the defensive became a sign of confidence, intelligence, and fortitude.

Southerners understood and justified why Lee had to assume a more defensive posture in his fighting with Grant. Not since Joseph Johnston's tenure

---

39. Robert E. Lee to Jefferson Davis, May 23, 1864, in *Lee Dispatches*, 195; "The Campaign," *Memphis Daily Appeal* (published in Atlanta), June 2, 1864. A number of Southern papers viewed Lee's retreat to Richmond and Joseph Johnston's gradual retreat to the outskirts of Atlanta as successes. See, for example, "The Campaigns in Georgia," *Richmond Sentinel*, May 18, 1864; "Similarity of the Campaigns in Georgia and Virginia," *Memphis Daily Appeal* (published in Atlanta), June 6, 1864; "What of the Hour," ibid., June 9, 1864; and "The Present Aspect," ibid., June 11, 1864.

in Virginia did they have to explain a dramatic Union advance, and for the first time they needed to reconcile why Lee was failing to achieve the bold feats of 1862 and 1863. In doing so they refused to believe that patriotism might have inspired the Army of the Potomac's hard fighting or that their own soldiers had become weak and effeminate. "Everything indicates that this is the supreme effort of the North to crush out the South," wrote a Confederate officer on June 10. "Never has their fighting been characterised by such desperation and recklessness."[40] Yet Lee did not fully appreciate that most Confederates had reoriented their thinking, that they demanded less aggression from their officers, and that the boldness of Union armies was perceived as a last-gasp effort by the "Black Republicans." Consequently Lee, though more defensive-minded than before, still attacked because he misunderstood how popular will had changed over the course of the war.

In the minds of many Southerners, Grant came to represent the dangerous excesses of aggression, the very perversion of courage, even though many Confederates had religiously upheld those same values early in the war. The *Richmond Daily Whig* described Grant as a mad bull so full of rage that he would continue to ram Lee's lines like a senseless beast, wild and deranged by the sight of his own blood. Confederates wrote off the extreme courage exhibited by the Army of the Potomac as the product of an ambitious, drunken general who could only motivate his soldiers with alcohol or a lucrative bounty. The *Memphis Daily Appeal* insisted that Lee's veterans preferred fighting Grant because "he makes his men drunk with whisky, and brings them to the muzzle of the guns in masses." The paper added, "In that state, men are insensible to danger, but are also incapable of fighting." In their rather ludicrous dismissals of Yankee heroism, Southerners were also redefining their own understanding of courage while validating a new model of behavior. For a Confederate soldier who fought behind the safety of breastworks, those at home still considered him brave and honorable as well as the officers who stood in the trenches with him.[41]

40. Richard Corbin to his father, June 10, 1864, in *Letters of a Confederate Officer to His Family in Europe, during the Last Year of the War of Secession*, by Richard W. Corbin (1902[?]; reprint, Baltimore: Butternut and Blue, 1993), 28.

41. "Grant's Progress," *Richmond Daily Whig*, May 21, 1864; "The War in Virginia," *Memphis Daily Appeal* (published in Atlanta), May 24, 1864. For other highly critical accounts of Grant's generalship during the Overland Campaign, see "From General Lee's Army," *Richmond Dispatch*,

In the end the Southern people wanted victories that were bought by conservative, defensive measures because such tactics saved their loved ones' lives while complementing the nation's strategic goals at a time when manpower was at a premium. More than anything, they wanted their armies to stay intact, their soldiers to remain behind breastworks, their generals to avoid unnecessary risks, and their despised enemy to continue attacking. Aggressive desires still burned in the hearts of many, particularly those in the ranks, but the military reality of the situation undercut any sustained enthusiasm for open warfare or frontal attacks.

During the final year of the war, Lee was not perfectly in tune with his constituency. It is true that his diminishing numbers virtually handcuffed him, allowing him little room to maneuver offensively. But when the opportunity presented itself, he launched costly assaults at the Wilderness on May 6, Harris Farm on May 19, the North Anna on May 23, Bethesda Church on May 31, and Cold Harbor on June 1.[42] At Petersburg he launched questionable counterattacks at the Weldon Railroad on August 21 and Fort Harrison on September 30. In the autumn of 1864, he sent Jubal Early to the Shenandoah Valley, urging him to attack when all Early needed to do was occupy Maj. Gen. Philip Sheridan's attention. Early's attempt to emulate the bold offensive movements of Jackson's 1862 Valley Campaign resulted in disaster, militarily and politically, helping seal the reelection of Abraham Lincoln. Lee's aggressive designs for Early actually undermined his efforts to erode Northern war spirit, one of the general's key aims. It is also a serious mistake to overlook the role of Grant's policy of exhaustion and overall strategy of simultaneous advances. Never had Lee faced such unrelenting pressure, and he never concocted the right antidote to save the dying Confederacy. Clearly Lee underestimated Grant, and the Army of Northern Virginia paid for it on the battlefield.

It is impossible to determine the exact political and military reasons be-

---

May 18, 1864; "Grant's Desperation," ibid., May 17, 1864; "The Struggle," ibid., May 18, 1864; "The Vicksburg Game," *Richmond Daily Whig*, May 31, 1864; "The Campaign," *Memphis Daily Appeal* (published in Atlanta), June 2, 1864; and "General Grant," *Richmond Sentinel*, June 7, 1864.

42. The best treatment of the fighting from Spotsylvania to Cold Harbor can be found in Gordon C. Rhea, *To the North Anna River: Grant and Lee, May 13–25, 1864* (Baton Rouge: Louisiana State University Press, 2000).

hind every one of Lee's closing tactical and operational offensives. Certainly a desire to strike a decisive blow against the enemy, to achieve that elusive victory of annihilation, must have motivated him during the early stages of the Overland Campaign. The belief that the Southern people craved offensive victories must have also entered his thinking. In the end he knew the odds were immense, nearly impossible to overcome. From the Petersburg trenches, Lee confided to Jefferson Davis, "I hope your Exc will put no reliance in what I can do individually, for I feel that will be very little. Still, we must try & defeat them."[43] Although achieving a complete victory was slim, Lee must have felt that he had no other option than to use those same offensive tactics that had once brought impressive victories.

The Army of Northern Virginia, consequently, sustained battlefield losses at a time when Confederate manpower should have been conserved. This criticism is not an indictment of Lee's generalship. More than any other Southern general, he came closer to bringing the Confederacy to the verge of independence. He deserves tremendous credit for trying something in 1864. Most generals in Lee's situation would have wasted all their energy pleading to the Davis administration that nothing could be done without more men. Still, Lee's offensive forays during the Overland and Petersburg Campaigns and Early's mission to the Shenandoah Valley nearly drained all the sand out of the Confederacy's hourglass. Lee should have avoided expensive battles and assumed a more conservative approach.

A defensive operational strategy afforded the best chance to ruin Lincoln's reelection bid while protecting Southern manpower. No one knows what would have happened if the Peace Democrats had swept the fall elections, but that appears to have been the South's last legitimate chance to independence. In the spring of 1864, everything depended on breaking the North's will to fight. Defensive tactics alone could have accomplished this goal. This criticism of Lee's generalship only makes sense when looking at the specific military and political conditions of the final year of the war. At that stage of the conflict, we are reminded that Confederate defeat was neither inevitable nor predetermined, that the Southern people still had the will to outlast the enemy if their generals preserved their armies through easy fighting and heavy victories.

43. Robert E. Lee to Jefferson Davis, June 21, 1864, in *Lee's Dispatches*, 254.

"The Siege of Richmond Was Raised"

Lee's Intentions in the Seven Days Battles

WILLIAM J. MILLER

F IVE WEEKS BEFORE he died in 1953, Douglas Southall Freeman, biographer of Robert E. Lee and George Washington, spoke to an audience
in Richmond, Virginia, about some of the problems facing writers of history.
Among the difficulties he identified was the necessity of judicious interpretation of data and the discipline to not jump to conclusions. The passionate
nature of his expressions suggests Freeman felt very strongly about the subject, especially about the emerging technique of "psychography," in which
the writer attempted to read a historical figure's thoughts and sought explanations for the man's actions and decisions through analysis of his mind and
spirit. "How dare a man say what another man is thinking," thundered Freeman, "when he may not know what he himself is thinking!" Freeman would
be pleased to know that psychohistory, as we now call it, is no more respected than it was in his last days half a century ago, though he would share
the chagrin of many historians that the technique is alive and is, perhaps,
more pervasive. Too few modern writers work in the spirit of Freeman's most
famous declaration: "Although I lived for twenty years with General Lee and
have lived for ten with General Washington, I am prepared humbly to submit
to you that I do not know what either of them ever was thinking at a given
moment unless he happened to have written it down himself. We cannot be
too sure."[1]

Despite his disavowals of any knowledge of what was in Lee's mind, Freeman did frequently suggest and even declare what the general was thinking
at a given moment. Most of the time he based his declarations on evidence
from Lee's words or writings, but occasionally he assumed too much and attributed to Lee intentions born in the brain not of the general but of the

---

1. Douglas Southall Freeman, "An Address," *Civil War History* 1 (1955): 10.

biographer. Freeman would have been a rare historian indeed if he did not sometimes press his own beliefs and analysis too far and impose them upon his subject. Had he been a less articulate man, less erudite, less forceful, and above all, a less persuasive writer, his assumptions—or presumptions—would have had far less influence on our understanding of Lee and his campaigns than they have. Freeman's interpretations, though sometimes ill founded, remain tremendously influential.[2]

Robert E. Lee said so little (and other writers have said so much more) of what occurred in his mind and heart during the Seven Days Battles, which makes it difficult to understand the general's designs and motivation during the campaign. Because of Lee's reticence, modern writers have filled the interpretive void, too often asserting supposition as fact and using such "facts" as the basis of further conclusions, making the task of understanding the campaign from Lee's perspective that much more difficult. Many writers have resorted unabashedly to the "psychography" Freeman so deplored and have rooted their interpretation of Lee's conduct of military operations in their psychoanalysis rather than in the circumstances under which the general made his decisions. So far as Lee's role in the Seven Days is concerned, the interpretive waters have been so muddied that they are badly in need of filtration. It is worthwhile, then, to reconsider the events and circumstances of that final week of June 1862 and to reexamine Lee's testimony in pursuit of an understanding of what he meant to do, might have meant to do, and did not mean to do.

The considerable literature on the 1862 Peninsula Campaign and the Seven Days Battles makes a review of events leading up to Lee's late-June offensive unnecessary. When Lee assumed command of the South's largest field army on June 1, the Confederacy's situation was dire. Southern forces had sustained a long series of defeats, from the Mississippi River to the Atlantic, and the largest army in American history to that point—more than one hundred thousand Federal soldiers commanded by Maj. Gen. George

2. On Freeman's influence on Confederate scholarship, see Gary W. Gallagher, "Shaping Public Memory of the Civil War: Robert E. Lee, Jubal A. Early, and Douglas Southall Freeman," in *Lee & His Army in Confederate History*, ed. Gary W. Gallagher (Chapel Hill: University of North Carolina Press, 2001), 255–82.

McClellan—lay just a dozen miles from the capital city, Richmond. Faced with these circumstances, Lee had but three choices: abandon Richmond and seek a favorable battlefield elsewhere; await McClellan's siege or assaults; or go on the offensive. Lee argued to his civilian superiors that the city should not be given up. He further declared to Pres. Jefferson Davis that Richmond could not survive a siege and that endeavoring to do so would merely postpone inevitable defeat. Very early in June, Lee decided that the best alternative, indeed the only alternative, left to him was to go on the offensive.[3]

McClellan's army lay divided by the Chickahominy River. Most of the Northerners stood behind fortifications south of the river, but the men of Brig. Gen. Fitz John Porter's Fifth Corps occupied the north bank. Lee recognized this great weakness in the Federal deployment, and he believed he could exploit it by moving around Porter's northern flank. Were he able by rapid movements to get past Porter's defensive line at Beaver Dam Creek and threaten the Federal supply line along the Richmond and York River Railroad, he would have forced McClellan to either withdraw from his advanced positions near Richmond and fall back toward his base or come out from behind his fortifications and fight on the open field. Neither alternative could please the Federal general, for both would disrupt his carefully pursued plan to lay siege to Richmond. Yet Lee's testimony indicates that he would be pleased with either development. His desire was to move McClellan or engage him where he could do so to advantage, perhaps both.

In the third week of June, Lee matured a plan for an offensive and presented it to his chief lieutenants: Maj. Gen. James Longstreet, Lee's senior field commander; Maj. Gen. Thomas J. "Stonewall" Jackson, fresh from his victorious diversionary campaign in the Shenandoah Valley; the aggressive and reliable Maj. Gen. Daniel Harvey Hill; and Maj. Gen. Ambrose Powell Hill, the youngest division commander in the army. Lee's plan was simple but daring. He would combine almost three-fourths of his army in an aggressive thrust toward Porter on the weak Federal right. Lee's stated target was McClellan's support structure—his supply line—the Richmond and York River Railroad. Jackson was to arrive with eighteen thousand men on the

3. See Clifford Dowdey and Louis H. Manarin, eds., *The Wartime Papers of R. E. Lee* (Boston: Little, Brown, 1961), 164.

Confederate left and drive eastward into the Federal rear. This movement was intended to force the Federals to withdraw from their strong position at Beaver Dam Creek. If Porter pulled back, he would have to abandon important bridges across the Chickahominy, and Lee could then send his three other columns, Longstreet and the two Hills, pouring across to the north bank to pursue or crush Porter as the opportunity offered. Jackson's was the key column, and on that general's performance hinged the prospects of victory and defeat. The Valley general's goal, according to Lee's written order, was the crossroads of Old Cold Harbor, whence good roads led to both Dispatch Station on the railroad and to Grapevine Bridge over the Chickahominy. Possession of Old Cold Harbor would put both the railroad and one of Porter's principal retreat routes in imminent danger and would, therefore, force the Federals to fight, withdraw, or both.

The daring of Lee's plan lay in two circumstances, either of which might prove fatal to the offensive. First, to concentrate the bulk of his force on the north bank against the smaller portion of the Federal army, the Virginian necessarily had to weaken his force on the south bank. Maj. Gen. John Magruder, with only twenty-five thousand men, was to hold the Richmond defenses in the face of the greater part of McClellan's immense army, some eighty-five thousand men. If the Union commander reacted passively to the movement against Porter and the railroad, Lee's plan could not fail to produce positive results. If McClellan reacted aggressively to the threat by reinforcing Porter and fighting for his supply line, Lee would have at least succeeded in negating the strong Federal defensive positions and forced the enemy to accept battle in the open. If, however, McClellan reacted to Jackson's turning movement by striking hard toward Richmond, Lee's plan might quickly collapse and the city might fall. Lee was willing to risk that McClellan would not be so bold, but never in the course of the first few days of this operation could he discount the possibility that the Federals might counterattack against his weakened right wing. His concern for Magruder and Richmond would play a dominant role in the way Lee conducted the first two engagements of his first campaign.

General Orders No. 75 was distributed to Lee's division commanders on June 24, and any investigation into Lee's intentions in the Seven Days must begin with them.

GENERAL ORDERS No. 75.

HDQRS. ARMY OF NORTHERN VIRGINIA,
June 24, 1862.

I. General Jackson's command will proceed to-morrow from Ashland toward the Slash Church and encamp at some convenient point west of the Central Railroad. Branch's brigade, of A. P. Hill's division, will also to-morrow evening take position on the Chickahominy near Half Sink. At 3 o'clock Thursday morning, 26th instant, General Jackson will advance on the road leading to Pole Green Church, communicating his march to General Branch, who will immediately cross the Chickahominy and take the road leading to Mechanicsville. As soon as the movements of these columns are discovered, General A. P. Hill, with the rest of his division, will cross the Chickahominy near Meadow Bridge and move direct upon Mechanicsville. To aid his advance, the heavy batteries on the Chickahominy will at the proper time open upon the batteries at Mechanicsville. The enemy being driven from Mechanicsville and the passage across the bridge opened, General Longstreet, with his division and that of General D. H. Hill, will cross the Chickahominy at or near that point, General D. H. Hill moving to the support of General Jackson and General Longstreet supporting General A. P. Hill. The four divisions, keeping in communication with each other and moving en échelon on separate roads, if practicable, the left division in advance, with skirmishers and sharpshooters extending their front, will sweep down the Chickahominy and endeavor to drive the enemy from his position above New Bridge, General Jackson bearing well to his left, turning Beaver Dam Creek and taking the direction toward Cold Harbor. They will then press forward toward the York River Railroad, closing upon the enemy's rear and forcing him down the Chickahominy. Any advance of the enemy toward Richmond will be prevented by vigorously following his rear and crippling and arresting his progress.

II. The divisions under Generals Huger and Magruder will hold their positions in front of the enemy against attack, and make such demonstrations Thursday [June 26] as to discover his operations. Should opportunity offer, the feint will be converted into a real attack, and should an abandonment of his intrenchments by the enemy be discovered, he will be closely pursued.

III. The Third Virginia Cavalry will observe the Charles City road. The Fifth Virginia, the First North Carolina, and the Hampton Legion (cavalry) will observe the Darbytown, Varina, and Osborne roads. Should a movement of the enemy down the Chickahominy be discovered, they will close upon his flank and endeavor to arrest his march.

IV. General Stuart, with the First, Fourth, and Ninth Virginia Cavalry, the cavalry of Cobb's Legion and the Jeff. Davis Legion, will cross the Chickahominy to-morrow and take position to the left of General Jackson's line of march. The main body will be held in reserve, with scouts well extended to the front and left. General Stuart will keep General Jackson informed of the movements of the enemy on his left and will co-operate with him in his advance. The Tenth Virginia Cavalry, Colonel Davis, will remain on the Nine-mile road.

V. General Ransom's brigade, of General Holmes' command, will be placed in reserve on the Williamsburg road by General Huger, to whom he will report for orders.

VI. Commanders of divisions will cause their commands to be provided with three days' cooked rations. The necessary ambulances and ordnance trains will be ready to accompany the divisions and receive orders from their respective commanders. Officers in charge of all trains will invariably remain with them. Batteries and wagons will keep on the right of the road. The chief engineer, Major Stevens, will assign engineer officers to each division, whose duty it will be to make provision for overcoming all difficulties to the progress of the troops. The staff departments will give the necessary instructions to facilitate the movements herein directed.

By command of General Lee:

R. H. CHILTON,
Assistant Adjutant-General.[4]

Writers and historians have offered a variety of interpretations of what Lee intended to do through General Orders No. 75. Joseph Harsh character-

4. U.S. War Department, *The War of the Rebellion: A Compilation of the Official Records of the Union and Confederate Armies*, 128 vols. (Washington, D.C.: GPO, 1880–1901), 11(2):498–99 [hereafter cited as *OR*; all references are to series 1].

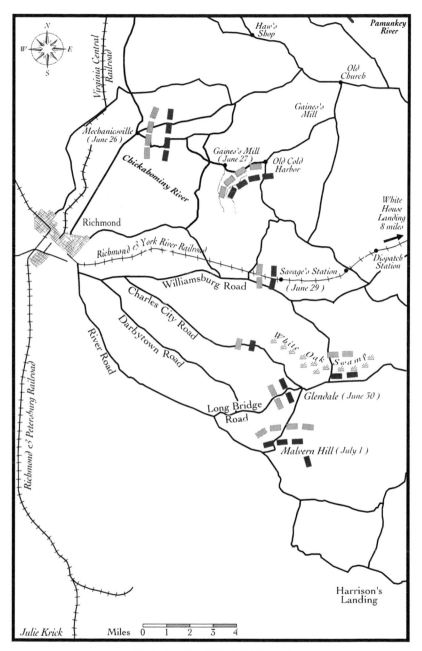

THE SEVEN DAYS BATTLES

ized the Virginian's movement north of the Chickahominy as a "sweeping attack" intended to "crush" Porter's force. Thomas Buell wrote that Lee wished Jackson to "come down surreptitiously from the north and kickoff a surprise attack, hitting Porter on the flank and rear. Simultaneously the other three commands would attack Porter's front. Together they would crush Porter's corps, then sweep down and occupy the north bank of the Chickahominy." John D. McKenzie saw General Orders No. 75 as Lee's plan to "destroy" Porter and suggested that "after destroying Porter, Lee planned to force the rest of the Union army to retreat from the suburbs of Richmond or face similar destruction." Are these reasonable interpretations of Lee's plan, or have writers read such aggressive designs into General Orders No. 75 because of hindsight, influenced, perhaps, by their knowledge of how Lee's offensive turned out?[5]

Nowhere do the words "crush," "destroy," or even "assault" appear in the orders. Instead Lee uses far-less-bellicose verbs to direct his divisions: "Proceed" (one instance), "advance" (three times), "move" or a derivative (four times), "cross" (three times), as well as "sweep," "press," and "bearing." The word "attack" appears twice, both times in section 2, in which Lee discusses operations south of the river. Both times the word is used as a noun—the first time in reference to the possibility of a Federal attack and the second time as a suggestion that Magruder and Maj. Gen. Benjamin Huger be alert for opportunities to profitably convert their feints and diversions at the Richmond defenses into real attacks. It may be significant that the language Lee employs to describe his plan is considerably less pugnacious than that of the writers who have sought to explain his intentions.

How much fighting did Lee intend or expect in making the movement north of the Chickahominy? Should the movement properly be termed an attack or something less specific, such as an "offensive," "advance," or "turning movement?" Maj. Walter H. Taylor and Col. A. L. Long, both of Lee's staff, wrote of the operation as an "attack," but both wrote long after the war and seem to have been using the word in the general sense of a forward

---

5. Joseph P. Harsh, *Confederate Tide Rising: Robert E. Lee and the Making of Southern Strategy, 1861–1862* (Kent, Ohio: Kent State University Press, 1998), 88; Thomas D. Buell, *The Warrior Generals: Combat Leadership in the Civil War* (New York: Three Rivers, 1997), 72; John D. McKenzie, *Uncertain Glory: Lee's Generalship Re-Examined* (New York: Hippocrene, 1997), 75–76.

movement. Lee purportedly used the same word in a discussion of the Seven Days after the war. In 1868 former Confederate colonel William Allan chatted informally with the general in Lexington, Virginia, and recorded for posterity his recollection of the conversation. Lee, according to Allan, explained that "he sent for Jackson to come to Richmond to see him, met him there, and arranged for the attack on McC's right." Lee related that "he prepared everything, & moved a part of his troops over at Mechanicsville to attack in conjunction with Jackson." We cannot be certain whether Lee uttered the word "attack" or Allan supplied it on his own based upon supposition, nor do we know if Lee might have used it casually in the sense of an offensive movement (Lee—or Allan—also used the word "movement" to describe the actions of the day) or specifically to refer to an assault on the Beaver Dam Creek position. E. P. Alexander, also of Lee's staff, likewise calls the movement an "attack" but is more explicit than his fellows in treating Jackson's movements, thereby amplifying points made in General Orders No. 75. Of the Beaver Dam Creek line, Alexander writes, "It had not been intended to attack it with infantry, but to threaten it with artillery, while Jackson passed to the rear and cut off the enemy's retreat." Alexander offers a variation on the same theme when he writes elsewhere that Jackson was to "march around the enemy's flank at Beaver Dam, & cross the creek above it & to take the enemy in rear." Once there Jackson could close the "trap" on the Federals and "completely cut off the retreat of Fitz John Porter's whole corps."[6]

Alexander's interpretation accords very well with Lee's language in General Orders No. 75. Both emphasize movement rather than fighting, and both call for Jackson to move *beyond* the Federal right flank at Beaver Dam Creek. In section 1, where Lee outlines the offensive part of his plan—his advance into enemy territory north of the Chickahominy—Lee calls not for combat

---

6. Walter H. Taylor, *General Lee: His Campaigns in Virginia, 1861–1865* (1906; reprint, Lincoln: University of Nebraska Press, 1994), 58–65; A. L. Long, *Memoirs of Robert E. Lee* (New York: J. M. Stoddert, 1887), 169–70; William Allan, "Memoranda of Conversations with General Robert E. Lee," in *Lee the Soldier,* ed. Gary W. Gallagher (Lincoln: University of Nebraska Press, 1996), 16 (Allan's memoranda resides in the Robert E. Lee Collection, Special Collections, James G. Leyburn Library, Washington and Lee University, Lexington, Va.); Edward Porter Alexander, *Military Memoirs of a Confederate* (New York: Charles Scribner's Sons, 1907), 119; Edward Porter Alexander, *Fighting for the Confederacy: The Personal Recollections of General Edward Porter Alexander,* ed. Gary W. Gallagher (Chapel Hill: University of North Carolina Press, 1989), 96, 100.

but for marching. Jackson was to move toward Cold Harbor and the York River Railroad. Once Jackson's movement triggered a Federal withdrawal from Beaver Dam, Longstreet and the Hills were to cross the river and advance down its northern bank. Twice did Lee suggest the likelihood of fighting, but in neither place, judging by his language, did he expect much resistance. At Mechanicsville the enemy was to be "driven" away from the hamlet and the bridge over the Chickahominy. Later at New Bridge, Longstreet and A. P. Hill were to "drive" the Federals away from their positions above that critical span. Officers routinely used the word "drive" to describe what was done to small forces of the enemy—pickets and skirmishers. Mechanicsville was one mile in advance of the main Federal line at Beaver Dam Creek, and Lee knew it was likely to be occupied by skirmishers rather than any heavy body of troops—indeed he could see as much for himself from the Confederate position at Chickahominy Bluffs, directly opposite Mechanicsville. The Federal position at New Bridge was an artillery emplacement, and infantry had vacated the area. These batteries above New Bridge, and the guns in them, faced southward toward the Confederate positions across the river and were intended to control access to the crossing. There were no defenses for infantrymen, so the few artillerymen at New Bridge would have been helpless against an advance from the west, whence Lee's men would come. The general knew all this from a cavalry reconnaissance a week earlier and from his own observations. Lee appears to have expected fighting at Mechanicsville or New Bridge to be short and slight. Surely he expected combat on June 26, 1862, but such does not appear to have been his goal. We must return again to General Orders No. 75 as our guide to what was in the general's mind. The final two sentences of section 1 seem to clearly express both Lee's goal and his chief concern: "The four divisions, keeping in communication with each other and moving en échelon on separate roads, if practicable, the left division [Jackson's] in advance, with skirmishers and sharpshooters extending their front, will sweep down the Chickahominy and endeavor to drive the enemy from his position above New Bridge, General Jackson bearing well to his left, turning Beaver Dam Creek and taking the direction toward Cold Harbor. They will then press forward toward the York River Railroad, closing upon the enemy's rear and forcing him down the Chickahominy."

These words are especially important when attempting to understand

Jackson's role. We cannot be certain what verbal instructions Lee gave to the Valley general, but far from suggesting that he was to attack the Federal flank at Beaver Dam Creek, Lee specifically states that Jackson was to stay to the left of the position; turn, or outflank, Porter's line; and continue in the direction of Cold Harbor and the railroad beyond. The key to the operation was for Jackson to get not just on the Federal flank but *beyond* and *behind* it. Lee emphasizes this point in a June 25 letter to Jackson in which he suggests specific routes by which he might move his command. Nowhere in this dispatch do the words "attack," "assault," or "fall upon" appear. Instead Lee explicitly stresses marching beyond Beaver Dam Creek *to Cold Harbor*. In speaking of one route, Lee writes that Jackson would be "in a good position either to take the road across Beaver Dam Creek by Walnut Grove Church and Gain's Mill to Cole Harbour; or to pursue the road by Old Raliegh, & Bethesda Church, to Cole Harbour; either of the latter routes would entirely turn Beaver Dam Creek."[7]

On the morning of the twenty-sixth, Lee's plan fell behind schedule immediately, not because of any complexity in General Orders No. 75 but because the normally dutiful and prompt Stonewall Jackson had failed to have his men at the right place on the twenty-fifth and was strangely dilatory in moving them the next morning. From his command post at Chickahominy Bluffs opposite the village of Mechanicsville, Lee waited long into the afternoon of June 26 to hear word of Jackson's arrival on Porter's right flank. The sound of firing to the north announced that Jackson was in contact with the enemy, as were A. P. Hill's skirmishers at Meadow Bridges, but the volume of fire was light, and Porter made no backward movements. Lee had reached

---

7. Robert E. Lee to Thomas J. Jackson, June 25, 1862, George and Catherine Davis Collection, Tulane University, New Orleans, cited in James I. Robertson Jr., *Stonewall Jackson: The Man, the Soldier, the Legend* (New York: Macmillan, 1997), 469. Gen. J. F. C. Fuller's analysis and articulation of the initial phase of G.O. 75 is exceptional for its clarity. Unlike most writers, Fuller views G.O. 75 as primarily a plan of movement to McClellan's rear rather than an assault on his front or flank. Although he also uses the word "attack" in describing the movement, plainly in the most general sense of an offensive movement, Fuller states that "Jackson was to outflank McClellan's position north of that river, and by turning his right and falling on his rear and severing his line of communications, compel him to retire. Then Longstreet and the two Hills would advance on Beaver Dam Creek and assail his retiring front." Fuller, *Decisive Battles of the U.S.A.* (New York: Harper & Brothers, 1942), 191.

a crisis even before his plan had begun to unfold, for he had lost any element of surprise he might have had that morning. He could no longer permit the thirty-three thousand men under Longstreet and the two Hills to lie idle, for the Federals might at any moment react aggressively. The Virginian appears to have adapted his plan to the new circumstances and ordered A. P. Hill to force his way across the Chickahominy and engage Porter.

By the time the firing died out that night, Lee had suffered a stinging defeat at Beaver Dam Creek. Porter's men had stood firm throughout the afternoon, raining bullets and shells upon Confederate attackers. Assault after assault broke upon the Federal positions, and Southern blood flowed freely. Lee had lost fourteen hundred men in the attacks, whereas Porter suffered about four hundred casualties. But while Beaver Dam Creek was a clear tactical defeat and represented a dismal beginning to Lee's efforts, the overall plan as laid out in General Orders No. 75 was alive and well. Lee learned that Jackson was in position behind Porter's flank—he had arrived hours late, well after Lee had unleashed A. P. Hill—and the entire army, save Magruder's holding force, was now north of the Chickahominy and in position to proceed according to plan.

In the aftermath of the defeat at Beaver Dam Creek, early historians groped for explanations as to what went wrong. Jed Hotchkiss of Jackson's staff blamed A. P. Hill and accused him of having "disobeyed orders." The old mapmaker wrote to Jackson's biographer in 1896 that Hill "had no business making an attack until after Jackson had attacked or he had heard his signals." Hotchkiss was predisposed to defend Jackson, especially in matters involving Hill, with whom Stonewall quarreled, but he was probably only voicing the prevailing opinion of his time. Jackson had a reputation for vigor and activity—and, of course, wore a martyr's halo by 1896—while Hill had become known as a temperamental officer given to rashness. Furthermore Hill's report strongly suggests that he had gone off on his own hook that day at Meadow Bridges. "Three o'clock having arrived, and no intelligence from Jackson or Branch," Hill wrote eight months after the battle, "I determined to cross at once rather than hazard the failure of the whole plan by longer deferring it."[8]

8. Jed Hotchkiss to G. F. R. Henderson, Apr. 6, 1896, Hotchkiss Papers, Manuscript Division, Library of Congress, Washington, D.C., Reel 34; OR, 11(2):835.

Unlike Hotchkiss and his contemporaries, however, most twentieth-century historians have tended, until recently, to blame Jackson first and Hill second for the bloody defeat. Recent authors have faulted Lee. In addressing the battle, John D. McKenzie writes, "Rather than calling a halt to the attack, Lee demonstrated his own tendency for direct assaults and supported Hill by ordering two other divisions to his aid in the attack." Edward Bonekemper thought Lee culpable on two points. After lambasting the general for making the bloody assault, he then faults him for not throwing more troops into the meat grinder, writing, "Lee had managed to get only 30 percent of his army involved in the assault." Bonekemper continues, "Mechanicsville provides a first opportunity to analyze the lethal effect of Lee upon the army of Northern Virginia."[9]

The "30 percent" of Lee's army engaged in the assaults at Beaver Dam was perhaps about 30 percent more than the general wished engaged. If the plan for the day was to turn the enemy position and force the Federals to abandon their line, not by frontal assaults but by maneuver, then Lee would have hoped that a very small percentage of his troops—most of them Jackson's—would be engaged in combat. Events did not proceed as he had hoped, however, and when Jackson was far behind schedule, Lee perhaps did give orders for his troops to attack. Most writers who have treated the events of June 26 have, in agreement with Hotchkiss and his compeers, portrayed A. P. Hill as a rogue who attacked without orders. Clifford Dowdey, for example, states that Hill's was "an impulsive act" and "constituted a personal interpretation" of General Orders No. 75.[10] This reading of events, almost universal, ignores the testimony of Maj. Joseph Brent of John Magruder's staff. Carrying news from his chief on the afternoon of the twenty-sixth, Brent found Lee waiting at Chickahominy Bluffs opposite Mechanicsville. The major was impressed with the army commander's anxiety, noting his "restless" eyes that had "the look of a man with fever." Brent delivered his message from Magruder and listened as Lee replied: "We were standing alone, with no one

9. McKenzie, *Uncertain Glory*, 78; Edward H. Bonekemper III, *How Robert E. Lee Lost the Civil War* (Fredericksburg, Va.: Sergeant Kirkland's, 1998), 46.

10. Clifford Dowdey, *The Seven Days: The Emergence of Lee* (Boston: Little, Brown, 1964), 178. See also Stephen W. Sears, *To the Gates of Richmond: The Peninsula Campaign* (New York: Ticknor & Fields, 1992), 201.

near us, when he said, 'I suppose you have come to find out the cause of our delay, as Genl. Magruder must be anxious. We have been waiting for Genl. Jackson, from whom I have not heard, but I cannot wait longer, and have just sent orders to Genl. Hill to cross at Meadow Bridge.' "[11]

Brent's testimony seems to be both reliable and supported by Lee's postwar discussions with Colonel Allan. After the war Allan recorded that Lee said he was, while at Chickahominy Bluffs, "uneasy for fear the enemy seeing his movement and the stripping of his Richmond lines, would push forward and reach the city, and so he attacked at Ellyson and Mechanicsville with what troops he had, and in spite of the formidable works, in order to occupy the enemy and prevent any counter movement." Brent's and Allan's testimony is not in violent opposition to any other account, and taken together with the reports of the principals, suggests the possibility that Lee ordered Hill to attack.[12]

Despite the unexpected and severe losses suffered at Beaver Dam Creek, Lee had every reason to be optimistic that all could yet be well. Reports in the early hours of June 27 told that Porter had abandoned the Beaver Dam Creek line and fallen back eastward. Lee pressed forward, with A. P. Hill's troops in pursuit. About 9:30 A.M Lee stopped at Walnut Grove Church, where he found Jackson. Neither man left a record of what they discussed, but subsequent events suggest Lee made only slight changes in his plans. General Orders No. 75 called for Jackson to move toward Old Cold Harbor, deep in the Federal rear, and when Jackson left Walnut Grove—strengthened by the ten thousand men of D. H. Hill's division—his target remained the same. The importance of this movement is obvious. While Lee directed A. P.

11. Joseph Lancaster Brent, *Memoirs of the War between the States* (New Orleans: Fontana, 1940), 161.

12. Allan, "Memoranda of Conversations with General Robert E. Lee," 16. Both Hill and Lee employed ambiguous language in their reports. Lee made no comment on Hill's statement, "I determined to cross at once rather than hazard the failure of the whole plan," but that declaration, even if interpreted literally to mean that Hill made the decision on his own, does not preclude the possibility that Lee sent orders to advance. We certainly have no reason to suspect Hill of deception (though knowing him as an ambitious young man, we might fairly conclude that he would be willing to appear in his superior's eyes as an energetic and aggressive commander unafraid to seize the initiative), but neither do we have reason to disbelieve Brent, who was a disinterested bystander. The two accounts do not seem irreconcilable.

Hill and Longstreet to advance against the Federals from the west, he sent more than half of his available troops on the north side of the river on another sweeping march, a turning movement, with the hope of falling upon the Union supply line and retreat route.

Around 2:00 P.M. A. P. Hill's men encountered resistance. Small creeks and their deep ravines cut the high plateaus north of the Chickahominy near where Dr. William Gaines maintained a mill on Powhite Creek. Lee had expected that the enemy would make a stand on the steep slopes of the creek, but as Hill's men pressed on, the Federal skirmishers steadily fell back. Lee realized that the enemy was not standing at Powhite, and not until Hill's men encountered the main Federal line in field works on Boatswain's Swamp did the Confederate commander know the location of his enemy. He brought Longstreet's division forward and deployed it on Hill's right. Tactically the situation was very similar to that at Beaver Dam Creek the previous day. Lee had strong forces in hand and in position on the enemy's front, awaiting the movements of Jackson's column endeavoring to turn the enemy's right flank. Once again Jackson was behind schedule.

After a long, confused march in which his column had taken an unnecessary detour, Jackson finally arrived at Old Cold Harbor and paused. In his report he admits that he was apprehensive because he was "unacquainted with the ground." When observing the existing battle lines, he feared that if he pressed forward, "our troops would be mistaken for the enemy and be fired into." Jackson was badly disoriented. In the conference at Walnut Grove Church, Lee apparently had not given him specific orders about what to do after reaching Old Cold Harbor. When the Valley general arrived at the intersection, he found no representative of Lee to assist him in deploying his troops (though the commander had sent staff officers for that purpose), so he acted in accordance with his understanding of Lee's intentions as expressed at the church. Jackson was under the impression that his was a reactionary force—a set piece that would respond to whatever transpired elsewhere on the battlefield. In his report he states, "hoping that Generals A. P. Hill and Longstreet would soon drive the Federals toward me, I directed General D. H. Hill to move his division [into position to cover] an open space, across which I hoped the enemy was to be driven."[13]

13. OR, 11(2):553.

In no case is our ignorance of what was said in the Walnut Grove meeting more frustrating. Jackson's assertion that he was to be the anvil upon which A. P. Hill and Longstreet were to smash the Federals seems born of a certainty about what Lee intended. This interpretation has influenced generations of historians, including Douglas Southall Freeman, Lee's principal biographer, and James I. Robertson, author of the definitive life of Jackson. We cannot be sure what Lee said to Jackson at Walnut Grove, but Jackson's interpretation stands in direct opposition to the intentions and expectations Lee expresses in his report, in which he speaks of Jackson's late arrival at Old Cold Harbor delaying "The attack on our left."[14] This statement, coupled with the outline of the plan expressed in General Orders No. 75, plainly suggests that Lee had in mind a drive southward toward the river and the railroad. Even if such a thrust by D. H. Hill and Jackson did not succeed in cutting the Federal supply line or McClellan's principal retreat route (Grapevine Bridge), any advance by Jackson would have kept the Northerners on the defensive—all advantages for Lee. Jackson was not the anvil, in Lee's view, but the hammer, and when he did not strike, he placed the Confederates in a bind.

Once again, while waiting for Jackson, Lee attacked with A. P. Hill. Through the long afternoon, Hill's regiments gallantly entered the thick woods north and west of Boatswain's Creek, and each time they came back bloodied and reduced. While Hill's men fought, Lee reserved his heavier blows. "The arrival of Jackson on our left was momentarily expected," he later writes, "and it was supposed that his approach would cause the extension of the enemy's line in that direction. Under this impression Longstreet was held back until this movement should commence."[15] Concealing portions of his strength and showing the Federals only what he wished them to see, Lee waited for his opponent to weaken himself by moving to meet the threat at Old Cold Harbor. If the Federals did as Lee wanted, he would unleash Longstreet to hit what he hoped would be the weakened Federal left.

The arrival of D. H. Hill's men, the advance portion of Jackson's column, at Old Cold Harbor did not lead to the hoped-for extension of the Federal line, and by the time Jackson arrived with the rest of his command, much of

14. Ibid., 492.
15. Ibid.

the day's light had fled. Delays had once again played havoc with Lee's plan, and he was forced to improvise. While Jackson's men were finally getting into position, Lee sent a message to Longstreet to ask that he make a feint to draw some of the pressure off of A. P. Hill. The general immediately moved forward, but when he saw the strength of the Federal position in the Boatswain's ravine, he realized that a half-hearted diversion would be futile. Longstreet decided at once to convert the demonstration into a full-scale assault. With the fading daylight, Lee apparently decided to force the issue and called for a general assault all along the line.

For the second successive day, Lee extemporized and suffered dearly. His army surged through the forests and ravines and in a few hours won a stunning victory, driving the Federals from the field, capturing thousands of prisoners, and forcing George McClellan to deal with what must have looked very much that evening like a strategic catastrophe. The Federal commander had all but lost his supply line and was forced to decide whether he would fight to save it or flee to safety.

Despite the clear Confederate victory, Lee's critics have focused instead on the cost: The Army of Northern Virginia lost more than nine thousand men killed, wounded, or missing. Gaines's Mill was, at the time it was fought, the second-largest bloodletting in American history, and some writers place the blame for that on Lee's shoulders. Thomas Buell, apparently writing of A. P. Hill's attacks through the afternoon, thought that "Lee continued to throw troops into the inferno incrementally, regiment by regiment, each was in turn consumed by the fire." In using Hill's men so roughly, was Lee merely gratifying what one writer has called "his own tendency for direct assaults"? This seems a difficult contention to support. A more reasonable explanation is the one Lee himself offered for the advance at Beaver Dam Creek to Major Brent a day earlier and to Colonel Allan six years later. With the element of surprise gone, the general was concerned that McClellan would discover and exploit the weaknesses in the Confederate deployment, specifically Magruder's gossamer-thin lines south of the Chickahominy. This concern was no less acute on June 27 at Gaines's Mill than it had been a day earlier, and in fact it might have conceivably been more so. He attacked with Hill to hold the enemy's attention and obscure his own weakness until Jackson was in position. In 1868 Lee explained to Allan that "he was forced to push forward and attack at Gaine's Mill with all his energy. Otherwise with a large part of his

army really farther from Richd. than McClellan was, disaster was to be appre-
hended." Lee did not have the luxury at Gaines's Mill of being extravagant
with time and chary of lives.[16]

The victory at Gaines's Mill brought to a close the first phase of Lee's
offensive. Two days of aggressive warfare had overthrown weeks of work by
McClellan and his officers. Lee had derailed the Federals' advance on Richmond and beaten them in a pitched battle. The cost had been great, but the
Northerners had suffered dearly as well. Yet not all writers have seen this
first phase as a victory for Lee. Edward Bonekemper believed that Lee had
planned a "complex, coordinated Mechanicsville attack" on Porter's force, in
which the general "hoped to drive it back, break the Union supply line from
White House on the York [sic] River to the Union army, and capture that
supply base, as well as the Union supply trains at Cold Harbor. Those goals
might have been achieved more efficiently and simply by going around the
north flank of McClellan's army instead of launching a complicated frontal
assault."[17] Going around the north flank of McClellan's army, however, is
precisely what Lee was attempting to do on June 26 and 27, as evidenced by

16. Buell, *Warrior Generals*, 79; Allan, "Memoranda of Conversations with General Robert E.
Lee," 16. In 1863, nine months after the battle, Lee wrote that on the afternoon of June 27, he
had believed that he had faced the "principal part of the Federal Army." He apparently thought
McClellan had reinforced the Federal force north of the Chickahominy, with the intention of
fighting for his supply line. What effect this belief had on Lee's intentions is difficult to know,
for he does not discuss the issue in his report. Calm reflection, of which Lee might not have had
the advantage, could have suggested to him that a strengthening of the Federals on the north
bank correspondingly reduced the immediacy of the threat south of the river. Lee's 1868 remarks, however, suggest that he did not see matters this way. Furthermore, even if McClellan
had strengthened his northern wing, such a move would not lessen the precariousness of Lee's
divided position. The Virginian's belief that "the principal part of the Federal Army" was before
him at Gaines's Mill could only have heightened his concern for both wings of his own army
and made him more impatient for swift action by Jackson. In fact the specter of Federal reinforcement of the north bank made a vigorous movement by Jackson upon the railroad beyond
the Federal right even more desirable, for while McClellan's reinforcement of the lines on Boatswain's Swamp made that position tactically stronger, it made his strategic situation more vulnerable. If Jackson could turn the enemy position and move upon his rear beyond Old Cold
Harbor, a greater proportion of the Federal army would have been turned, endangered, and
forced to retreat by the few available bridges over the Chickahominy. *OR*, 11(2):492.

17. Bonekemper, *How Lee Lost the Civil War*, 45.

GAINES'S MILL
Courtesy Library of Congress

his orders to and deployment of Jackson's and D. H. Hill's divisions. While
Lee did launch frontal assaults on both days (whether they were "complicated" is open to debate), he had neither planned nor wished for either and
ordered them, by his own testimony, only because his efforts to turn the Federal northern flank were unsuccessful.

Having abandoned his line of communications, McClellan had two options. He could fall back eastward, down the Peninsula, whence he had come
six weeks earlier, and reestablish a supply base at Cumberland Landing or
even Yorktown, or he could hasten southward from the Chickahominy to the
James and establish a new base under the protection of U.S. Navy gunboats.
Lee could not divine which option the Federal commander would choose.
The Virginian knew McClellan had his men on the move—he could see the
clouds of dust above the trees south of the Chickahominy—but he did not
know where the Federals were bound. If McClellan moved eastward, Lee's
army was in a good position to pursue along the north bank of the Chickahominy. For this reason, Lee wrote later, he deemed it "injudicious" to shift

the Army of Northern Virginia "until the intention of General McClellan was discovered."[18]

While he waited, Lee sent detachments to watch Bottoms Bridge, Long Bridge, and other crossings on the lower Chickahominy, and he urged his troops south of the river to be vigilant. The thick forests and McClellan's fortifications near Seven Pines kept prying Southern eyes at a distance, so not until the morning of June 29 did Lee receive the cheering news that Mc-Clellan had abandoned his works there. If Lee had retained any lingering suspicions that the Federals might launch an assault on Richmond, he could now dismiss them. McClellan was in retreat. Soon came the valuable news that McClellan had made no move during the night toward the crossings leading east over the Chickahominy, so sometime early that morning Lee concluded that the Army of the Potomac was headed for the James, and he began to plan accordingly.

Lee never revealed his intentions for June 29, and so historians have guessed at them. Not surprisingly Freeman has been the most influential of the theorists. More surprising, however, is that in synthesizing his theory, Freeman violated his own rule against presuming to know what was in the general's mind. His explication of the Seven Days, especially the second phase of the operation, seems to rely significantly upon Longstreet's *From Manassas to Appomattox*. While the memoir of a key participant is very often a dependable source in understanding a series of events, the reliability of Longstreet's book seems questionable, at least with respect to the Seven Days. The general wrote thirty years after the war, when he was in his seventies and in very poor health. He employed an editor or ghostwriter to produce the manuscript, and we do not know the extent of that man's influence on the general's historical testimony. Furthermore Longstreet could not help but emphasize his own column's participation in the operation, especially, perhaps, at the distance of more than three decades. The questionable worth of the old general's testimony thus impugns the value of Freeman's interpretation.

Longstreet's perception of the pursuit on June 29 and 30 seems to turn on the idea that his was the key column and that attacking and cutting off

18. *OR*, 11(2):493.

the enemy en route to the James was the army commander's chief goal. Lee, he says, "decided to intercept the enemy in the neighborhood of Charles City cross-roads [that is, Glendale]." His column, Longstreet writes, was dispatched "to interpose between the enemy and the James River." He believed that Lee wished to capture or destroy the Federals short of the river, writing, "General McClellan's army was in his [Lee's] power and must be our prize, never to reach the new base." The possibility of hurting the Federals undoubtedly animated Lee, but where and with which of his columns to do this we must admit remains uncertain.[19]

Lee's deployment of his columns on the morning of June 29 suggests that he wished to lose no time in pursuing and striking the enemy. His units were to advance in a broad arc, all moving on generally convergent paths. Jackson, with D. H. Hill, was to push south and cross the Chickahominy and pursue the Federals toward White Oak Swamp. Magruder and Huger, who had been holding the Richmond defenses, were to strike eastward to Savage's Station and on the Charles City Road respectively and press the retreating enemy in its rear and flank. Longstreet, with A. P. Hill, was to countermarch from Gaines's Mill to New Bridge, sweep behind the advancing Magruder, and march southeastward on the Darbytown Road toward McClellan's route to the James. It was a good plan, sending three large columns in pursuit on four different roads, but while Lee clearly articulated this plan of pursuit, he was less clear about what he hoped to accomplish by it. Where was the heavy blow to land and when?

Here Freeman stepped into the breach. The Richmonder believed Lee intended that Longstreet's would be the main column—the striking column—and implied it was Lee's intention to "get in front of McClellan's moving army." Freeman suggested that Lee must have realized when he was formulating his plans on June 29 that time was too short to interdict the Federal column anywhere on its route that day. In a vaguely conceived surmise, he went on to declare that on the morning of the twenty-ninth, "there

19. James Longstreet, "'The Seven Days,' Including Frayser's Farm," in *Battles and Leaders of the Civil War*, ed. Robert Underwood Johnson and Clarence Clough Buel, 4 vols. (New York: Century, 1887–88), 2:399; James Longstreet, *From Manassas to Appomattox* (Philadelphia: J. B. Lippincott, 1896), 131, 148.

were then two battles to be planned—first the attack on the rear guard that day and a general engagement on the 30th."[20]

This thesis begs two questions. First, why would Lee intend to deliver his crushing blow south of White Oak Swamp, ignoring the great advantage the swamp gave to him? A military engineer of long experience, Lee would certainly have recognized the potential of the swamp as a barrier to McClellan— wide belts of thick, wet woods on both sides of the stream with few crossings (three common fords and one bridge all served by narrow roads or mere trails). Second, why would Lee ignore that he had before him a beaten and disorganized army in retreat over unfamiliar roads through a densely forested pocket of land obstructed on three sides by thick swamps? It seems reasonable to expect that he would have been eager to turn the swamp to his advantage, just as he would later use the Wilderness to trap the Army of the Potomac at Chancellorsville and during the opening rounds of the Overland Campaign. Because defeat in the White Oak Swamp pocket would likely shatter McClellan's army, jam the few crossings, and compel thousands to surrender and thousands more to flee in chaos through the swamp, it seems likely that Lee would have considered the advantages of thrusting at McClellan's rear in the pocket of land formed by the sickle-shaped wetland. Those Federals who did escape to the south side of White Oak would find Longstreet and Hill in position to rout any remaining organized force and scoop up the tide of fugitives headed for the James.

Allowing the Federals to escape White Oak Swamp would have surrendered significant advantages that Lee, due to his experience and training, would not have wanted to relinquish. Thus the plan of operations that Longstreet and Freeman attribute to the commanding general seems unreasonable. Nothing from Lee's mouth or pen supports the Longstreet-Freeman thesis that he wished to permit the Federals to safely cross to the south side of the swamp before attacking them, that he had planned two battles, or that he wished to fight the decisive battle south of White Oak Swamp on June

20. Douglas Southall Freeman, *R. E. Lee: A Biography*, 4 vols. (New York: Charles Scribner's Sons, 1934–35), 2:167. Clifford Dowdey does not cite the sources of his conclusions in *The Seven Days*, but, writing after Freeman, he too argues that Lee planned to fight the principal battle on June 30 south of White Oak Swamp in the vicinity of Glendale. Dowdey, *Seven Days*, 261.

30.[21] In fact, evidence suggests that just the opposite might have been true—that Lee hoped to land the heavy blow on June 29 north of White Oak Swamp.

When disposing his army on the twenty-ninth, Lee retained more than half of his troops—all of Jackson's and D. H. Hill's and most of Magruder's divisions—north of the swamp, all with orders to drive vigorously eastward or southward into the concave pocket formed by the Chickahominy and its tributary swamp. Scarcely a quarter of the troops under Lee's command made the looping march southward with Longstreet and A. P. Hill to intercept the Federal retreat at Glendale near Frayser's Farm. Surely Lee would not have massed his most powerful force north of White Oak Swamp if he intended to deliver his knockout blow south of it.

Magruder and Jackson were to converge near Savage's Station, and Lee's language in his report suggests he expected significant results from the collaboration. After the movement failed—Magruder attacked haltingly and Jackson not at all—Lee wrote that the Federals were able to withdraw at their own pace and "cross White Oak Swamp without interruption." Clearly he had wished for the Federal retreat to be "interrupted" north of the swamp, and when Magruder failed to do so, Lee openly expressed his displeasure. Nine months later, when writing his report, Lee hinted that he had hoped for great results at Savage's Station, stating that although Magruder's troops had fought well and hurt the Federals, "the result was not decisive."[22]

In consideration of Lee's intentions on June 29, a dispatch from army headquarters to Brig. Gen. J. E. B. Stuart that day deserves special consideration. Sometime probably after noon, Lee's assistant adjutant general, Robert H. Chilton, wrote to the cavalry general, then operating on Jackson's left: "The Gen'l Comd'g requests that you will watch the Chicahominy as far as Forge Bridge, ascertain if any attempt will be made in that direction by the enemy, advising Genl. Jackson, who will resist their passage until reinforced.

---

21. In writing to Jefferson Davis to explain the situation and his plans on June 29, for example, Lee gave no special emphasis to the movement of Longstreet's column. Robert E. Lee to Jefferson Davis, July 2, 1862, in *Wartime Papers of Robert E. Lee*, 206.

22. *OR*, 11(2):494; Robert E. Lee to John B. Magruder, June 29, 1862, in *Wartime Papers of Robert E. Lee*, 205.

If you find that they have passed down below where they cannot cross, leave a force to watch movements which may be made & recross yourself to this side for further operations."[23]

Jackson might be excused for not knowing just what he was to do. According to Lee, Jackson had orders to "push pursuit vigorously" south of the river. How, Jackson might have wondered, was he to pursue vigorously south of the Chickahominy and at the same time cooperate with Stuart in resisting the passage of the Federals north of it? The Valley general apparently did not seek a clarification from Lee but arrived at his own interpretation, apparently deciding that circumstances had changed and Lee no longer wished him to pursue the enemy. Instead he was to maintain his position on the north side of the river and hold his command in readiness to cooperate with Stuart. Jackson endorsed the dispatch at 3:45 P.M.: "Genl. Ewell will remain near Dispatch Station & myself near my present position."[24]

Jackson was obviously confident that his interpretation of the dispatch was correct, despite that it had not explicitly changed any previous orders to him from Lee. The order was vaguely worded enough that Jackson's reading of it seems reasonable, and we might assume, as perhaps Jackson did, that some new development during the day had caused Lee to adapt his plan. Later in the day, however, when he learned that Jackson had not moved, Lee seems to have been flummoxed. He wrote Magruder: "I learn from Major Taylor that you are under the impression that General Jackson has been ordered not to support you [in the movement at Savage's Station and on toward White Oak Swamp]. On the contrary, he has been directed to do so, and to push pursuit vigorously." This clarification came in a note in which Lee upbraided Magruder for having made "so little progress" in pursuit of the enemy and declared that "the pursuit should be most vigorous. I must urge you, then, again to press on his rear rapidly and steadily. We must lose no more time or he will escape us entirely."[25]

In light of this almost frantic appeal for vigor and zeal to one commander in the enemy's rear, it seems inconceivable that Lee would have consciously

23. R. H. Chilton to J. E. B. Stuart, June 29, 1862, doc. SA 71, J. E. B. Stuart Papers, Huntington Library, San Marino, Calif., cited in Robertson, *Stonewall Jackson*, 488.

24. Ibid.

25. *Wartime Papers of Robert E. Lee*, 205.

ordered the other commander in that sector, Jackson, into idleness for the better part of the afternoon. Far more likely is that Jackson was completely led astray by Chilton's words, or that Chilton misunderstood Lee's meaning or words during dictation. Given the clarity of his wishes as expressed in his evening dispatch to Magruder, Lee could not have wished the possibility of Jackson's cooperation with Stuart to take precedence over his orders to cooperate with Magruder. It seems plain that Jackson, Chilton, or both misunderstood Lee's intentions, emphasized the wrong option in the commander's design, and in so doing wrecked his plan for June 29.

Lee certainly wished to hit McClellan wherever he could do so to advantage, so it seems unlikely that he would have let such an opportunity pass on June 29 by planning, as Freeman suggests, a mere rear-guard action north of the swamp. Where he wished his "main blow" to land we cannot tell, but Freeman's supposition that he intended it to fall south of the swamp, though possibly correct, seems ill founded. Lee's deployments, his remarks in his report, his open disappointment with Magruder's performance at Savage's Station, and the obvious topographical significance of White Oak Swamp as an obstacle all have been largely ignored as indicators of what Lee's intentions might have been that day, while Freeman's interpretation has been accepted unquestioningly. These factors conspire to at least suggest that events north of the swamp on that day were far more important—and disappointing—to Lee than Freeman and others have guessed.

If we cannot be sure of Lee's intent on the twenty-ninth, we can feel more certain of his goals the following day. Three columns—Jackson's, Huger's, and Longstreet's (with A. P. Hill in tow)—moving on three roads were to converge on the Federals south of White Oak Swamp in the vicinity of Glendale. We do not know how much Lee knew about the topography of the area or what he understood of the road network south of White Oak Swamp, but he certainly knew that the Federals would have to pass through Glendale en route to the James and that that passage could not be rapid enough to deny the Confederates the opportunity to strike a blow. Jackson was to continue pressing on the Federal rear in the hope of inducing haste and confusion. Huger likewise was to seize or threaten the crossroads, interdicting the Federal escape route and, at least, compelling the Northerners to devote troops to its defense. Longstreet and A. P. Hill were in position to threaten the rear of any force opposing Huger or Jackson. Although the Federals had the advantage of interior lines in opposing Jackson, Huger, and Longstreet, Lee had good reason to believe that those defensive positions were makeshift and the troops in them were harried, weary, and vulnerable. A breakthrough by any of the three converging columns might collapse the entire Federal line and lead to a rout. Longstreet and Hill on the Federal flank and rear were in position to, if all went well, deliver a coup de grâce somewhere near the crossroads.

Lee met with Jackson on the morning of June 30 at Savage's Station. The two men stood in the dust by the Williamsburg Road, and Lee again gave his junior orders for the day. Although neither general recorded what was said, Lee later wrote that he ordered Jackson "to pursue the enemy on the road he had taken." This road led to the principal bridge over White Oak Swamp. Was Jackson to merely follow the enemy column? Was he to press it vigorously to and beyond the swamp? After the campaign Lee wrote in his report that Jackson on that day had "been unable to force the passage of White Oak Swamp . . . ," a statement that seems to leave little doubt that he expected vigor out of Jackson and wished him on the south bank of White Oak rather than on the north.[26] In the course of events, however, when Jackson reached the swamp late in the morning of June 30 and found the bridge destroyed and the enemy in strong force on the south bank, he settled into an artillery duel, rejected opportunities to get his infantry across the stream, and so passed the day in a stalemate. Whatever the reasons for Jackson's restraint on June 30, it seems clear that Lee did not order it.

The Confederate commander, meanwhile, spent the afternoon southwest of the Glendale intersection with Longstreet's and A. P. Hill's troops. He could hear Jackson engaged with the enemy. He could hear Huger engaged on the Charles City Road. Yet as the afternoon passed, the Federals did not weaken their positions around Glendale. Longstreet's artillery dueled with the Federals and his infantry lightly probed the enemy position, but Lee held the two divisions back until he better understood what was happening with Jackson and Huger. Late in the afternoon Lee personally reconnoitered Malvern Hill, some three miles south of Glendale and just north of the James, and saw that the Federals had crowned the hill with artillery, battery after battery of rifled guns, including 20- and 24-pounders. How this information

26. *OR*, 11(2):495.

affected Lee's decisions that day is difficult to know, except for the obvious realization that Malvern Hill was a much stronger position than the enemy occupied at Glendale. If Lee hoped to reap any advantage out of the Federals' chaotic flight, he would almost certainly have to do so before they reached the protection of the guns at Malvern Hill.

After his reconnaissance Lee rejoined Longstreet on the Long Bridge Road and soon thereafter ordered the Georgian to send his men against the Federal positions. It was late in the afternoon; perhaps five hours of daylight remained. Lee's report makes clear that he had not intended, nor did he wish, to attack only with Longstreet and Hill at Frayser's Farm. Although the two divisions were in position early in the day, Lee waited for hours before he sent them forward, hours in which he hoped for success from Jackson and Huger in the rear of the Federals opposing Longstreet. He was confident that had Huger and Jackson cooperated in the attack by Longstreet and Hill, "the result would have proved most disastrous to the enemy."[27] Instead Longstreet and, for the third time in five days, Hill suffered severe losses, and the enemy escaped to fight again.

Lee met informally with his commanders early on July 1 and learned that McClellan had strengthened his already strong position on Malvern Hill, and he pondered what to do next. His juniors offered opinions about what course to follow: D. H. Hill stated that McClellan should be left alone in his powerful position; Longstreet is said to have favored an attack. Lee knew the Federals had suffered severely at Glendale and had lost a large number of guns (sixteen). He had seen the battlefield at Glendale, on which nearly sixty-five hundred men had become casualties (making the fight the fifth largest battle in American history to that point). The general had every reason to suspect that the Federals were nearer the breaking point than ever before, and he undoubtedly wished to take advantage of the opportunity to push them beyond that point. He decided to investigate whether an opportunity existed for decisively defeating McClellan at Malvern Hill.

Other writers have treated the battle at Malvern Hill well, though not yet fully. What seems clear is that after preparing for action, deploying his infantry, and testing the Federal position with a converging artillery fire, Lee decided an attack was not feasible. Miscommunication and misunderstandings

27. Ibid.

then intervened. Only when reports led him to believe that his artillery bombardment had been successful in weakening the Federal line, that probes by the infantry held promise, and that portions of the Federal line were retreating did he authorize an infantry assault. All this proved incorrect, however, and the Confederate troops marched into a slaughter rarely matched in the history of modern war.

Writers have had just cause in criticizing Lee's performance at Malvern Hill. He mishandled the tactical arrangements, and few commanders can expect laurels for such a defeat. That Lee might be responsible for some of these errors of command is not disputed, but it seems difficult to fault his intentions that day. He wished to strike the defeated enemy one more time and had reason to believe that such a blow could pay immense dividends, possibly leading to the destruction of the Federal army. Lee prepared to deliver the blow but withheld it when he could find no way to strike to advantage. That he later attacked based on erroneous information and with disastrous result is irrelevant when considering what he meant to do.

And what did he mean to do? By far the most influential sentence in the literature of the Seven Days Battles is Lee's summation in his report: "Under ordinary circumstances the Federal Army should have been destroyed."[28] This simple statement has led historians to surmise that Lee's intention, beginning with General Orders No. 75 and continuing with every battle from Mechanicsville to the James, was to destroy McClellan's army. Because Lee hammered at McClellan for a week, he gave the impression that he was attempting to destroy his enemy, and his later statement that the enemy *should have been* destroyed only reinforces the assumption. This seems a difficult interpretation to support, chiefly because it rests to a large degree upon supposition.

Lee certainly did attempt to annihilate McClellan's army during the Seven Days. He attempted to destroy a portion of it at Gaines's Mill, and he attempted on three consecutive days—June 29, June 30, and July 1—to destroy the fleeing Federals south of the Chickahominy. But to say that Lee attempted this during the week-long operation is not to say that he set out with that goal in mind, nor is it to say that he was, from first to last, transfixed by the idea of destroying McClellan. A contemporaneous reading of

28. Ibid., 497.

General Orders No. 75—that is, a reading devoid of hindsight—reveals a plan for a turning movement, a maneuver designed primarily to *move* the enemy army rather than destroy it. On June 28, after two days of operations, Lee found that he had succeeded in moving the enemy. As he writes in his report: "The siege of Richmond was raised, and the object of a campaign, which had been prosecuted after months of preparation at an enormous expenditure of men and money, completely frustrated."[29] From this perspective the campaign could be judged a success. But on June 29 Lee found that he had not only succeeded in dislodging McClellan's army and delivering Richmond but also created a situation from which he might reap an even greater victory. With the Federals in retreat, cut off from their supplies, and moving over unfamiliar roads and through swamps on a line of march generally across Lee's front, the Virginian saw that he had the chance to inflict great damage on, and perhaps even destroy, the enemy force. A series of mishaps, miscommunications, and personal failures by subordinates on those three critical days south of the Chickahominy prevented Lee from landing what might have been a killing blow at Savage's Station, Frayser's Farm, or Malvern Hill. These occurrences were what Lee considered extraordinary circumstances, and he believed they had cost him a precious opportunity to annihilate the enemy—an opportunity not inherent in the design of General Orders No. 75 but serendipitously presented by the execution of it.

Can we declare that we know what was in the mind of Robert E. Lee in the last week of June 1862? We can read his report and those of others. We can consider supplementary evidence and say with confidence that we possess some clues to what he was thinking and trying to do. And we can say that he wished to avert the impending siege of Richmond by disrupting Federal operations. Lee developed a bold plan that would dislodge the Union army and permit him to damage it if the opportunity arose. After having both moved and injured McClellan's forces, thereby deranging the Federals' plans, Lee realized he had the opportunity to inflict even greater damage on the enemy. He believed it possible to destroy the Federal army, and he intended to try, developing a plan of pursuit designed to land heavy blows. But we can only theorize about where he wished those blows to fall, and there we must stop. We must at some point admit the limits of our knowledge, and in con-

29. Ibid.

sidering Lee during the Seven Days, we are perhaps wise to admit our limit sooner rather than later. Douglas Southall Freeman, despite his presumptions about Lee, was frank enough to confess his own weaknesses. To his audience in Richmond just weeks before his death, Freeman said: "You can, as a rule, gentlemen, tell the student from the man who is pursuing just a simple, momentary delight by the humility of the student as compared with the confidence of the man who has read or studied very little. It is not an encouraging thing to say, but the more you probe, the less confident you are that you know precisely what occurred."[30]

30. Freeman, "Address," 10.

Lee, Grant, and "Prescience" in the Overland Campaign

GORDON C. RHEA

R OBERT E. LEE'S contemporaries and subsequent generations of historians have rightly placed the Army of Northern Virginia's commander
in the foremost rank of American generals. Portraits of Lee as tactician invariably invoke the Virginian's facility to divine his opponents' intentions.
Frequently cited is his ability to fathom Ulysses S. Grant's plans during the
Overland Campaign. In May 1864 the Southern war correspondent Peter W.
Alexander wrote from the bloody fields of Spotsylvania Court House that the
"way in which [Lee] unravels the most intricate combination of his antagonist, the instinctive knowledge he seems to possess of all his plans and designs, the certainty with which he moves his own army and makes his own
dispositions, is truly wonderful." Lee's skill, Alexander suggested, stemmed
from "prescience," and proof of this talent, Alexander asserted, could be seen
in the Southern commander's anticipation of Grant's attack in the Wilderness and of the Federal army's shift three days later to Spotsylvania Court
House. Writing home that same month, Lee's aide Walter H. Taylor marveled
that the general "seemed to divine [Grant's] intention." Expounding on this
theme after the war, Taylor claimed that the "faculty of General Lee, of dis-
covering, as if by intuition, the intention and purpose of his opponent, was
a very remarkable one."[1]

John B. Gordon, one of Lee's lieutenants, fuelled the myth of Lee's prescience when he penned his memoirs nearly forty years after the war. On the

1. Peter W. Alexander Despatch, May 18, 1864, *Daily (Columbia) South Carolinian*, May 29,
1864; Walter H. Taylor to Bettie, May 23, 1864, in *Lee's Adjutant: The Wartime Letters of Colonel
Walter Herron Taylor, 1862–1865*, ed. R. Lockwood Tower (Columbia: University of South Carolina Press, 1995), 162; Walter H. Taylor, *General Lee: His Campaigns in Virginia, 1861–1865, with
Personal Reminiscences* (Norfolk, Va.: Nusbaum, 1906), 238.

morning of May 7, 1864, Gordon wrote, Lee informed him that Grant "will move his army to Spotsylvania Court House." Gordon noted that his postwar examination of Union records established that Lee had foretold Grant's plans at the very moment that Grant was issuing orders for the movement. "Let it be remembered that this announcement by General Grant of his purpose was made at 6:30 A.M. on the 7th," Gordon reminded his readers, "and that General Lee's prediction was uttered on the same morning and at nearly the same hour, when there was no possibility of his having gained any direct knowledge of his antagonist's intentions." The Georgian attributed Lee's clairvoyance to his capacity of thinking as his opponent thought. "Grant stood in his own place and calculated from his own standpoint," Gordon explained. "Lee put himself in Grant's place and calculated from the same standpoint; and both found the same answer—Spotsylvania." Lee's eminent biographer, Douglas Southall Freeman, built upon Gordon's theme. "The accurate reasoning of a trained and precise mind is the prime explanation of all these achievements," he posited. As Freeman saw it, Lee would collect all available information, visualize the military problem at hand, and "project himself mentally across the lines to the position of his adversary." Once in his opponent's shoes, Lee would then imagine the "logical thing" for his antagonist to do.[2]

The idea that Lee possessed an uncanny ability to fathom the plans of his opponents—whether from divine inspiration or from the workings of a precise and logical mind—has become an accepted part of the Lee tradition. Alexander, Taylor, Gordon, Freeman, and a host of other writers have sug-

2. John B. Gordon, *Reminiscences of the Civil War* (New York: Charles Scribner's Sons, 1903), 268–70; Douglas Southall Freeman, *R. E. Lee: A Biography*, 4 vols. (New York: Charles Scribner's Sons, 1934–35), 4:170–71. Gordon embellished many stories in his memoirs, including this one. He undoubtedly rode and spoke with Lee on May 7, though not until the afternoon. While Lee might have predicted to Gordon that Grant was planning to advance to Spotsylvania Court House, Lee could not have done so at 6:30 A.M., when Grant was writing his dispatch. See U.S. War Department, *The War of the Rebellion: A Compilation of the Official Records of the Union and Confederate Armies,* 128 vols. (Washington, D.C.: GPO, 1880–1901), 36(2):790 [hereafter cited as *OR*; all references are to series 1 unless otherwise noted], which states that "the General is now starting to visit Ewell's lines." See also Franklin Gardner Walter Diary, May 7, 1864, Fredericksburg and Spotsylvania National Military Park Library, which says, "In the afternoon rode with General Lee along our line to the left. Found Gen. Ewell's headquarters."

gested that the Virginian's augury reached its highest state of evolution in his dealings with Grant. "Grant's bludgeoning tactics and flank shifts [Lee] quickly fathomed," Freeman flatly asserts, "but he was progressively less able to combat them as his own strength declined."[3]

The first three weeks of combat between Grant and Lee provide fertile ground for exploring whether Lee in fact "quickly fathomed" the working of Grant's mind. These blood-drenched days of relentless maneuver and combat, from May 4, 1864, through May 25, 1864, encompass the Wilderness, Spotsylvania, and North Anna River actions. They include Grant's and Lee's meeting engagements and most of their major battles of mobility. On close inspection they reveal a pattern counter to conventional wisdom. On at least six critical occasions, Lee was either puzzled over Grant's intentions or altogether misread the Union general's plans. His failure to grasp his opponent's design led him to act in ways that placed his army in peril. Fumbling by Federal commanders sometimes saved Lee from his own mistakes; other times, good fortune intervened. The picture that emerges is not that of a general who "quickly fathomed" his enemy. Rather, the Lee that comes into focus is a man who frequently misconceived his antagonist's strategy. His strength—a trait often overlooked by his biographers—was his remarkable ability to rescue his army from seemingly irredeemable predicaments and to turn those unfavorable situations to his advantage.

During the Overland Campaign, Lee fended off an army double the size of his own that was vastly superior in weaponry, supplies, and sundry accoutrements of war. This was no mean feat. My aim is not to minimize that accomplishment but rather to correct the overly simplistic, generally accepted version of how Lee achieved it. I also hasten to add that a comparably critical companion essay could be written about Grant's failure to exploit Lee's mistakes. Both men were able and resourceful commanders, but each had limitations. Understanding those limitations does not diminish their stature; it simply gives us a more complete understanding of their martial achievements.

Lee and his Army of Northern Virginia spent the winter of 1863–64 behind imposing earthworks lining the Rapidan River's southern bank. The Confederate Second Corps, commanded by Lt. Gen. Richard S. Ewell, held

---

3. Freeman, R. E. Lee, 4:172.

the right wing of the river line; Lt. Gen. Ambrose P. Hill's Third Corps the left wing; and Maj. Gen. James E. B. (Jeb) Stuart's cavalrymen patrolled the country beyond both ends of the formation. Late in April 1864 Lt. Gen. James Longstreet rejoined Lee with two divisions of his First Corps. Lee positioned Longstreet in reserve along the Orange and Alexandria Railroad near Cobham Station, fifteen miles south of the Rapidan. Altogether Lee marshaled about 65,000 soldiers.

Grant assumed command of the Federal war effort in March and laid plans to launch multiple offensives in Virginia. Maj. Gen. George G. Meade's Army of the Potomac, supplemented by Maj. Gen. Ambrose E. Burnside's Ninth Corps—a combined force of some 118,000 soldiers—was to cross the Rapidan and engage Lee in battle. Simultaneously a force of some 30,000 soldiers under Maj. Gen. Benjamin F. Butler was to advance up the James River from Fortress Monroe, threatening Richmond and Lee's rear. Two more Union armies were to press into the Shenandoah Valley, menacing Lee's left flank and closing that strategic pathway to the Confederates.

Lee monitored the Federal buildups with concern. The Army of the Potomac alone outnumbered him two to one. His instincts told him to seize the initiative. Shortages in food and fodder, however, ruled out an extended campaign of maneuver. In addition Lee realized that he might be called upon to send troops to Richmond to help fend off Butler. That eventuality required him to stay near the rail line. For the time being, Lee saw no option but to remain on the defensive. Above all, he wanted to avoid retiring to Richmond, where he would forfeit his ability to maneuver. The war then would become a siege that the North must necessarily win. "If I am forced to retire from this line," he warned the Confederacy's president, Jefferson Davis, "either by a flank movement of the enemy or the want of supplies, great injury will befall us."[4]

On May 2 Lee met with his subordinate commanders at the Confederate signal station atop Clark's Mountain. Grant's camps were clearly visible across the river on the plain below. It was apparent the Federals were about to move. But what route would they take? A frontal assault was unlikely, as the enemy knew the strength of Lee's fortifications along the river. Turning movements around one or both of the Confederate flanks were possibilities.

4. OR, 30(1):1283.

Lee discounted the likelihood of a maneuver upriver, to his west, for that would raise supply problems for the Union force and sever Grant's communications with Butler. Grant was more likely to cross east of the Army of Northern Virginia, Lee decided, and he informed his subordinates of his conclusion. As Ewell later put it, Lee "gave it as his opinion that the enemy would cross by some of the fords below us, as Germanna or Ely's." After the war Lee confirmed that he had "believed that Grant would cross the Rapidan on our right, and resolved to attack him whenever he presented himself."[5]

Grant's probable route afforded the Confederates a unique opportunity. Once across the Rapidan at Germanna and Ely Fords, the Union army would become ensnared in the Wilderness of Spotsylvania. Lee was intimately familiar with the ground, having fought the battle of Chancellorsville there the previous spring. This was a blighted area that had been cleared during colonial times for charcoal to feed the voracious appetite of local foundries. Thick stands of impenetrable second growth covered the land. Roads were few and clearings scarce. The dense foliage would thwart the deployment of infantry, deny discernable targets to artillery, and render cavalry virtually useless. Altogether the Wilderness promised to nullify the Union advantage in numbers and material and offered Lee's smaller army a perfect setting for fighting Grant's juggernaut. Lee could not have invented a better place to do battle.

The fact that Grant's route would take him into the Wilderness, however, did not guarantee that the Federal force would stop there. It was within the ability of Union commanders to pass through the forest and reach more-open country in a day's march. If Lee wanted to ensure that he fought Grant in the Wilderness, he needed to take affirmative steps to hold him there. He had to place across Grant's path a force sufficient to retard the Union army's progress until he could bring up the rest of his troops.

Surprisingly Lee did nothing to increase his chances of intercepting Grant in the Wilderness. He dispatched not a single brigade from Ewell or Hill to impede the Federal advance. And he directed Longstreet to leave half of his

5. OR, 36(1):431–32, 1070; Robert E. Lee to William Smith, July 17, 1868, copy in Fredericksburg and Spotsylvania National Military Park Library. Ewell's account is the only first-hand record of Lee's pronouncement on Clark's Mountain. A similar version appears in Jedediah Hotchkiss, "Virginia," in Confederate Military History: A Library of Confederate States History . . . Written by Distinguished Men of the South, ed. Clement A. Evans, 13 vols. (Atlanta: Confederate Publishing, 1899), 3:431–32. Hotchkiss makes it clear that he was not present.

corps at Cobham Station, well over a day's march from the Wilderness, and to advance the other half toward Liberty Mills, a Rapidan crossing located in the opposite direction from the Wilderness.[6]

Why did Lee neglect to post a force in the Wilderness to delay Grant? His concern about Richmond was part of the reason. Until he better understood the threat posed by Butler, he felt constrained to keep Longstreet near the rail line. But anxiety for Richmond's safety does not completely explain Lee's behavior. Why did he move half of Longstreet's corps toward his upriver flank, away from the Wilderness? And why did he not extract parts of Ewell's and Hill's corps from their entrenchments and dispatch the troops to the Wilderness to delay Grant?[7]

Lee's actions spoke louder than his words. Had he been truly convinced that the Wilderness was Grant's destination, he would have taken every feasible step to ensure that the campaign's opening—and perhaps final—encounter took place in that woodland. The fact that Lee did not do so suggests that he harbored serious doubts about the direction of Grant's march, notwithstanding his prophecy on the mountaintop. The only reason that Lee would send half of Longstreet's corps toward the left of his line was because he feared the Federals might attack that flank. And he did not forward troops from Ewell and Hill to the Wilderness because he was not persuaded they would be needed there.

As events transpired, Grant unwittingly gave Lee the opportunity to fight him in the Wilderness. The windfall for the Confederates was the consequence, not of anything that Lee did but rather of temerity on Meade's part. The Union army clearly had the capacity to pass through the Wilderness in a single day's march. Meade, however, feared that his supply wagons could not keep up. Assuming that Lee could not reach the area before morning, Meade convinced Grant to overnight the army in the woods. By tarrying, Grant gave Lee the advantage that the Confederate commander had neglected to secure for himself.[8]

6. John Bratton to wife, May 3, 1864, John Bratton Collection, Emory University, Atlanta; OR, 36(2):940.

7. On April 19, 1864, Lee told Pres. Jefferson Davis that he was holding Longstreet in reserve because of the threat to Richmond. OR, 30(1):1326.

8. Details of the Union decision to halt in the Wilderness are in Gordon C. Rhea, The Battle of the Wilderness, May 5-6, 1864 (Baton Rouge: Louisiana State University Press, 1994), 49-58.

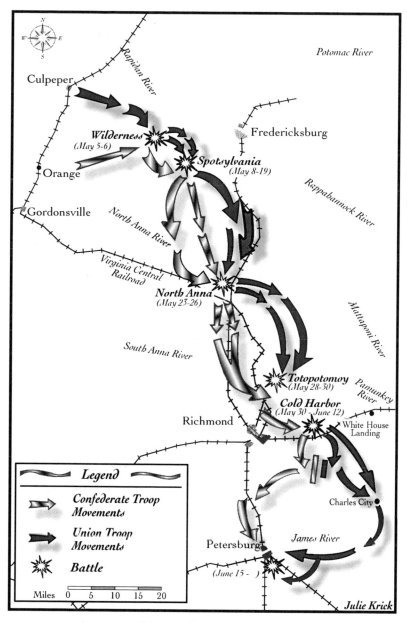

THE 1864 OVERLAND CAMPAIGN

Once Lee received word that the Army of the Potomac was heading into the Wilderness, he rushed to exploit the opportunity. The next morning elements from Ewell's and Hill's corps caught the enemy before they could escape the woodland. Furious combat raged all that day and the next, when Longstreet arrived. The result was a draw. The First Corps's artillery chief, Edward P. Alexander, questioned whether Lee had forfeited the chance for a decisive victory by failing to shift troops toward the Wilderness before the campaign opened. "In view of the great probabilities that Grant would move upon our right flank very early in May," Alexander observes, "it does not seem that there would have been any serious difficulty in having both Hill and Ewell out of their winter camps and extended a few miles in that direction and Longstreet's corps even as far down as Todd's Tavern." Had that been done, speculates Alexander, Lee could have hit Grant with the full force of his army. "What proved a drawn battle," Alexander contends, "might have proved a decisive victory." The converse is also true. Had the Union army not overnighted in the Wilderness, decisive victory might well have belonged to the Federals.[9]

Morning dawned on May 7 to illuminate a smoke-enshrouded landscape of carnage. Lee regarded the previous two days of fighting with satisfaction. He had deflected the Union army's blows and thrown telling punches of his own. While he had failed to defeat Grant, he had brought the Union monolith to a standstill. The Confederates occupied strong defensive ground and had held the Federals near the Rapidan, as Lee had hoped.

What would Grant do next? Lee reviewed the possibilities. A year before, Lee had fought essentially the same Union army—commanded on that occasion by Maj. Gen. Joseph Hooker—on essentially the same ground. Hooker had retreated across the Rapidan after suffering fewer casualties than had Grant. Perhaps Grant would follow Hooker's example. It was also possible that he would renew his attacks or that he would withdraw and sidle south. If Grant chose the latter course, two routes were likely. The Federal army could retire fifteen miles to Fredericksburg and descend toward Richmond

9. Edward Porter Alexander, *Fighting for the Confederacy: The Personal Recollections of General Edward Porter Alexander*, ed. Gary W. Gallagher (Chapel Hill: University of North Carolina Press, 1989), 348. See also Gary W. Gallagher, *Lee and His Generals in War and Memory* (Baton Rouge: Louisiana State University Press, 1998), 88.

THE WILDERNESS: "LEE TO THE REAR"

From Angelina V. W. Winkler, The Confederate Capital and Hood's Texas Brigade
(Austin: Eugene Von Boekmann, 1894)

along the Richmond, Fredericksburg, and Potomac Railroad. Or it could slice directly south from the Wilderness to Spotsylvania Court House, the intersection of an important road network.

Lee collected information to evaluate Grant's probable course. Cavalry probes disclosed that the Federals had abandoned the roads north to Germanna and Ely Fords. Grant clearly had no intention of withdrawing the way he had come. At first, Union cavalry under Maj. Gen. Philip H. Sheridan seemed to be falling back in the direction of Fredericksburg. Shortly after 3:00 P.M., however, the Federal horsemen returned and launched a massive push down Brock Road toward Spotsylvania Court House. Lee honed his judgment. "The general thinks there is nothing to indicate an intention on [Grant's] part to retire, but rather that appearances would indicate an intention to move toward Spotsylvania Court House," wrote Lee's aide Taylor. Noting that the Federals had relinquished the roads north, Taylor continued, "the general thinks they may move toward Fredericksburg or Spotsylvania Court House and must open some new way of communication."[10]

10. OR, 36(2):966, 967, 969–70.

Late in the day Lee stopped at the Chewning farm, site of Hill's headquarters. A lookout atop the Chewning house reported Federal guns rolling south. "It was no doubt simply confirmatory of numerous other reports from the cavalry and other points of the line, that General Grant was moving to Spotsylvania C. H.," one of Hill's aides later wrote. In fact Lee was not sure what Grant had in mind. Fredericksburg remained as likely a destination for the Union host as did Spotsylvania Court House. Efforts by Federal cavalrymen to clear Brock Road southward were susceptible to two readings: the riders might be paving the way for Grant's army, or they might only be ridding the sector of Confederates so that Grant could shift to Fredericksburg without harassment from that quarter.[11]

Anticipating that he might have to march toward Spotsylvania Court House on short notice, Lee assigned his artillery chief, Maj. Gen. William N. Pendleton, to cut a road from the lower Confederate flank south through the woods, paralleling the potential Union route south along Brock Road. Striking Catharpin Road west of Todd's Tavern, Pendleton's makeshift trail enabled the Confederates to either access Brock Road at Todd's Tavern or proceed along a more roundabout way to Spotsylvania Court House via Shady Grove Church Road.[12]

Shortly before night Lee directed Maj. Gen. Richard H. Anderson, who had replaced the seriously injured Longstreet as head of the First Corps, to start toward Spotsylvania Court House along Pendleton's trail. Anderson was to withdraw "as soon after dark as you can effect it," then to march to the rear and let his men sleep. "I have reason to believe that the enemy is withdrawing his forces from our front and will strike us next at [Spotsylvania Court House]," Anderson later reported Lee as saying. "I wish you to be there to meet him, and in order to do so, you must be in motion by three o'clock in the morning."[13]

11. William H. Palmer to William L. Royall, May 11, 1908, in *Some Reminiscences*, by William L. Royall (New York: Neale, 1909), 35.

12. *OR*, 36(1):1041.

13. Richard H. Anderson's Report, Richard H. Anderson Collection, Duke University Library, Durham; Anderson to Edward R. Robins, May 1, 1874, in Charles L. Peirson, "The Operations of the Army of the Potomac, May 1–7, 1864," *Papers of the Military Historical Society of Massachusetts*, 14 vols. (Boston: Military Historical Society of Massachusetts, 1881–1918), 4:229.

Despite his language to Anderson, Lee remained uncertain whether Grant was heading for Spotsylvania Court House or Fredericksburg. In a companion missive Lee's aide Taylor alerted Ewell to prepare to follow Anderson "should it be discovered that the enemy is moving in that direction, or should any change in [the enemy's] position render it advisable." Until further notice, Ewell and Hill were to remain in the Wilderness. Had Lee been convinced that Grant was marching to Spotsylvania Court House, he would have sent his entire force to intercept him. Instead he set in motion only his smallest corps under an untested commander. Even more tellingly, Anderson needed at least five hours to reach Spotsylvania Court House on the assigned route. If Lee had genuinely attached urgency to this mission, he would never have advised the general to wait eight hours before starting but would have sent him on his way immediately and hurried reinforcements close behind.

In fact Grant was heading his whole army toward Spotsylvania Court House. Once again mistakes by the Union high command saved Lee. Meade and Union cavalry chief Sheridan were not on speaking terms. Orders went awry, and Sheridan, rather than clearing Brock Road to Spotsylvania Court House, rested his men for the night at Todd's Tavern, frittering away precious hours. Snafus among Union infantry commanders delayed the advance still further. And as luck would have it, fires, smoke, and the stench of death persuaded Anderson to leave the Wilderness early. Unable to find a suitable resting place, he kept on, stopping at sunrise near the Po River. Hollywood could not have orchestrated a more timely appearance. Alerted to Grant's approach, Anderson double-quicked two brigades to assist Stuart's belea-guered Confederate cavalrymen opposing the Union advance. This small force blunted the Union drive, enabling Anderson to rush the rest of his men into place in the nick of time.

Once again—through luck rather than by guile—Lee had thwarted Grant. Surprisingly, even after Anderson was locked in combat, Lee persisted in his suspicion that Grant might really be retiring to Fredericksburg. The First Corps, he thought, might be fighting a Union rear guard sent to protect the main body as it withdrew. "The enemy has abandoned his position and is moving toward *Fredericksburg*," Lee reported to Richmond that morning. "This army is in motion on his right flank, and our advance is now at Spotsyl-vania Court House." Not until 10:00 A.M. did Lee understand that Anderson was opposing the head of Grant's advance and dispatch Ewell and Hill to assist him.[14]

Lee's failure to grasp Grant's intentions and to act accordingly had almost cost him the campaign. If Anderson had followed Lee's instructions and delayed his march, or if the Union army's machinery had worked with even moderate efficiency, Grant would have won the race to Spotsylvania Court House. A powerful Federal force would have stood between the Army of Northern Virginia and Richmond, placing Lee at a serious disadvantage.

Once the Spotsylvania Campaign began in earnest, Lee again misread his adversary after the initial confrontation near the courthouse. Late on May 8 Ewell began extending Anderson's line across the fields and woods east of Brock Road, following the terrain. A bulge, half a mile wide and just as deep, jutted forward in the center of the Confederate formation. The soldiers named the protrusion the Mule Shoe, after its shape. Salients such as the Mule Shoe were difficult to defend. Lee decided, however, that the need to control high ground justified the blister in his line, and he packed the Mule Shoe with artillery to strengthen it. "Our men did not like it at all," wrote a Southerner in Maj. Gen. Edward "Allegheny" Johnson's division of Ewell's corps, which occupied the salient. "It was so liable to be enfiladed by artillery and would be a dangerous trap to be caught in should the line be broken on the right or left."[15]

For three days Grant launched a welter of attacks against the entrenched Confederate line, all of which failed. Finally on May 11 he formulated a major offensive aimed at the Mule Shoe. At 4:00 A.M. the next morning, Maj. Gen. Winfield Scott Hancock's Second Corps, supported by the Ninth and Sixth Corps, was to charge en masse against the salient's broad tip. Grant had to shift his forces to prepare for the attack since Hancock was posted on the right end of the Union line, four miles from the staging area. He directed Hancock to wait under nightfall, then march into place under cover of darkness. A heavy rain helped conceal the troop movement.

Sifting information from his scouts, Lee surmised that something was

---

14. OR, 36(2):874.

15. William J. Seymour, *The Civil War Memoirs of Captain William J. Seymour: Reminiscences of a Louisiana Tiger*, ed. Terry L. Jones (Baton Rouge: Louisiana State University Press, 1991), 119–20.

afoot. General Lee's son Maj. Gen. William H. F. "Rooney" Lee, who commanded a cavalry division, reported that Burnside's Ninth Corps seemed to be withdrawing toward Fredericksburg. The Southern newspaperman Alexander related a rumor that Grant was "retiring in the direction of Fredericksburg and Germanna Ford."[16]

Late in the day Lee met with several of his generals. "Gradually, the conviction spread that [the Federals] were retiring toward Fredericksburg," Ewell's aide Campbell Brown reported of the conference. "My opinion is the enemy are preparing to retreat tonight to Fredericksburg," Maj. Gen. Henry Heth recorded Lee as saying. "I wish you to have everything ready to pull out at a moment's notice." Anderson's aide G. Moxley Sorrel jotted in his notebook, "Toward evening, indications are apparent of the intended withdrawal of the enemy and preparations are made to move after him."[17]

Lee had been searching for opportunities to take the offensive. Grant's withdrawal seemed to offer the perfect occasion. But for Lee to catch Grant on the move, the Army of Northern Virginia had to be ready to give chase. Rain was rapidly dissolving the trails and farm tracks that linked the entrenched formation to the main roads. Lee accordingly directed his artillery chief Pendleton to remove from the front any guns that might be difficult to withdraw later "so that everything might be ready to march at any hour." Pendleton in turn instructed his subordinate commanders to prepare for a "swift and silent movement during the night, should one prove necessary." Alexander left the First Corps's guns in place but made certain to clear paths to the rear. Brig. Gen. Armistead L. Long, commanding Ewell's artillery, faced a more difficult situation. Most of his ordnance was ensconced in the

---

16. Jedediah Hotchkiss, *Make Me a Map of the Valley: The Civil War Journal of Stonewall Jackson's Topographer*, ed. Archie P. McDonald (Dallas: Southern Methodist University Press, 1973), 203; *OR*, 51(2):916–17; Cadmus M. Wilcox's Report, Virginia Historical Society, Richmond; Peter W. Alexander Despatch, *Richmond Daily Dispatch*, May 18, 1864.

17. Campbell Brown Memoir, Campbell Brown and Richard S. Ewell Papers, Tennessee State Library and Archives, Nashville; Henry Heth, *The Memoirs of Henry Heth*, ed. James L. Morrison Jr. (Westport, Conn.: Greenwood, 1974), 186; G. Moxley Sorrel Journal, May 11, 1864, Eleanor Brockenbrough Library, Museum of the Confederacy, Richmond. See also Taylor, *General Lee*, 242; and Charles S. Venable, "The Campaign from the Wilderness to Petersburg," in *Southern Historical Society Papers*, ed. J. William Jones et al., 52 vols. (1876–1959; reprint, with 3-vol. index, Wilmington, N.C.: Broadfoot, 1990–92), 14:528–29 [hereafter cited as *SHSP*].

Mule Shoe. Only a few tortuous trails led to the rear, and those were fast becoming impassable. Out of an abundance of caution, Long decided to evacuate the battalions of Lt. Col. William Nelson and of Maj. Richard S. M. Page, which had been stationed along the Mule Shoe's tip. He left in place only Lt. Col. Robert A. Hardaway's battalion along the Mule Shoe's western leg, which had convenient access to decent roads.[18]

Never had Lee made a more egregious miscalculation. Grant was not retreating—he was preparing to attack. And he had targeted for his offensive the tip of the Mule Shoe, the very segment of fortifications that Lee was fatally weakening. Bereft of artillery, Allegheny Johnson's men would be at the mercy of the Federals.

As midnight approached, Confederate pickets reported disturbing levels of Union activity near the Mule Shoe. Johnson—who had been surprised to discover his line stripped of artillery—sent an aide to Ewell to complain of his exposed situation. The general brushed off the aide, so Johnson visited Ewell himself and finally convinced the corps commander that the enemy was girding to assault. Ewell alerted Lee's headquarters, and orders went out for the guns to return. The directives, however, were not delivered with urgency commensurate to the danger. Not until 3:30 A.M. did word reach the gunners. Valuable time ticked by as tired men and animals hauled the pieces along dark, rain-slicked trails.[19]

At 4:30 A.M., as morning's first sun set swirling fog aglow, Hancock's thousands swarmed across intervening fields and catapulted over the Mule Shoe's tip. Some guns pulled up just in time to be captured. Within minutes Hancock had driven Johnson from his entrenchments, captured thousands of Confederates, and was pressing into the interior of the salient. From the east Burnside joined the attack. Lee scrambled to mend the breach by thrusting fresh troops into the endangered sector. Again Federal bungling saved the Army of Northern Virginia from a catastrophe precipitated by Lee's erroneous reading of Grant. The Union commanders had neglected to bring up

18. OR, 36(1):1044, 1086; Alexander, Fighting for the Confederacy, 374; Robert A. Hardaway, "Extracts from the Diary of an Officer of Gen. Lee's Army," Richmond Whig, May 23, 1864.

19. Robert Hunter, "Major Hunter's Story," in SHSP, 33:337; OR, 36(1):1080; McHenry Howard, Recollections of a Maryland Confederate Soldier and Staff Officer under Johnston, Jackson, and Lee (Baltimore: Williams & Wilkins, 1914), 294–95 n14.

THE BLOODY ANGLE

From Robert Underwood Johnson and Clarence Clough Buel, eds., Battles and Leaders of the Civil War *(New York: Century, 1887–88)*

fresh troops, and the attacking force lost all semblance of order. Comparatively small bodies of Confederates were able to clear the enemy from the Mule Shoe's interior, and the battle deteriorated into a bloody face-to-face melee, with substantial portions of each army ensconced on opposite sides of the same earthworks. "At every assault and every repulse new bodies fell on the heaps of the slain, and over the filled ditches the living fought on the corpses of the fallen," a survivor recounted. "The wounded were covered by the killed, and expired under piles of their comrades' bodies." The focal point of the fight, a spot where the earthworks made a slight bend, was aptly named the Bloody Angle.[20]

A patchwork of Confederate brigades held the Union army at bay while

20. Alanson A. Haines, *History of the Fifteenth Regiment New Jersey Volunteers* (New York: Jenkins & Thomas, 1883), 177–78. For details of the fight of May 12, see Gordon C. Rhea, *The Battles for Spotsylvania Court House and the Road to Yellow Tavern, May 7–12, 1864* (Baton Rouge: Louisiana State University Press, 1997), 232–307; and Robert K. Krick, "An Insurmountable Barrier between the Army and Ruin: The Confederate Experience at Spotsylvania's Bloody Angle," in *The Spotsylvania Campaign*, ed. Gary W. Gallagher (Chapel Hill: University of North Carolina Press, 1998), 80–126.

the remnants of Johnson's division labored to construct new defenses along the Mule Shoe's base. By 3:00 A.M. on May 13, the new line was complete, and the beleaguered defenders dropped back. The Union assault had failed, but Lee had paid a steep price. Johnson's division, one of the best in the army, was wrecked, and Lee had lost about eight thousand soldiers.

The Virginian readily admitted that he had misjudged Grant's intentions. His "fatal mistake," he conceded, was "in removing the artillery on our line." Alexander later remarked that he had never seen "an occasion where artillery would have done such execution." He was certain that had Ewell's artillery been in place, "the charge would not have been successful." In Alexander's unimpeachable opinion, "nowhere else, in the whole history of the war, was such a target, so large, so dense, so vulnerable, ever presented to so large a force of artillery." In his view the Federals would have had no recourse but flight, "with phenomenal loss for the time exposed to fire." Lee's misapprehension of Grant's design had cost him a priceless opportunity and seriously weakened his own army.[21]

While the armies recovered from the relentless fighting, Grant cast about for ways to resume the offensive. He correctly identified Lee's Achilles' heel as the triangle of land on the extreme Confederate right bounded by the Fredericksburg and Massaponax Church Roads. He estimated that by striking there in strength, he could overrun the southern flank of the Rebel army and break into Lee's rear. A newspaperman summarized the thinking at Grant's headquarters. "Taking advantage of the storm and darkness, we expected to surprise the enemy, at least such of him as remained about Spotsylvania Court House, and re-enact the brilliant affair of [May 12]."[22]

Lee was mindful that the southern end of his line was weak. He did not believe, however, that the Federals intended to attack in that sector since the Union army was concentrated predominantly to the north. It never dawned on him that his adversary had targeted the region for a crushing assault before morning's first light.

Grant's scheme entailed a few uncomplicated movements. After dark he planned to take the Fifth and Sixth Corps from the northern end of his for-

---

21. William W. Old, "Personal Reminiscences," in *SHSP*, 33:24; Edward P. Alexander, *Military Memoirs of a Confederate* (New York: Charles Scribner's Sons, 1907), 520.

22. "The Campaign in Virginia," *Philadelphia Sunday Dispatch*, May 22, 1864.

mation, swing them behind the Second and Ninth Corps, and paste them onto the southern end of his line. By morning, assuming everything went as he anticipated, the Union army would stand oriented along a north-south axis. The maneuver would climax with an assault by the Fifth and Sixth Corps, now constituting the army's southern wing. At 4:00 A.M. on May 14, "if practicable," they were to charge west along the Fredericksburg and Massaponax Church Roads, converge on Spotsylvania Court House, and pierce the Confederate line.[23]

Darkness, rain, and mud conspired against the maneuver's success. "I'll do the best I can," promised Maj. Gen. Gouverneur K. Warren, heading the Fifth Corps, "but very difficult things are being attempted on these night movements over such roads." For hours Warren's troops floundered in muck. The Sixth Corps—Maj. Gen. Horatio G. Wright's outfit—fared no better. "A terrible piece of work, dirt up to our knees, rain from above," a Federal grumbled. "Many have their shoes stuck fast in the mud and march in stockings or barefoot." A participant wrote home that he "never knew such a horrible night, all mud, rain, darkness and misery." At 4:00 A.M., the time Grant had set for the attack, Warren had only twelve hundred bleary-eyed soldiers in place, and Wright's men were still mired several miles to the rear. Shortly after 7:00 Grant dashed off a note to Washington. "The very heavy rains of the last forty-eight hours have made it almost impossible to move trains or artillery," he wrote. "Two corps were moved last night, in the night, from our right to the left, with orders to attack at 4:00 A.M., but owing to the difficulties of the road have not fully got into position." He was not optimistic. "This," he concluded, "with the continued bad weather may prevent offensive operations to-day."[24]

Not until daylight did Lee receive reports that something was amiss. Union forces were concentrating toward the battlefield's southern sector. The deployments puzzled Lee. Was Grant initiating another turning movement? Was he planning to attack? Was he simply undertaking a diversion to disguise his real intentions? Lee needed more information before he felt comfortable formulating a response. "The enemy is making movements here

23. OR, 36(2):700, 732.

24. Ibid., 721, 746; John Chester White Journal, May 14, 1864, Library of Congress, Washington, D.C.; George M. Barnard to father, May 14, 1864, Massachusetts Historical Society, Boston.

which are not yet to be fully understood," his aide Charles S. Venable wrote in a dispatch reflecting the Confederate commander's quandary. "He seems to be extending to our right," Venable went on, "having occupied the position at the Beverly house [on Fredericksburg Road], and the [Myers house], on this side of the river."[25]

Lee could easily have borrowed troops from the northern portion of his formation and shifted them south to oppose Grant's concentration. He remained oblivious to the danger and did nothing. By late morning Grant had his troops in place. The day was well advanced, however, and he assumed that Lee had learned of his deployment and had taken steps to meet it by strengthening his southern flank. Grant could ill afford another round of massive casualties with no discernible gains. Persuaded that Lee must have taken steps to counter his movement, Grant withheld his blow.

The Union commander in chief would have been astounded to learn that the Virginian had done nothing. Not until midafternoon did Anderson inform Lee that Grant had evacuated the battlefield's northern sector, and only then did Lee fully realize what had happened. "Can you find out anything on your front," he asked Ewell. "Should you find that the enemy is changing his line be prepared to draw out to follow him."[26]

Grant's concentration clearly heralded a major Union offensive. Alerted at last to the danger, Lee directed Anderson to withdraw a division from Laurel Hill and rush it to the southern Confederate flank. By nightfall Fredericksburg Road and Massaponax Church Road lay securely in Confederate hands, firmly closing the back door to Spotsylvania Court House that had stood ajar all day.[27]

May 14 was a significant lapse on Lee's part. As the Confederate artillerist Alexander later conceded, Grant had "devised an attack which would have had a very fair chance of taking us quite by surprise, had he been able to make it." Alexander later thanked "darkness and mud" for delivering the Confederates, but caution on Grant's part was their real savior. Adverse weather, it is true, delayed the Union march and forced Grant to postpone his attack. But by 10:00 A.M. Grant had secured the very advantage he had

25. OR, 51(2):929–30.

26. Ibid., 929.

27. G. Moxley Sorrel Journal, May 14, 1864; Anderson's Report.

hoped to attain at daybreak. He cancelled the assault on the assumption that the Rebels must have brought up reinforcements. Lee, however, failed to grasp Grant's design and took no serious countermeasures until late afternoon. The Confederate general had unwittingly exposed his army to serious peril. Once again mistakes by his enemy had saved him from disaster.

Grant probed Lee's defenses for several days, launched another futile assault on May 18, and concluded that it was time to maneuver once again. He decided to use the stratagem he had employed after the Wilderness, shifting east and south in an attempt to interpose his forces between the Confederate army and Richmond. Topography figured prominently in his scheme. A few miles east of Telegraph Road, the Ni, Po, and Matta Rivers merge to form the Mattaponi River, which flows due south. By marching east from Spotsylvania Court House, Grant could slide above the bothersome streams, then turn south and descend along the Mattaponi's far side. Under this scenario the river network would work in Grant's favor, shielding him from attack and forcing the Confederates to cross the irksome tributaries in the inevitable race south.

Grant began by pushing Hancock east to Guinea Station, then along the Mattaponi's far side through Bowling Green and Milford Station. If Lee left his earthworks and attacked Hancock, Grant intended to fall on the Confederate rear. If Lee ignored Hancock, then the Second Corps was to continue on to the North Anna River, paving the way for the rest of the army to follow. Hancock left Spotsylvania Court House on his circuitous march after dark on May 20. Lee learned of his departure and suspected that the Federals might be preparing to shift south along Telegraph Road. To block the Union advance, Lee filed Ewell's men into formidable earthworks at Stannard's Mill and Mud Tavern across Telegraph Road. The move was a masterstroke. Ewell not only closed Telegraph Road to the Federals but also was handily situated to march east and sever Hancock from the rest of the Union army. "The enemy is apparently again changing his base," Lee asserted with confidence. "I am extending on the Telegraph Road, and will regulate my movements by the information of his route."[28]

Lee selected Hanover Junction as the best point to concentrate his army

28. *OR*, 36(3):812. For the time of Ewell's departure, see "Army Correspondence, May 23, 1864," *Richmond Sentinel*, May 25, 1864.

to counter Grant's likely deployments. This junction of the Virginia Central Railroad and the Richmond, Fredericksburg, and Potomac Railroad was a short distance below the North Anna River, about twenty miles south of Ewell's position across Telegraph Road. It was both a critical link in the Confederate supply network and a strategic point from which Lee could monitor Federal movements. If Grant tried to advance along Telegraph Road, the Army of Northern Virginia would stand directly in his path. If Grant pursued a wider arc to the east, Lee could slide east below the North Anna and Pamunkey Rivers to oppose him, all the while keeping between the enemy and Richmond. Grant, however, had left two corps—Warren's and Wright's—in front of Spotsylvania Court House, which prevented Lee from withdrawing without exposing his rear to attack. Until the Federals evacuated their entrenched line, Lee saw no option but to leave a substantial force at Spotsylvania.[29]

Lee spent an anxious afternoon. Word arrived that Warren had left Spotsylvania and was following in Hancock's wake. Did Hancock and Warren constitute a raiding party, or was Grant launching a wide sweep toward Richmond? At 3:00 P.M. Lee sent forays to probe the Union earthworks. Wright and Burnside were still in place. "Unless we can drive these people out, or find out where they are all gone," Lee wrote in frustration, "we are detained here to our disadvantage."[30]

Concerned about his own situation, Lee failed to notice that Grant had dispersed his army across a twenty-mile front. Wright and Burnside remained at Spotsylvania Court House, Warren was at Guinea Station, and Hancock was at Milford Station, too scattered to assist one another. Years later, when Grant penned his memoirs, he acknowledged his predicament on the afternoon of May 21. "Lee now had a superb opportunity to take the initiative either by attacking Wright and Burnside alone, or by following the Telegraph Road and striking Hancock's and Warren's corps, or even Hancock's alone, before reinforcements could come up," he explained. Grant thought that Lee "never again had such an opportunity of dealing a heavy blow." Grant's aide Adam Badeau later claimed that "if Lee ever meant to assume the offensive,

29. William N. Pendleton to wife, May 22, 1864, in *Memoirs of William Nelson Pendleton, D.D.*, ed. Susan P. Lee (Philadelphia: J. B. Lippincott, 1893), 335.
30. *OR*, 36(3):815.

this was the moment, with Grant on the arc of the circle of which he held the chord; one national corps at Milford, another at Guinea, and two at Spotsylvania, and all in motion by different roads with which they were unacquainted, while the rebels knew every plantation path and every ford, and every inhabitant was a friendly guide for them and a spy on Grant." A Confederate cavalryman aptly quipped, "Old Ewell says [Grant] puts him in mind of a measuring worm, and the time to strike him is when he has just lengthened out his line." May 21 was just such a time, but Lee missed it. The specter of Grant's beating him to the North Anna had blinded him to the offensive opportunities that Grant's movement offered.[31]

To concentrate his scattered corps, Grant withdrew Burnside and Wright from Spotsylvania Court House. Seizing the chance to slip away to the North Anna, Lee dispatched Anderson down Telegraph Road, in Ewell's wake, and Hill along a more westerly route. Lee accompanied Anderson. The Rebel chieftain assumed that the entire Union force was on its way to Bowling Green, following Hancock. He was very wrong. Camping for the night near Guinea Station, Warren had thrust strong elements west toward Telegraph Road. Brig. Gen. Samuel W. Crawford's division had pitched its tents near Mud Tavern, and Col. J. Howard Kitching's brigade, augmented by a cavalry detachment, had bivouacked near Nancy Wright's Corner, three miles south of Mud Tavern. Crawford's and Kitching's outposts were no more than a mile from Telegraph Road.

Lee had presented Grant a rare opportunity. All night Anderson's corps marched unsuspectingly past Warren's camps. By catapulting Warren into Lee's flank, Grant stood to sever the Confederate column and open the way for Burnside and Wright to attack from the north. Consistent with the campaign's invariable pattern, Union fumbling saved the unwitting Lee from disaster. Warren's outposts listened to the sound of Rebel feet marching by but neglected to notify their superiors. Not until after daylight on May 22, after the last of Anderson's wagons had passed, did Warren discover to his dismay what had happened. "Such opportunities are only presented once in a cam-

31. Ulysses S. Grant, *Personal Memoirs of U. S. Grant,* 2 vols. (New York: Charles L. Webster, 1885–86), 2:562–63; Adam Badeau, *Military History of General Ulysses S. Grant,* 3 vols. (New York: Appleton, 1881), 2:220; Joseph F. Waring Diary, May 21, 1864, Southern Historical Collection, Wilson Library, University of North Carolina, Chapel Hill.

paign and should not be lost," Warren's aide Washington Roebling lamented.[32]

During the morning of May 22, the Army of Northern Virginia crossed the North Anna River and threaded into camps along the Virginia Central Railroad near Hanover Junction. Early in the day Lee admitted to President Davis that he was uncertain about the Union army's whereabouts. He believed that Grant was "endeavoring to place the Mattapony River between him and our army, which secured his flank, and by rapid movements to join his cavalry under Sheridan to attack Richmond." So far as Lee could gauge, Bowling Green and Milford Station marked the farthest point of the Federal advance. "As soon as I can get more positive information concerning the movements of the enemy, I will forward it to you," the general promised. Later in the day Lee conceded, "I have learned as yet nothing of the movements of the enemy east of the Mattapony."[33]

The Confederate commander remained perplexed over Grant's intentions, which made it difficult for him to formulate his next move. If Grant meant to advance along the Telegraph Road axis, Lee was at the right place to intercept him. But if he intended to follow a more easterly route to the Pamunkey, as Lee suspected, the Confederates would have to shift considerably to their right. Data available to Lee supported the inference that Grant intended to march to the Pamunkey. Hancock had initiated the Union advance by skirting the upper bank of the Mattaponi, and so far as Lee could ascertain—he remained unaware of his close call the previous night—the rest of the Union army had followed suit. Grant was also establishing a new supply depot at Port Royal, which lent credence to the scenario as Lee understood it. Finally the pattern of Grant's generalship during the campaign suggested a Union movement to the Pamunkey. Grant had initiated the campaign by swinging southeast of Lee, and his answer to stalemate in the Wilderness had been another turning movement to the southeast. After conceding deadlock at Spotsylvania Court House, the Federals had once again sidled off to the southeast. Grant's invariable behavior made it unlikely

32. Washington A. Roebling's Report, Gouverneur K. Warren Collection, New York State Library, Albany; OR, 36(3):88.

33. R. E. Lee to Jefferson Davis, May 22, 1864, in The Wartime Papers of R. E. Lee, ed. Clifford Dowdey and Louis H. Manarin (Boston: Little, Brown, 1961), 746–47.

that he would venture a frontal attack against Lee on the North Anna. If the past offered guidance, he would try to turn Lee's flank by crossing to the east. "I think it probable [Grant] will make still another move to the right," Lee's aide Taylor wrote home, echoing his boss's conclusion.[34]

Lee elected to rest his troops in anticipation of a hard march to the Pamunkey and made no preparations to fight Grant at the North Anna River. In fact Grant was heading directly Lee's way. Warren, Wright, and Burnside, after passing through Guinea Station, had veered back to Telegraph Road, and Hancock was moving to join them there as well. Once again Lee had misinterpreted Grant's movement and was leaving undefended the very sector that the Union general had targeted. It remained to be seen whether fortune would intercede.

The next morning—May 23—Lee persisted in his conviction that Grant intended to stay east of the Mattaponi. He made no preparations to receive the Federals at the North Anna and left a brigade of South Carolina troops under Col. John Henegan in a redoubt north of the stream. "At present, all my information indicates that the movement of General Grant's army is in the direction of Milford Station," Lee wrote President Davis. He echoed that belief in a letter to his wife, informing her that Grant had "become tired of forcing his passage through us" at Spotsylvania Court House and had shifted toward Bowling Green, "placing the Mattaponi River between us."[35]

Lee could not have been more mistaken. All morning Grant's juggernaut advanced toward the North Anna. Hancock's corps materialized in front of Henegan's position, and Warren's corps forded the river two miles upstream at Jericho Mills. Wright and Burnside came close behind. Most of the Southern soldiers rested complacently in their camps along the Virginia Central Railroad. Lee rode to the river to investigate. Looking across at the Federals collecting in front of Henegan, he announced, "This is nothing but a feint, the enemy is preparing to cross below."[36]

34. Taylor, Lee's Adjutant, 162.

35. Ibid.; Robert E. Lee to Jefferson Davis, May 23, 1864, in Wartime Papers of R. E. Lee, 747–48; Robert E. Lee to wife, May 23, 1864, in ibid., 748.

36. George N. Neese, Three Years in the Confederate Horse Artillery (New York: Neale, 1911), 274–75. A newspaperman wrote, "When the enemy arrived on the north side of the North Anna, the impression prevailed in certain official and private circles that his demonstration on our left was merely a feint to cover an intended movement further down the river, perhaps to the Peninsula." Report of Special Correspondent, May 26, 1864, Richmond Enquirer, May 27, 1864.

Lee's miscalculation cost him dearly. Warren secured a bridgehead on the southern bank, repulsed an attempt by Hill to drive him back, and thrust his entire corps across the river. Hancock overran Henegan and secured the bluffs controlling Chesterfield Bridge. The Army of Northern Virginia faced a dire crisis. That evening Lee met with his generals. Warren's position on the Confederate left rendered the river and railroad untenable. Lee rose to the occasion, however, and devised a bold and ingenious plan. The Army of Northern Virginia would take up a line shaped like an inverted V, its left leg anchored on Little River, its apex at Ox Ford, and its right behind a swamp near Hanover Junction. The tip of the formation, resting on precipitous bluffs, was virtually impregnable. And the Virginia Central Railroad, which connected the two feet of the inverted V, enabled Lee to shuttle troops from one side of the formation to the other. Adversity, it developed, had afforded Lee a marvelous opportunity. By pulling his troops back from the river to form the legs of the V, Lee would create the illusion that he was retreating. Grant would doubtless throw his army across in pursuit. The Confederate position would divide the Federal force into three parts, and neither segment could readily assist the others. Lee, however, could leave a skeleton force to hold one leg, concentrate the mass of his army along the other leg, and fall upon the enemy there with overwhelming strength. "Our holding a half mile of river made the Federal line very bad," noted Porter Alexander, who attended the conference.[37]

Lee had redeemed a desperate situation fostered by his misreading of Grant. But fate was to deny him the opportunity to play his deadly trick to conclusion. Grant reacted precisely as Lee had anticipated, thrusting his force across the river and dividing it on either side of the inverted V. But before Lee could act, sickness incapacitated him. Confined to his tent, he was too ill to strike, and he lacked confidence in his subordinates to let them act on their own initiative. By evening Grant had discovered Lee's snare and began entrenching. Close inspection of the Confederate formation persuaded him that it was invulnerable. Conceding that Lee had checked him once again, Grant crossed back over to the river's northern bank and initiated another broad turning movement east.

A close examination of the first weeks of the Overland Campaign under-

37. Alexander, *Fighting for the Confederacy*, 390.

scores two points. By no stretch of the imagination was Lee able to "divine" Grant's intentions. On multiple occasions he was either unsure about Grant's plans or plainly wrong. What saved Lee was his facility to respond to emergencies and turn bleak situations to his advantage. He was a master at improvising, and the pressure of a crisis only served to sharpen his wits. He took inadequate steps to catch Grant in the Wilderness but moved boldly once he recognized the opportunity offered by the Union commander's decision to overnight in the dense woodland. Lee left his army vulnerable at Spotsylvania Court House by withdrawing artillery from the Mule Shoe but staved off defeat by waging a determined defense, deftly shuttling forces to endangered sectors until he could construct a new line. And at the North Anna he inadvertently permitted the Federals to breach the river but rebounded by devising the cleverest defensive configuration of his career.

Luck was also in Lee's corner. Each time he blundered and left his army vulnerable, the Federals blundered as well. The campaign would have been irretrievably lost to the Confederates had Grant pushed through the Wilderness on his first day of marching; had Sheridan pounded his way to Spotsylvania Court House; had Hancock's attack at the Mule Shoe been properly supported; had the Union Fifth and Sixth Corps assaulted Lee's right flank on May 14; had Warren realized that Lee was passing along Telegraph Road the night of May 21–22; or had Grant exploited his advantage on May 23 at the North Anna River before Lee could reconfigure his formation.

The pattern set in the Wilderness, at Spotsylvania Court House, and at the North Anna River was to continue. Following a costly assault at Cold Harbor on June 3, Grant undertook to shift his army across the James River and strike Petersburg before Lee could respond. During the earlier stages of the maneuver, Lee remained uncertain whether Grant meant to attack north of the James or cross the river. Lacking resources to cover both eventualities, he remained north of the James. Grant boldly crossed his army on ferries and pontoons and stole a march on Lee. Predictably, a parade of mistakes by the Union commanders delivered the Confederates from defeat and led to another ten months of war in Virginia.

"The Great Tycoon" Forges a Staff System

ROBERT E. L. KRICK

GOOD GENERALSHIP IS FOUNDED on the mastery of the many dozen elements that comprise a commander's job. While most evaluations of Civil War officers look exclusively at battlefield performance, a more balanced assessment requires an investigation of the roles that commanding generals perform away from the front. In the case of Robert E. Lee, his relationship with the large class of men who comprised the Army of Northern Virginia's staff corps remains a largely unexplored field. An examination of that relationship quickly divides into two connected lines of inquiry, each of which deserves separate attention before reuniting to form the whole. The first is Lee's philosophy on the selection and employment of both his personal staff and the other staff at army headquarters. The second explores Lee's move toward the development of a general staff for the entire army and how his ideas developed over the course of the war. Did he ever recognize that such a body of officers would bring a greater degree of training and professionalism to the daily duties of managing the Army of Northern Virginia?

Lee failed on all those counts, according to a popular premise, which suggests that by maintaining a small personal staff instead of cultivating a larger professional body, he showed an inability to adapt to the stern demands of modern war. Lee did in fact realize the inadequacy of his army's staff system and took what steps he could to improve the utility and professionalism of the staff corps at every level. Nor did he ignore the qualifications of the immediate staff around him. Unlike many of his fellow generals, Lee did not make a habit of installing boyhood chums, men of the same religious faith, or his wife's cousins into key staff positions.

The insufficiency of R. E. Lee's personal staff is a recurring theme in Army of Northern Virginia literature. Some writers identify too few staff officers at army headquarters as a contributing factor in the poor communication, bad maps, and occasional problems with marching and supply that plagued the army. Such a line of reasoning is too simplistic. Just because Lee kept a small supporting cast, one should not conclude that he did not value the role of staff or understand its importance. Many historians, however, have made such an argument without ever looking behind the numbers and evaluating Lee's own ideas about the role of a general staff and his relationship with the men who served him.

While Lee should have had more attendees at army headquarters, this criticism has been overplayed by the endless procession of ill-informed modern authors pretending to give a "fresh" view of Lee's generalship, chiefly by citing one another as proof or by latching on to a few anti-Lee remarks by soldiers and expanding from there. Critics of the general's staff work have drawn most of their fodder from Col. Walter H. Taylor, who spent his entire military career as Lee's principal staff officer. He wrote incessantly about the inadequate number of men available to staff the headquarters apparatus, attributing some of that scarcity to Lee's unwillingness to take men from the battlefield and give them bureaucratic posts. Taylor's complaint about too few staff officers deeply influenced Lee biographer and historian of the army Douglas Southall Freeman. He repeatedly echoed Taylor's line of thought, saying once that Lee's mania about economy of force went too far when it came to staff officers and that, "beyond question," Lee and the army "would have been better served if he had had two or three more staff officers." It should be noted that most of Lee's critics have stayed close to Freeman's contention that the general should have expanded his staff, never looking beyond the thinly supported assertion of Lee's most influential biographer.[1]

Several additional factors contributed to Lee's unflagging determination to limit the size of his staff. While other generals welcomed volunteers and

1. Walter H. Taylor, *Lee's Adjutant: The Wartime Letters of Colonel Walter Herron Taylor, 1862-1865*, ed. R. Lockwood Tower (Columbia: University of South Carolina Press, 1995), 68–69, 88–89, 140–41; Douglas Southall Freeman, "Morale in the Army of Northern Virginia," in *Douglas Southall Freeman on Leadership*, ed. Stuart W. Smith (Shippensburg, Pa.: White Mane, 1993), 75; Edward Porter Alexander, *Fighting for the Confederacy: The Personal Recollections of General Edward Porter Alexander*, ed. Gary W. Gallagher (Chapel Hill: University of North Carolina Press, 1989), 236. A recent example of the ill-informed reiteration regarding Lee's staff is Edward H. Bonekemper III, *How Robert E. Lee Lost the Civil War* (Fredericksburg, Va.: Sergeant Kirkland's, 1998), 203.

part-time help, Lee strove to limit his own staff to what the law allowed, no doubt viewing the subject through the same narrow lens he used in almost every matter involving army personnel. Such strict adherence to the rules proved useful on occasion. Within days of assuming command of Virginia's military forces in 1861, Lee refused to provide a friend's youthful kinsman a staff position in Richmond. "It is necessary that persons on my staff should have a knowledge of their duties and an experience of the wants of the service to enable me to attend to other matters," Lee explained on April 25. "It would otherwise give me great pleasure to take your nephew." This was more than a diplomatically worded repulse; it was a succinct statement of Lee's philosophy on staff officers. He was determined to surround himself with qualified men regardless of their connections and what influence they could bring to bear. His first crop of staff officers in that frantic spring of 1861 consisted of men selected for him, appointed to that duty by representatives of Virginia's wartime governor, John Letcher.[2]

Lee's unswerving adherence to a Spartan lifestyle and modest public comportment clearly helped shape his preference for a small personal staff. During the war's early years, he frequently came in close contact with generals who rode about the lines accompanied by enormous parties of aides. Many of the latter were short-term volunteer staff officers—often men with political or business connections to their patron general. Their presence cluttered the battlefield without noticeably improving operations. The most astonishing case is that of Maj. Gen. John Bankhead Magruder, whose entourage might have reminded some observers of a wedding party, so vast and wasteful was his collection of assistants. Ostentatious excess always annoyed Lee, and the examples of Magruder, J. E. B. Stuart, and other generals inordinately fond of martial display perhaps reinforced his insistence on maintaining a painfully thin personal staff.[3]

2. Robert E. Lee to [?], Apr. 25, 1861, in *The Wartime Papers of Robert E. Lee*, ed. Clifford Dowdey and Louis H. Manarin (Boston: Little, Brown, 1961), 12; Walter H. Taylor, *General Lee: His Campaigns in Virginia, 1861–1865, with Personal Reminiscences* (Norfolk, Va.: Nusbaum, 1906), 21.

3. A careful search of the Compiled Service Records and other official sources shows that during his thirteen months in Virginia, General Magruder had about fifty different staff officers, a rate of accretion never threatened by any other Confederate general in the East during the war. The author of this chapter has in preparation a detailed biographical register of the twenty-

Lee's distaste for military decoration won him admiration in some circles. Many soldiers noticed and appreciated the low-key atmosphere around army headquarters. When most of Lt. Gen. James Longstreet's corps transferred to Tennessee in the last quarter of 1863, its soldiers frequently drew comparisons between what they were accustomed to in Virginia and what they saw in the Army of Tennessee. Lee's frugal use of a personal staff became apparent to one officer in Maj. Gen. Lafayette McLaws's division only after seeing Gen. Braxton Bragg ride along the lines, "his staff and escort very large . . . , quite different" from General Lee's conservative appearance back in Virginia. The following year, during the battle of Cold Harbor, a North Carolina infantryman saw Lee for the first time and marveled that his chief "had none of the innumerable staff or retinue of officers and couriers along with him which is always to be seen with other General officers." This was surprising, for "of course Gen. Lee must have a very numerous staff." The correspondent supposed that Lee "uses them as necessity requires and not as parasites."[4]

Among the various irregularities and imperfections in the Army of Northern Virginia's staff system, perhaps none invaded the most remote corners of the high command so thoroughly as did nepotism. This pervasive habit infected most generals in Lee's army, and like a virus it rarely bred positive results. Few generals were immune to its influence. Lee himself had kinsmen on his staff at various times, but all were of such distant relation as to deflate quickly any accusations on that point. A man of Lee's lineage, connected to virtually every old family in Virginia, could hardly move through the army without encountering cousins of varying familiarity. But in most other parts of his organization, Lee could see more clearly defined cases of nepotism at every level, from corps commanders downward. In a nation and an era where influence and connection carried enormous weight, the Confederate Congress did nothing to arrest the progress of nepotism. Lee recognized it, complained of it, but never took measures to exterminate it. While begging Jefferson Davis for a more powerful general staff, Lee took the opportunity

---

one hundred men who served as Army of Northern Virginia staff officers. The statements in this note and in note 32 are based directly on that research.

4. Robert P. Myers Diary, Sept. 21, 1863, Eleanor Brockenbrough Library, Museum of the Confederacy, Richmond [repository hereafter cited as EBL]; Letter of "Alexander," (*Fayetteville, N.C.*) *Weekly Intelligencer*, June 14, 1864.

ROBERT E. L. KRICK

to add that he hoped to fill that body with "proper officers—not the relations and social friends of the commanders, who . . . are not always the most useful." When Mrs. Lee pestered her husband about a staff position for their son Rob (R. E. Lee Jr.), the general reminded her of the impropriety of it. "It is wrong in principle," he lectured, and not "for the public good." More specifically, Lee told her, "I am opposed to officers surrounding themselves with their sons & relatives."[5]

Wrong or not, it occurred with alarming regularity in the Army of Northern Virginia. Some generals managed to place as many as seven relatives on their staff at different times during the course of the war, and many had at least one staff officer reaping the rewards of familial patronage. Lee never managed to stamp out what one historian has called "the nests of nepotism" built up by some generals.[6]

The need for every able-bodied man to be in the ranks provided another incentive to Lee. He complained often about his inability to press into service everyone who was eligible and persisted in seeking out and breaking up situations where overfed and underworked men virtually sat out the war in "bombproof" positions. His constant clamoring about ensuring that every healthy man was in the field left Lee little room to pad the numbers of his own staff, even had he been so inclined. The horde of energetic assistants needed to ride herd on the army's movements necessarily would have depleted the fighting cadre. The general felt, reiterated his great biographer Freeman, "that it was incumbent upon him to set an example of economy of force, even to the extent of economizing on staff officers." In fact there is

5. U.S. War Department, *The War of the Rebellion: A Compilation of the Official Records of the Union and Confederate Armies*, 128 vols. (Washington, D.C.: GPO, 1880–1901), ser. 4, 2:448 [hereafter cited as *OR*; all references are to series 1 unless otherwise noted]. Despite Lee's grumbling on the subject, he contemplated installing his son Custis Lee as his chief of staff when Chilton left. *Wartime Papers of R. E. Lee*, 686, 695. Young R. E. Lee Jr., rebuffed by his father and too young to be a regularly commissioned staff officer anyway, eventually served with the rank of cadet on the staff of his brother, Brig. Gen. W. H. F. Lee.

6. Douglas Southall Freeman, *R. E. Lee: A Biography*, 4 vols. (New York: Charles Scribner's Sons, 1934–35), 2:490. Nepotism figures, based on the author's research, show that nearly half of the 204 Confederate generals that served in Virginia during the war managed to install at least one relative onto their staff. Undoubtedly the number should be higher, but not all family connections are apparent at a glance. J. E. B. Stuart was the officer with seven kinsmen on his staff.

reasonable doubt that Lee really understood how undermanned his staff was or even recognized that he had too few personal staff officers to help him administer the army. At the same time, it is pertinent to wonder to what extent a larger personal staff would have improved operations. There is no obvious evidence that things around J. E. B. Stuart's bloated cavalry corps headquarters functioned with a smoothness not found at Lee's, at least administratively. It was on the battlefield or on the march that the extra staff would have proved most beneficial.[7]

For most of his three years in command of the Army of Northern Virginia, Lee had no more than six personal staff officers attached to his field headquarters. These men traveled with him, camped with him, and carried the power of his authority in time of battle. Lee's adjutant general, Col. Walter H. Taylor, is the best known of the group, in part because he wrote two books postbellum. The recent publication of his splendid war letters has directed even more attention toward this influential man. Habitués of Confederate records recognize Taylor's signature at a glance; his endorsement appears on countless thousands of army documents, from furlough requests to battlefield dispatches. His affable efficiency was well known throughout the army. Men seeking an audience with Lee first had to penetrate the vigilant screen erected by Taylor, who soon became adroit at shielding the general from needless interruptions. J. E. B. Stuart, in the course of recommending some other officer for his own staff, held Taylor up as the standard, writing, "With the exception of Major W. H. Taylor, of General Lee's staff, I know no one equal to him as an Assistant Adjutant General in the field." Taylor appears to have been one of the most able bureaucrats in Confederate history.[8]

---

7. OR, 33:1294–95; Charles B. Dew, *Ironmaker to the Confederacy: Joseph R. Anderson and the Tredegar Iron Works* (New Haven: Yale University Press, 1966), 231–33, 237, Freeman, "Morale in the Army of Northern Virginia," 75. Lee's reaction to the pleas of his friend J. R. Anderson, director of the vital iron works in Richmond, is stunning evidence about how gravely the commanding general viewed his manpower problems. In one instance Anderson asked by name for two skilled men to help at Tredegar, and Lee refused to detail them from the army.

8. J. E. B. Stuart to "General," Jan. 15, 1864, in *The Letters of General J. E. B. Stuart*, ed. Adele H. Mitchell (N.p.: Stuart-Mosby Historical Society, 1990), 359–60. Moxley Sorrel held the same position on Longstreet's staff that Taylor did on Lee's and was especially well suited to judge Taylor's worth. Writing after the war, Sorrel characterized the army's adjutant general as "ex-

Charles S. Venable, Charles Marshall, Robert H. Chilton, T. M. R. Talcott, and Armistead L. Long also served extensively as members of Lee's private staff, and nearly a dozen others held similar positions for shorter periods. In time of battle each man ultimately became a high-ranking courier. It mattered little, for instance, that Chilton was a member of the adjutant general's department, with administrative and disciplinary responsibilities. On the battlefield he toted messages, drafted orders, and supervised movements, as did the others. Lee used everyone at hand, regardless of their official niche, to prosecute his aims and spread his influence. This disregard for the finer points of a staff officer's job description was not unique to R. E. Lee. Most Confederate generals seem to have adopted similar practices, glad to have any authoritative representative on the battlefield to implement and supervise their tactical designs.[9]

Each staff officer had a specific rank and assignment under Lee, but in practice they all seem to have been nearly interchangeable off the battlefield as well. They frequently shared duties and performed each other's tasks instead of adhering only to the specific requirements of their offices. This stemmed in part from the imbalance between the workload and the number of staff officers on hand and in part from Lee's somewhat helter-skelter system. Early in his tenure at the army's head, he customarily met with his entire staff every morning and assigned chores to them after breakfast, much the way a schoolteacher would pass around random projects to a room of students. In a sense this system mirrored Lee's laissez-faire style on the battlefield, in which he would assemble the parts and let his generals build the final product.[10]

In his desire to improve efficiency, Lee began in the late summer of 1862 to overhaul his relatively open system of governing staff officers into one that gave him more control and forced his subordinates to be more accountable. He may have felt dissatisfaction at the performance of his staff officers early in the war, or perhaps the enormity of the daily workload forced a corrective. Soon a more regular system emerged to deal with the never-ending official

tremely efficient" and observed that "better could not be found for this important post." G. Moxley Sorrel, *Recollections of a Confederate Staff Officer* (New York: Neale, 1905), 77–78.

9. Freeman, *R. E. Lee*, 3:228–29.

10. Taylor, *General Lee*, 56.

chores. Lee designated Walter Taylor as the paperwork czar. A. L. Long and then Charles Marshall more rigorously carried out the duties of the position of Lee's secretary, drafting most of his correspondence and working on his battle reports. Venable and Talcott, as Lee's primary aides-de-camp, ran errands and accompanied their chief on his daily rides around the army's line and camps. R. H. Chilton regularly used the title of chief of staff, but his daily duties are less apparent from this distance. Despite this gradual drift toward better-defined roles, the parts still proved easily switched. Whenever Taylor sneaked away for a day or two of recreation, poor Venable stepped in behind what he called Taylor's "miserable desk" to wage war with the pile of papers that confronted army headquarters every morning.[11]

None of the officers among Lee's personal stable of assistants had qualifications that made them specially suited for their chores. Walter Taylor did not aspire to staff duty. It came to him in 1861, and he adapted to it. Whatever administrative skills he demonstrated during the war were ones he learned in the course of his work. One year at the Virginia Military Institute and some time as a banker in Norfolk, Virginia, hardly fitted twenty-three-year-old Taylor to be the lead staff officer in any army, especially one as sizable and active as the Army of Northern Virginia. Venable and Marshall both had developed into first-rate scholars in the decades before the Civil War, but neither man showed any interest in the army as a profession; they were products of a strictly nonmilitary environment. T. M. R. Talcott came from a military family, but his prewar experience as an engineer included civilian projects only. A. L. Long and Robert H. Chilton alone had prewar experience as soldiers (Chilton was a paymaster). That four of the army commander's six primary staff officers—and the best four by most calculations—could emerge from such markedly civilian backgrounds hardly seems credible. Of the six men, at least five brought exceptional intelligence to their staff duties. It was about the only common denominator among them.[12]

11. C. S. Venable to "My own darling," Jan. 11, 1864 [5], McDowell Family Papers, Alderman Library, University of Virginia, Charlottesville [repository hereafter cited as UVA].

12. All six men are easy to learn about today. Walter Taylor's life is ably documented in Tower's introduction to Taylor, *Lee's Adjutant*. Charles Venable is the subject of a good biographical profile (including a rarely seen postwar photograph) in Harry Clemons, *Notes on the Professors for whom the University of Virginia Halls and Residence Houses are Named* (Charlottesville: University Press of Virginia, 1961), 138–43. A summary of Robert H. Chilton's life can be found

Lee only infrequently pulled strings to secure the services of any staff officer. He generally accepted what he was given. This did not always prove to be in the best interests of the army, nor was it beneficial to harmony at headquarters. Robert H. Chilton offers the most pertinent example. The Adjutant General's Office in Richmond appointed Chilton as Lee's chief of staff in June 1862. The two men had been acquainted before the war but are not known to have been particularly close. Lee must have viewed Chilton's prewar administrative experience as welcome seasoning for the green crop of younger men already on the staff. Instead of acting as the keystone, however, Chilton seems to have become the weakest link in the chain. In Douglas Southall Freeman's delicate phrasing, Chilton "was not a man who gave himself with special cooperative spirit to his duties." His awkwardly written order at Malvern Hill apparently played some role in flogging the army into an attack it did not wish to make and should not have attempted. Worse still, Chilton exceeded the boundaries of propriety and launched a witch hunt after that battle, eventually forcing General Magruder into court on grounds of incompetence. Although historians know less about this episode than we could wish, it seems unlikely that Lee used Chilton as a stalking horse. He supported Chilton during the proceedings, when pressed to do so, but it would have been uncharacteristic for Lee unofficially to approve of his chief of staff's unilateral actions. Chilton's mangling of an oral message from Lee to Maj. Gen. Jubal Early at Second Fredericksburg in May 1863 stands as the army's greatest known piece of specific incompetence by a staff officer (except perhaps Special Orders No. 191 during the Maryland Campaign, the precise culprit remaining unidentified in that case). Chilton seems to have had a fair number of enemies in the army, some of whom inexplicably referred to him as "Aunt Jenny."[13]

in William C. Davis, ed., *The Confederate General,* 6 vols. (Harrisburg, Pa.: National Historical Society, 1991), 1:184–85. Talcott's papers are at the Virginia Historical Society in Richmond, and a brief biographical sketch of him exists in the *Richmond News Leader,* May 7, 1920. Long wrote a popular biography of his chief, entitled *Memoirs of Robert E. Lee: His Military and Personal History* (New York: J. M. Stoddert, 1877). Charles Marshall is best discovered in *An Aide-de-Camp of Lee: Being the Papers of Colonel Charles Marshall,* ed. Frederick Maurice (Boston: Little, Brown, 1927).

13. Longstreet's own chief of staff reported that, though Chilton was "sometimes called chief of staff . . . Lee really had no such chief about him." Sorrel, *Recollections,* 78. See also Freeman,

Why Lee endured Chilton so long is a mystery. It may have resulted in part from Lee's stubborn unwillingness to burden the overworked authorities in Richmond with his own problems, though one well-placed government official reported to his wife in October 1862 the rumor that the general recently had asked for a new chief of staff. Nearly eighteen months later, when Chilton expressed dissatisfaction and a desire to leave, Lee offered no obstacle. His farewell letter to Chilton displays a considerable courtliness, even when judged against the general's usual standard. "I shall miss your ever ready aid & regret your departure," Lee wrote. "You have been untiring in the discharge of your duties, honest in your purpose & earnest in your efforts." Nonetheless, he told Chilton that Richmond would be a more suitable billet for him than the field—strange advice to a man who had been the army's chief of staff for nearly a year and a half.[14]

Intelligence and zeal made up for whatever professional inadequacies Lee's personal staff officers brought to their new occupations. At least one observer identified Charles S. Venable as the general's closest confidant on the staff. Freeman attributed this to Venable's "age, dignity, and station." Venable completed his thirty-third year the very week the war started in 1861 and had compiled a prestigious academic record since graduating from Hampden-Sidney College at age fifteen. His credentials included participation in an astronomical expedition to the Labrador coast. By 1861 the Virginian was teaching mathematics at the University of South Carolina, and he immediately enlisted in a local unit to fight for the South. Venable summarized his views on the war in a belligerent October 1861 letter: "My only

"Lee as a Leader," in *Freeman on Leadership*, 150. The fullest account of the Chilton-Magruder controversy is Richard Selcer, "Conduct Unbecoming," in *Civil War Times Illustrated* 34 (Mar.–Apr. 1995): 60–69. Chilton and Lee had been acquainted before the war in San Antonio. Unattributed biographical sketch of Chilton, n.d., Robert H. Chilton Papers, Folder C-191, EBL. The "Aunt Jenny" quote comes from S. Bassett French to J. Bankhead Magruder, May 25, 1863, in T. J. Jackson's Compiled Service Record (M331), Roll 139, National Archives, Washington, D.C. [repository hereafter cited as NARA].

14. Jeremy F. Gilmer to "My dear Loulie," Oct. 8, 1862, Gilmer Papers, Southern Historical Collection, Wilson Library, University of North Carolina, Chapel Hill; Lee to Chilton, Mar. 24, 1864, Box 1, R. E. Lee Collection, EBL. According to Gilmer, Lee requested Gen. William W. Mackall, a man with both field and staff experience, who was just then returning South after a few months in a Federal prison. Chilton was announced as the Army of Northern Virginia's new chief inspector that same month, perhaps not coincidentally.

feeling is that no decent man with a revolutionary mind has any right to sit on his tail in these times & teach fifty boys." After brief stints as an engineer officer and adjutant in the western part of the Confederacy, Venable received a transfer to Lee's staff in June 1862. In an unusual step Lee asked specifically for Venable, submitting his request "without having an opportunity to consult you beforehand," Lee wrote in April. For the next thirty-four months, they were closely connected as part of the same military family.[15]

Like others on the staff, Venable parlayed his glamorous job as a Lee confidant into an influential postwar role in affairs relating to Lee and the Army of Northern Virginia. He and Walter Taylor became generally accepted as arbiters in disputes large and small. Their important staff positions gave them credibility and a level of prestige unavailable to others. So great were their reputations that anything they wrote after the war was of immediate interest and, rightly or wrongly, seems to have been viewed as virtually coming from Lee himself. A North Carolina veteran seeking details on Gettysburg wrote to Venable in 1889 and added, "It is needless for me to say that any fact coming from you will have peculiar and justly great weight." Crusty veteran Jubal Early felt the same way. Admonishing Venable after the war about some historical dispute, Early wrote Venable, "Very naturally what one of General Lee's staff officers says will be taken as historically correct." In addition to mediating disputes, Lee's surviving staff emerged after the war as some of the leading spokesmen for the Lost Cause, waxing eloquently about their commanding general's virtues, often at the expense of other officers' reputations. Taylor, Long, and Marshall all wrote favorably of their old commander, and extensively. Venable provided occasional material, all positive in tone, and William Nelson Pendleton of the general staff is better known even today for his hagiographic efforts than for his generalship.[16]

Available wartime correspondence from members of Lee's staff confirms that their respect for him, and for the most part their affection, were not the product of postwar pressures to be a good Southerner. The same evidence

15. R. K. Charles, "Events in Battle of Fredericksburg," *Confederate Veteran*, 14 (1906): 65; Freeman, *R. E. Lee*, 3:229; C. S. Venable to Thomas S. Fleming, Oct. 8, 1861, in Venable's Compiled Service Record (M331), Roll 254, NARA; Robert E. Lee to C. S. Venable, Apr. 26, 1862, McDowell Family Papers.

16. Joseph J. Davis to C. S. Venable, July 30, 1889; and Jubal A. Early to C. S. Venable, Oct. 3, 1879, Charles S. Venable Papers, Virginia Historical Society, Richmond.

also shows, however, that the difficulties of working under Lee somewhat tempered their admiration. They claimed that he failed to recognize the extent of his demands upon them and that their unnecessary workloads could have been solved without injury to the service by the addition of another one or two staff members. Walter Taylor, who is the authority for the fact that Lee's staff privately called him "The Great Tycoon," struggled most of all to maintain a consistently pleasant relationship with his general. More than once during the war years, Taylor admitted that while he respected and admired Lee, "I might serve under him for ten years to come and couldn't *love* him at the end of that period." Frequently Lee's temper sparked unrest among his staff. "He is so unreasonable and provoking at times," complained Taylor in August 1864. Venable talked of leaving the staff just before Gettysburg for the same reasons, saying, "I am too high-tempered to stand a high-tempered man."[17]

At least three major quarrels between Lee and Venable are on record. On the banks of the Potomac in July 1863, Venable interrupted Lee during a conference with two other generals in order to render a report "in an abrupt and rather loud tone of voice." Lee replied "rather sharply" to Venable, "you had as well make your report to the whole army." The general later tried to repair Venable's damaged feelings by offering him a glass of buttermilk, but the aide remained only partially mollified. At the North Anna River, when dysentery and squandered tactical opportunities combined to fray Lee's nerves, Venable reportedly visited the general's sickbed and, in the course of an argument, "told the old man that he is not fit to command this army, and that he had better send for Beauregard." In addition to demonstrating Venable's lack of military acumen, this vignette confirms the earlier observation that the two men had a closer, less formal relationship. E. Porter Alexander told of yet another episode, this one in October 1864, when Lee felt especially testy and delivered an unwarranted rebuke to Alexander. Not finding that general contrite enough, Lee turned on an innocent bystander—Charles Venable. Alexander learned from Venable later that "for two weeks the general never addressed him except officially" as a result of this spat. Still, Venable recognized that "the old man has much to annoy and worry him and is very

17. Taylor, *Lee's Adjutant*, 83, 175, 182; C. S. Venable to "My own dear wife," June 21, 1863, McDowell Family Papers.

kind and considerate after all." Even Lee's legendary self-control could crack, and those closest to him bore the brunt of his eruptions.[18]

Outside of his own headquarters entourage, Lee did indeed have a numerous staff, but most of its members were part of the general staff and not seen around him on a daily basis. The distinction in the Confederate army between a personal staff and the general staff was a potentially confusing concept. It would be wrong to think of it as a sort of mathematical formula, with a beginning, an end, and a few benchmarks along the way. Indeed each general seems to have defined their staff's positions in whatever way suited him. One bill debated in Congress in the fall of 1862, entitled "An Act for the Establishment and Organization of a General Staff of the Army of the Confederate States of America," even asserted that only men with the function of aide-de-camp would be considered part of the personal staff of a general. All others were to be wed to the military organization, regardless of its commander. In practice, of course, nearly all staff positions—general or personal—were perceived as part of a commander's entourage. General Lee seems rarely to have interfered with the constant shuffling and rearranging common to most brigade and division staffs, nor did he evince any desire to standardize the terminology.[19]

Critics have contended that R. E. Lee never adapted to a more modern mode of warfare. His general staff, argues respected scholar T. Harry Williams, "was not, in the modern sense, a planning staff."[20] The army included thousands of animals and wagons and from thirty-five thousand to eighty-five thousand men. It marched hundreds of miles every year, forded dozens of streams and rivers, operated in unfriendly territory on more than one occasion, and fought the most violent large-scale battles in American history. A military machine of that size, and with commensurate requirements, clearly required a general staff with an infrastructure that could accommodate extensive and diverse needs. The Army of Northern Virginia did not have that support system to an ideal degree, but Lee was not entirely to blame for this

18. Venable Papers; H. B. McClellan Papers, cited in Freeman, *R. E. Lee*, 3:359; Alexander, *Fighting for the Confederacy*, 482; C. S. Venable to "My own dear wife," June 21, 1863, McDowell Family Papers.

19. *Daily Richmond Examiner*, Sept. 30, 1862.

20. T. Harry Williams, *Lincoln and His Generals* (New York: Alfred A. Knopf, 1952), 313.

void. He perceived at least some of the fundamental deficiencies in the staff apparatus of his army and frequently tried to use his influence to improve the situation. Lee's manifesto on this subject appeared in the text of a letter he wrote to Jefferson Davis on March 21, 1863. In noting that some Army of Northern Virginia divisions at that time were larger than Winfield Scott's entire army during the battles for Mexico City in the last war, Lee showed that he understood the increased demands placed upon army headquarters. His own unwieldy army had produced a fresh set of problems that needed solving.

The language of Lee's plan to deal with this issue should forever absolve him from any charges of inflexibility or lack of vision: "The greatest difficulty I find is in causing orders and regulations to be obeyed. This arises not from a spirit of disobedience, but from ignorance. We therefore have need of a corps of officers to teach others their duty, see to the observance of orders, and to the regularity and precision of all movements. This is accomplished in the French service by their staff corps, educated, instructed, and practiced for the purpose. The same circumstances that produced that corps exist in our own Army. Can you not shape the staff of our Army to produce equally good results?" Lee's proposal included reducing the number of an army commander's aides in favor of more assistants to the department heads, else "they will never be able to properly attend to their outdoor and indoor work." Most importantly he asked that the standardization be forced into the army at the division and brigade level as well, "giving each a complete organization in itself, so that it can maneuver independently." The official implementation of these suggestions did not occur until much later in the war, but in the Army of Northern Virginia, the broader designs became policy almost at once and were enforced incrementally when opportunities arose.[21]

The absence of a professional body of staff officers in the army cannot be traced to indifference, a lack of imagination, or to the unseemly hand of politics. In this as in many other institutional matters, the Confederate nation suffered the consequences of youth. "General Lee had no general staff to start with," cautions Freeman; "he had to build it up as best he could." A general staff, trained to manage an army, could not be plucked from a hat. Like every other part of the professional military environment, ideally it is cultivated in

21. *OR*, ser. 4, 2:447–48.

years of peace to excel in days of war. But unlike combat, which cannot be duplicated in training, good staff work can be achieved through practice and exercises. Moving and feeding an army, implementing its framework of discipline, and managing its personnel are peacetime skills that carry over into war.[22]

The old army of the 1840s and 1850s virtually ignored the concept of a general staff, at least as it came to be defined during the Civil War. Very few veterans of that peacetime force entered the Confederate service with any knowledge of a modern staff officer's duties. Although one historian has estimated that in 1860 nearly one-third of the U.S. Army's officers were engaged in staff duties, the raw number still was only about 350 men. One can suppose that fewer than 100 of that number found their way into the Army of Northern Virginia, and the skills they brought were not necessarily the ones they would need for a war exponentially larger in every way than anything they had seen before. The antebellum army's small size, lack of unity, and scattered nature of its many outposts prevented aspiring young soldiers from learning how to practice a staff officer's trade as it would become defined in the 1860s. Most of those 350 antebellum staff officers filled jobs that involved extensive paperwork and administrative duties. Very few of them had practical experience in logistics or maneuver—skills that would prove most desirable and scarce in the Civil War. Confronted with relatively large, untrained volunteer armies in 1861 and 1862, the few weathered veterans with their old-army skills must have seemed nearly useless.[23]

Although Lee's army lacked a carefully inculcated general-staff system, that does not mean officers of that service were altogether absent. The demands of a large army in the field forced adaptation, and soon the govern-

---

22. Freeman, "Lee as a Leader," in *Freeman on Leadership,* 149.

23. William B. Skelton, *An American Profession of Arms: The Army Officer Corps, 1784–1861* (Lawrence: University Press of Kansas, 1992), 135, 222–23; T. Harry Williams, *Americans at War: The Development of the American Military System* (Baton Rouge: Louisiana State University Press, 1960), 36. The one exception to this blanket statement about experience is the Engineer Corps. Lessons learned during the Mexican War and endless work on the coastal defenses were sufficient seasoning for officers in that branch. T. Harry Williams has argued that the general staff in the Mexican War had a positive effect on operations, especially in matters of supply. Even if that assertion is true, the lessons learned in that war do not seem to have allowed the Army of Northern Virginia's staff officers to hit the ground running in 1861 and 1862.

ment had organized branches specializing in ordnance, commissary, and quartermaster functions. In the Army of Northern Virginia, Lee so narrowly defined the boundaries of his own staff that many of the department heads who ran the various bureaus within the army must be considered members of the general staff more than of Lee's own military family. The best examples within this category are Lt. Col. Robert G. Cole, the army's chief commissary officer; Lt. Col. James L. Corley, the chief quartermaster; Lt. Col. Briscoe G. Baldwin, who supervised the army's ordnance department; Brig. Gen. William N. Pendleton, the well-known chief of artillery; and the several men who occupied the position of chief engineer for the army. In the organizational plan of almost any other Confederate commander, those men would have been considered part of the general's staff. In Lee's case these officers and their many assistants moved and camped separately from him. They still reported directly to "The Great Tycoon," but the scope of their duties and the nature of their commissions excluded them from Lee's private circle of staff officers.[24]

Lee granted more latitude to his personal staff than to the department heads who occupied the general-staff positions. He was less tolerant of the supply chiefs and held them to a more rigorous accountability. While it is true that no other officer of similar rank and responsibility displayed as many imperfections as Pendleton and yet retained his office, beyond that anomaly Lee demonstrated displeasure with some of the others quite regularly. He never did find a fully satisfactory engineer. At different times during the war, Jeremy F. Gilmer, Martin L. Smith, William P. Smith, and Walter H. Stevens filled that role. Gilmer soon moved into Richmond and exercised a greater control over nationwide engineering matters. The other three served spells as the army's chief engineer, but they all learned that Lee already understood military engineering. What he wanted was someone to assist in reconnaissance while performing the primary duty of supervising the sizable body of assistant engineers in place throughout the army. Stevens and the two Smiths each had strong points, but none seemed able to win the general's complete confidence.[25]

24. Taylor, *General Lee*, 57; Taylor, *Lee's Adjutant*, 219; Freeman, *R. E. Lee*, 1:638–43.

25. The deficiencies of the engineer branch, both in numbers and organization, seem to have plagued many other generals too. The best example of Lee's desire for a controlling hand can be found in his wistful remarks from March 1863 in *OR*, 25(2):686. See also *OR*, 11(3):586.

Little is known of Lee's relationship with Lt. Col. James L. Corley, the army's chief quartermaster. Corley attained that lofty general-staff position without much work, being assigned to it in June 1862 after serving as a field officer for five months. He had graduated from West Point in 1850 and had twelve years of experience in the old army—some of it as a quartermaster—but nothing in his known record made him especially suitable for his important duty with Lee. The little evidence that survives tends to reflect on Corley's personality more than his ability. One junior quartermaster in the army wrote of Corley in midwar that he "has the reputation of being a straight-laced West Pointer and rather gruff." Another staff officer put it less obliquely, calling him "that fool of a Chief Quartermaster."[26]

Chief Commissary Lt. Col. Robert G. Cole was another significant figure on the army staff. As the primary representative of Commissary General Lucius Northrop, Cole must have suffered by association. Lee fought constantly, almost daily, with Northrop about feeding the Army of Northern Virginia; they never did approach harmony in their views. Like Corley and A. L. Long, Cole was a member of the class of 1850 at West Point. When he joined the armies of the South in 1861, Cole reported that "nearly the whole of my eleven years service has been with my company on the frontier of Texas." Somehow the authorities in Richmond managed to ignore those credentials and, instead of making Cole an infantry officer, converted him into probably the most important general-staff officer in the Army of Northern Virginia, with daily responsibilities for keeping the men fed. Cole and Corley were unusually young for their positions. Both were in their mid-thirties when Lee surrendered at Appomattox.[27]

Lee never publicly commended Cole and Corley, and it is tempting to conclude that the commanding general was dissatisfied with their performance. At one point in the fall operations of 1863, however, the general called for John A. Harman and Wells J. Hawks (formerly Stonewall Jackson's quar-

26. Edgeworth Bird to Sallie Bird, Sept. 9, 1864, in *The Granite Farm Letters: The Civil War Correspondence of Edgeworth and Sallie Bird*, ed. John Rozier (Athens: University of Georgia Press, 1988), 200; Oscar Hinrichs Notebook, 70, typescript in possession of R. K. Krick, Fredericksburg, Va.

27. Robert G. Cole to unknown, n.d., in Cole's Compiled Service Record (M331), Roll 59, NARA; F. B. Heitman, *Historical Register of the United States Army* (Washington, D.C.: GPO, 1890), 194, 201, 416; *Savannah Morning News*, Nov. 8, 1887.

termaster and commissary officer respectively) "and told them that the success & safety of the enterprize depended on them." Legendary mapmaker and staff officer Jedediah Hotchkiss jotted down that anecdote shortly after it happened and added his own observation that Lee's remarks were "Strange when he had Corley & Cole." Despite that tale, the lamentable absence of source material on Lee's dealings with his quartermaster and commissary make it difficult to assess their relationships. An investigation of whether the army was properly fed and supplied is beyond the scope of this essay. Events elsewhere in the South, beyond the control of men like Cole and Corley, frequently determined the success or failure of their work.[28]

Not only did the Confederacy labor under the disadvantages of starting afresh, but by 1862 when Lee took command in Virginia, little had been done to lay a good foundation of staff work. The system he inherited from Gen. Joseph E. Johnston only compounded Lee's problems. Douglas Southall Freeman sheds his usual diplomacy when he labels Johnston "a wretched military administrator." He insists, "The service of supply in all its branches was disorganized, feeble, and confused." But Lee did not passively accept what he inherited. He immediately set about to reshape, invigorate, and make more efficient the army's staff system. Joseph L. Brent, chief ordnance officer on the staff of General Magruder in 1862, offered a vivid testimonial on the organizational transformation that Lee inspired and oversaw. Most of the junior ordnance officers under Brent's supervision in May and June 1862 "were not any better qualified than I, and some of them had not the interest and ambition to learn that I had." Immediately after Lee's ascension to command, Brent watched his environment change. E. P. Alexander, as the army's chief of ordnance, was able to use Lee's "great powers" to "convert a paper skeleton into a living body." Brent wrote later, "Under the new impulse from Genl. Lee's headquarters, enormous progress was made, defects were supplied, and . . . we had an Ordnance system organized in the field which functioned with reasonable efficiency." From the start Lee proved he could reshape a staff department to suit the army's needs.[29]

28. "Incidents Relating to the Life of Gen. Jackson Compiled by Jed. Hotchkiss Capt. & Top. Engr. 2nd Corps A.N.Va.," UVA. Hotchkiss scribbled these random notes—not all of them pertaining to Jackson—in the blank pages of an 1857 catalogue for Mossy Creek Academy.

29. Freeman, "Morale in the Army of Northern Virginia," in *Freeman on Leadership*, 87; Joseph Lancaster Brent, *Memoirs of the War between the States* (New Orleans: Fontana, 1940), 152.

Despite these innovations enacted prior to the Seven Days Campaign, the armywide shortage of staff officers forced Lee to perform many headquarters chores himself during his tenure as commanding officer. T. Harry Williams insists that these duties, many dealing with seemingly insignificant matters, "should have fallen to his staff." Writing in the 1950s, Williams believes that Lee focused on too many details because he did not have a mind attuned to modern war and "because it was traditional for the commanding general to do it in older armies." Lee habitually "looked to the past in war," writes Williams. There may be some merit in that line of argument, but it presumes to answer the question of just how modern a war Lee was fighting in the 1860s. A march of twenty miles was still a good day's work, and everyone moved by horse or on foot. Operationally at least, Lee's war bore more resemblance to the Revolution than to World War I. Still, even if Lee handled responsibilities that should have been left to subordinates, one must be impressed by his willingness to reconfigure his staff to meet the evolving and ever-changing needs of his army.[30]

A pair of enormous gaps remained unfilled in the makeup of Lee's general staff. The absence of any officer designated to control operations stands out. Modern staffs have men trained to move armies from place to place, to calculate the time and roads needed to accomplish the maneuver, and to get soldiers to the part of the battlefield where their presence is in accord with the general's wishes. That office was not only unfilled in the Army of Northern Virginia but also unknown. Pressed to identify the man most closely associated with those duties in the army, one would have to answer R. E. Lee—he acted as his own operations officer, sometimes with success.

Likewise no staff member filled the role of intelligence officer. The duty of coordinating reconnaissance reports and preparing appreciations of the enemy's movements and strengths is one of the most vital of all staff positions. In the Army of Northern Virginia, this was nearly a one-man operation—the same one man, Lee, who also assumed the duties of operations officer. Historians frequently point to the Virginian's ability to divine his enemies' intentions as one of his most consistent talents as a general. An endless sifting of information, most of it provided by intelligence-minded cavalry chief J. E. B. Stuart, kept Lee conversant with enemy strengths and options. Ideally an army commander should concentrate his energies on preparing his

---

30. Williams, *Lincoln and His Generals*, 313.

own army for battle rather than investigating the details of his opponent. This is not to say that an able general should not spend time studying the psyche and habits of his counterpart, an essential skill prized by commanders through many eras. But poring over enemy newspapers or gathering and piecing together other clues is a chore more suitable for some trained officer of the staff, not the commanding general of the army.[31]

Although basic staff work in the Army of the Potomac seems not to have been any better than in the Army of Northern Virginia, the many commanders of that invading force enjoyed one noticeable advantage. For much of the war, the Federal army in Virginia had officers at army headquarters who excelled in planning. The elaborate, multilayered operations on the Peninsula in 1862, at Gettysburg and Mine Run in 1863, and from the Wilderness through Petersburg in 1864 all required meticulous preparation. Their success, particularly on the march from Cold Harbor to the James River and later in the offensives below Petersburg, is the best evidence imaginable of the chasm between the two armies in operational matters.

Many men besides Lee recognized the need for a large, adequately trained army staff. "The great defect in our army," wrote Lafayette McLaws in 1895, "was in staff organization & its practices." William W. Chamberlaine, himself a staff officer, agreed, identifying the "lack of staff officers to communicate orders and information" as one of the army's principal early war weaknesses. E. Porter Alexander gave a practical example of this when he wrote about the time in late July 1863 that the three corps of the army marched on the same road. Because no staff officer had calculated the length of the columns or predicted the time it would take for each corps to push its many brigades into line of march, the whole process took far longer than it should have and entailed endless waiting at the tail of the column. Alexander pointed out that the episode demonstrated "how important in a big army is the detail, which only a large & well trained staff can supply."[32]

---

31. Despite the long-held belief among historians that Lee enjoyed considerable talent as a prognosticator, recent scholarship (at least for the 1864 campaign) has downplayed this. Gordon Rhea contends elsewhere in this volume that Lee's ability to predict his enemy's movements broke down in 1864.

32. Lafayette McLaws to "My Dear McBride," July 3, 1895, A. J. McBride Papers, Atlanta Historical Society, Atlanta; William W. Chamberlaine, *Memoirs of the Civil War between the Northern and Southern Sections of the United States of America, 1861–65* (Washington, D.C.: Byron S.

Porter Alexander's observations on the importance of staff officers and their duties are especially germane. He served as a staff officer at army headquarters, as the chief of artillery for a corps, and as a battalion commander in the line. Having seen all sides of the prism, his conclusions bear extra weight. Alexander argued in favor of bulk—not more-efficient staff officers, but more numerous ones: "Scarcely any of our generals had half of what they needed to keep a *constant & close supervision on the execution of important orders.*" This point was not lost on Lee during the war, who complained in 1863 that his chief need was "a corps of officers to . . . see to the observance of orders, and to the regularity and precision of all movements."[33]

Ultimately the real gauge of a staff's efficiency is in the field. If an army is well supplied, adequately clothed, properly disciplined and armed, and otherwise prepared for battle, the general staff has done its job. For almost the entire war, the Army of Northern Virginia entered each campaign in fighting trim. The engine house of this formidable, imposing war machine was managed with admirable efficiency by Lee's staff officers. It is not surprising that many of the specific complaints about bad staff work at army headquarters related to the Seven Days Battles, Lee's first operation as commander of the Army of Northern Virginia. A close study of that campaign shows that Lee harbored unrealistic expectations for the operational ability of his army. Long-distance marching, turning movements, and other maneuvers involving cooperation among different columns proved too difficult. Failed opportunities to bring timely combinations to the battlefields contributed to what Lee viewed as a squandered chance to destroy the Union army. Certainly the best-known example of bad staff work during that campaign occurred at Malvern Hill, where Chilton signed a message to the division commanders that ordered a frontal assault based on nothing more tangible than the yelling of certain troops. A staff that could produce that sort of order, contends British historian G. F. R. Henderson, "must have been utterly incapable of directing the intricate movements devised by Lee to ensnare McClellan." Freeman

---

Adams, 1912), 135; Alexander, *Fighting for the Confederacy*, 273. Yet Moxley Sorrel writes that Lee had a staff that "was small and efficient," and he makes no mention of any need for more officers to assist the commander. See Sorrel, *Recollections*, 77.

33. Alexander, *Fighting for the Confederacy*, 236–37; *OR*, ser. 4, 2:448.

agrees: "There might as well have been no headquarters staff for all the good it did."[34]

Writing with the analytical perspective of a professionally trained European officer, Henderson feels strongly that poor staff work actually contributed to the chaos that kept the Confederate victory during the Seven Days Campaign from being total. Referring to the staff system as a whole, Henderson terms it "too small," "too inexperienced," and "insufficiently trained." Reflecting on the same subject, Freeman judges the Seven Days as a campaign that "will always remain a tragic monument to defective staff work." He maintains, "A detailed list of the errors of the staff would be a review of the campaign."[35]

The disappointments of June and July 1862 did not deflate Lee's hope that he could achieve a grandiose victory over the enemy. While he employed less intricate tactical formations at Second Manassas, Sharpsburg, and Fredericksburg, his operational maneuvers remained complex. What campaign could possibly have been more taxing on an army's staff than the invasion of Maryland? At Chancellorsville, nearly a full year after the Seven Days, Lee again arranged his army in a manner that would have challenged any veteran corps of staff officers. Admittedly as the war progressed, at least two of Henderson's three criticisms of the staff corps became less valid. Its inexperience diminished with each passing day, of course, and presumably its competence increased with practice as well. The number of staff officers, once deemed too small, had grown by midwar. Lee deserves some credit for the manifest improvements. His outspoken support of a staff overhaul in the winter of 1862–63 helped standardize the regulations, ensuring that each general had, in theory, enough full-time commissioned staff officers to conduct his brigade, division, or corps effectively. Only then, by midwar, would Henderson judge the army's staff as "trustworthy." Another Englishman, Garnet Wolseley, visited the army in the last quarter of 1862 and was told that al-

---

34. *OR*, 9(2):497; G. F. R. Henderson, *The Science of War* (London: Longmans, Green, 1905), 218–19; Freeman, *R. E. Lee*, 2:233–34. Archer Jones agrees that during the Seven Days, "Lee and his staff, in their first campaign together, showed their inexperience." See Jones, *Civil War Command and Strategy: The Process of Victory and Defeat* (New York: Free Press, 1992), 70.

35. Henderson, *Science of War*, 218–19; Freeman, *R. E. Lee*, 2:233–34.

ready the army's staff system had undergone significant improvement in the few months since the Seven Days. Wolseley claimed that "every one in the South" knew that poor implementation of Lee's orders during that summer campaign had been a principal cause of George McClellan's escape.[36]

By the summer of 1864, the Army of Northern Virginia's staff system finally had reached a level that Lee probably found satisfactory. A centralized system of quartermaster and commissary officers allowed for greater control and efficiency in gathering and distributing supplies. Lee had stamped out many of the irregular practices of his generals, forcing them to travel, camp, and go to battle with staffs corresponding in size and duty to the requirements of the law. Brigades, divisions, and corps had foundations that allowed them to operate as separate forces, with a body of staff officers attached to the organization rather than to a specific general. These beneficial changes came gradually and were for the most part too late to aid the army in its operations during the glory years of 1862 and 1863.

It is no exaggeration to assert that improving the army's efficiency stood at the top of R. E. Lee's perpetual list of chores. In winter quarters or in the field, he regularly issued directives to the army and wrote gently wheedling dispatches to the authorities in Richmond, all designed to improve the organizational integrity of the Army of Northern Virginia. His concerns ranged from excessive personal baggage in the wagon train to straggling on the march, from batteries with mismatched ordnance to cavalry regiments with sore-backed horses. To enforce and regulate the issues he found so crucial, Lee took pains to install a staff system that could achieve the results he wanted. In this he must be judged almost completely successful.

His scorecard is less positive in matters of battlefield staff work. Lee's compulsive economizing and pervasive conservatism injured the army's performance on some battlefields. Communication among the three primary branches of the army never could be called good, and liaison between Lee and his subordinates often was worse. Although the Seven Days established

36. OR, ser. 4, 2:448; Henderson, *Science of War*, 225–26; An English Officer [Garnet Wolseley], "A Month's Visit to the Confederate Headquarters," *Blackwood's Edinburgh Magazine* (Jan.–June 1863): 12. Shirley M. Gibbs offers a dissenting voice to Henderson, arguing that Lee never understood the origins of his problems during the Seven Days and that he did not take steps to improve staff work. See Gibbs, "Lee's Command Procedures" (M.A. thesis, Duke University, 1962), 120–22.

an unchallenged nadir at the start, this issue proved to be a thorny problem on many subsequent battlefields. When a corps commander exclaims, as did Lt. Gen. Richard S. Ewell on the road to Gettysburg, "Why can't a Commanding General have some one on his staff who can write an intelligible order?" then clearly the headquarters of the Army of Northern Virginia cannot be said to have been a smoothly functioning military machine. Poor communication remained a nagging, unsolved problem until the end of the war. Lee seems either not to have noticed this point or failed to give it adequate weight among his priorities.[37]

By every account, his personal staff was underdeveloped and overused during his entire three years in command of the army. Although some generals around him practiced excess, Lee remained unaffected. He was determined to make the best of his situation rather than change it. A tireless advocate of reform and improvement in his own army, Lee's recommendations and complaints never seemed to apply to himself. Had the size of his staff doubled, it is unlikely that anyone would have accused Lee of maintaining a bloated throng of rear-echelon lackeys, and undoubtedly the daily work of army headquarters would have become more manageable. That is a step Lee should have taken.

Strangely he seems not to have shown much interest in shaping the composition of his personal staff. He wanted a few of the men filling those posts, but some of the others seem to have been assigned to him unsolicited. When Lee took over the army on June 1, 1862, he kept many of Joe Johnston's own staff officers indefinitely rather than replacing them with men he knew and trusted, and there is no evidence that he ever tried to ease out unwelcome or marginally inept officers from his staff. Despite this apparent indifference to his surroundings, Lee did at least know how to use the men he had. He converted Walter Taylor from a bank clerk into a staff officer widely respected throughout the army, an amazing accomplishment when most bureaucrats were held in such low esteem. Charles Venable and Charles Marshall earned entirely spotless wartime records, and their ability as representatives of the army commander is well known. Nearly every man proved to be an ideal fit for Lee and his command style; that is more of a compliment to him than to them.

37. I. R. Trimble to John Bachelder, Feb. 8, 1883, Bachelder Papers, New Hampshire Historical Society, Concord.

R. E. Lee cannot be judged to be an innovator in matters of staff work. He introduced nothing in his army that carried over into the postwar military establishment. Lee does, however, deserve more credit than he usually gets for having an understanding of what was needed to manage a modern army. If he mistakenly took too much responsibility upon himself, it was because he felt, more keenly than most, the importance of setting the tone for his subordinate generals. In an armywide sense he knew what should be done, yet it proved beyond his powers to establish a system to achieve it thoroughly. Profiting from a combination of his vast experience, his considerable reputation, and the incredible effect of his personality, Lee did at least steadily manage to improve the staff organization of his army under the most difficult circumstances. Deficiencies existed until the end, but they were not the consequence of negligence. When the Army of Northern Virginia stacked its arms for the last time in April 1865, it had a staff corps that was a more robust and useful thing than any previous model in the army's history.

The General and the Governor

Robert E. Lee and Zebulon B. Vance

MAX R. WILLIAMS

I N THE LULL BEFORE the 1864 spring campaign, North Carolina governor Zebulon B. Vance, a former Confederate colonel, visited his state's
troops in Virginia. His tour of the Army of Northern Virginia initiated a lasting and working partnership with Robert E. Lee that continued for the rest
of the war. The reputations of both men are clouded by a complexity between
their own words and their deeds, the representations of their contemporaries, and the construction of historians. But the intercourse between Lee and
Vance in the spring of 1864 and during the last months of the war begins to
cast doubt on what scholars think they know of both men. A close inspection
of the wartime relationship between the general and the governor suggests
that the characterizations of Lee as the American military model of submission to civilian authority and of Vance as a narrow champion of states' rights
is far too simplistic.

Elected in 1862, Governor Vance, formerly a staunch Unionist, had
sought to uphold North Carolina's rights against perceived encroachments by
the administration of Jefferson Davis while supporting Confederate military
efforts. But events in the South and in North Carolina had resulted in a substantial peace sentiment in the state. Erstwhile Vance ally William W.
Holden, longtime influential editor of the *North Carolina Standard,* had decided to contest Vance in the August 1864 gubernatorial election as a peace
candidate, claiming that the army favored peace overwhelmingly. Since
North Carolina soldiers in the field could vote, the colorful young Vance
came to "review" his troops and to campaign, an activity at which he excelled.

The Army of Northern Virginia was a fertile ground for garnering votes
in the North Carolina election. The soldier vote, if decisively for either Vance
or Holden, would probably determine the outcome of the election. In late

March, when Vance reached Lee's army, thirty-five North Carolina regiments were organized into eight brigades. Most were encamped near Orange County Court House. In the absence of Lt. Gen. James Longstreet's corps, which had two artillery batteries from the state but no regiments, North Carolina men composed more than half Lee's numbers. Even when Longstreet returned from Tennessee, approximately one-fifth of the Army of Northern Virginia came from the Old North State.[1]

The North Carolina brigades were encamped at intervals along the Rapidan or in the nearby countryside, with the commands of Brig. Gens. Stephen D. Ramseur and James Henry Lane on the right and left respectively. Vance reached Ramseur's position on March 26, welcomed by generals Robert E. Lee, Jeb Stuart, and other notables. For the next ten days, he moved along the line of North Carolina brigades. One observer described the governor as "about six feet high—inclined to stoutness—with long black hair, which of late has commenced to turn gray." Lane noted: "He is a large, fine-looking man and one of marked intelligence. In him is happily blended true eloquence and sound reasoning, with an inexhaustible fund of anecdotes."[2]

Vance's progression from place to place proved a triumph. A marvelous extemporaneous speaker, he attracted large crowds wherever he went. When word spread of his passion and eloquence, soldiers from other states joined the North Carolinians in hearing him. Area civilians swelled the crowds. Walter H. Taylor, Lee's adjutant, noted: "Gov Vance of No Caro is here on a visit to his troops. Speech making, tournaments and reviews are the order of the day. There will be a review tomorrow and if the weather is favorable no doubt there will be as many ladies present as soldiers."[3]

The governor's style was inimitable and infectious. A correspondent of

1. U.S. War Department, *The War of the Rebellion: A Compilation of the Official Records of the Union and Confederate Armies*, 128 vols. (Washington, D.C.: GPO, 1880–1901), 36:1021–27 [hereafter cited as *OR*; all references are to series 1].

2. *Fayetteville (N.C.) Observer*, Apr. 11, 1864; James H. Lane, "Glimpses of Army Life in 1864," in J. William Jones and others, eds., *Southern Historical Society Papers*, 52 vols. (1876–1959; reprint with 3-vol. index, Wilmington, N.C.: Broadfoot, 1990–92), 18:408 [hereafter cited as *SHSP*].

3. Walter H. Taylor to Bettie, Mar. 25, 1864, in Walter H. Taylor, *Lee's Adjutant: The Wartime Letters of Colonel Walter Herron Taylor, 1862–1865*, ed. R. Lockwood Tower (Columbia: University of South Carolina Press, 1995), 143–44.

ZEBULON B. VANCE AFTER THE CIVIL WAR

Courtesy of the North Carolina Office of Archives and History, Raleigh, North Carolina

the *Fayetteville (N.C.) Observer* explained his inability to describe a Vance speech adequately by admitting that his attempts to take notes failed, "I was so full of daughter [laughter] and so fascinated that I was unable to proceed further." In humorous language worthy of the governor himself, the correspondent described Vance's style: "He commenced with a joke, went on with a joke, joked a little while longer, and then told another joke; got his audience in an excellent humor with themselves, with their Governor, with the ladies, and with everybody else, when he commenced to discuss the condition of the country and spoke of the politics in North Carolina."[4]

In substance Vance's speeches were much the same. He acknowledged the desire for peace by "everyone in the Confederacy," thought it impossible to negotiate with the enemy, and opposed separate state action for peace as unconstitutional. Although skeptical of the outcome, he expressed a willingness "to send commissioners whenever it was thought necessary." Anticipating rejection of peaceful overtones by the Lincoln government, Vance said "that he was willing to bear the humiliation, that Europe and the world might see that the bloodshed and misery caused by this war was not of our making, and that the United States government alone was responsible therefore." He contended that the only way "to obtain peace honorably was by fighting for it."[5]

Warning that his hearers should not be misled by the "syren [sic] voice of evil minded men," Vance sought to energize the troops with patriotism and purpose. He said, "if we would only stand by our colors, maintain our organization and discipline and continue to strike boldly in the future as in the past—for home, freedom and independence—the sun of peace would soon rise in the east and shed its benign rays over our war-worn land." He believed that "Any other course would lead to disaster, dissolution and ruin." To reassure the North Carolina troops that Holden had overestimated the peace sentiment in the state, the governor denied that there was serious dissension in North Carolina and said that there was no more than "one man out of twenty" in the state "but whose whole heart was devoted to the cause, and would do anything in their power for their soldiers in the field." While acknowledging that North Carolinians "sometimes honestly differed from other

4. *Fayetteville (N.C.) Observer*, Apr. 11, 1864.
5. *Raleigh Daily Confederate*, Apr. 4, 1864.

people in matters of public policy and propriety," he assured the troops that the state's "popular heart beat in unison with her soldiers, and her determination was as strong as theirs to fight this war through to victory and independence."[6]

Formerly the popular colonel of the Twenty-Sixth North Carolina Infantry, Vance relished these days with his troops. His enthusiasm rose, and his speeches became more passionate and more patriotic as he moved from one encampment to another. Always stimulated by responsive audiences, he must have been ecstatic at his reception. There was considerable "pomp and circumstance" wherever he went. For example, on March 28 Lee reviewed the brigades from the Old North State, which "were out in full force, and presented a splendid appearance, in military bearing, as well as in every thing else that the most ardent well-wisher could desire." These "children of old Rip Van Winkle—battle scarred veterans . . . stood in long line almost as far as the eye could reach, with their arms glistening in the light of the noonday sun."[7]

On another occasion Vance enjoyed the rare honor of reviewing the Army of Northern Virginia with General Lee. Bands played and cannons boomed. Finally, "General Lee and Governor Vance appeared, and amid a storm of enthusiastic cheers and an avalanche of friendly greetings, rode slowly along the excited lines." One observer noted that on this stirring occasion the grand "confederate yell" hailed Lee and his "honored guest." Later Vance spoke from an elevated platform to thousands of civilians and soldiers from various states. While addressing Gen. Alfred Scales's brigade, Vance "brought tears to the eyes of many of the old battle-scarred veterans." An observer noted, "It was an interesting sight to witness these old heroes wipe away tears, and a few minutes later be convulsed with laughter." Maj. Gen. J. E. B. Stuart followed Vance from place to place "and seemed to be completely carried away with his speeches." It was reported on one or two occasions that General Lee "forgot his usual dignity and laughed heartily at his anecdotes."[8]

If Vance's purpose was to secure the army vote, he succeeded beyond his

---

6. Ibid.

7. Ibid.

8. Edward Warren, *A Doctor's Experiences in Three Continents* (Baltimore: Cushing & Bailey, 1885), 314–15; Lane, "Glimpses of Army Life in 1864," 408.

expectations. One old soldier remembered, "He received an ovation wherever he went and captured the army in toto." James A. Graham wrote, "Every body seemed to be perfectly delighted with the Governor and a large majority of the soldiers will support him in the coming campaign." A straw poll was conducted in the Fourteenth North Carolina Infantry. After several speeches Vance was unanimously chosen—"with shouts of up with Vance and down with the traitor."[9]

Apparently Vance's visit revivified much of the Army of Northern Virginia. Dr. Edward Warren, a member of the governor's staff with him in Virginia, reportedly "heard General Lee remark that Governor Vance's visit to the army has been equivalent to its reinforcement by fifty thousand men." This hyperbolic statement was extravagant for the reserved Lee, but he was surely impressed with Zeb Vance, as were his "lieutenants." Stuart heard all his speeches. Of one Vance effort he proclaimed, "If the test of eloquence is its effect, this speech was the most eloquent ever delivered." Vance later stated that he was "encouraged" by what he had seen of Lee's army. He had found "their condition . . . splendid, their provisions good, and their spirits buoyant."[10] Both Vance and those whom he had inspired in Virginia had benefited from his sojourn there. Soon, however, the Army of Northern Virginia would be confronted by a superior army imbued with the determination of Lt. Gen. U. S. Grant, now commander in chief of all Federal armies, who would accompany Maj. Gen. George G. Meade's Army of the Potomac across the Rapidan River and into the Wilderness. The ensuing battles would be bloody and desperate. Governor Vance was largely forgotten except by North Carolinians after he returned to his state to confront significant challenges: Holden and the peace movement, a shortage of supplies for both the army and the home front, and encroachments, though of a different kind, by both the Federal and Confederate governments. The memories of his visit to Virginia dimmed for Vance as they did for the beleaguered Army of Northern

9. Walter Clark, ed., *Histories of the Several Regiments and Battalions from North Carolina in the Great War, 1861–65, Written by Members of the Respective Commands*, 5 vols. (Goldsboro, N.C.: Nash Brothers, 1901), 2:46; James A. Graham to Mother, Apr. 2, 1864, in *The James A. Graham Papers*, ed. H. M. Wagstaff (Chapel Hill: University of North Carolina Press, 1928), 184; *Fayetteville (N.C.) Observer*, Apr. 11, 1864.

10. Warren, *Doctor's Experiences*, 316; James A. Graham to Mother, Apr. 2, 1864, in Wagstaff, *Graham Papers*, 184; *Fayetteville (N.C.) Observer*, Apr. 25, 1864.

Virginia. But his visit to the Old Dominion had at least one lasting consequence of importance: Governor Vance and General Lee forged a relationship
based on mutual respect and common purpose.

At first consideration Lee and Vance would seem to have had very little
in common. Descended from the Lees and Carters of Virginia, Robert Edward Lee was fifty-seven years old. Son of a country farmer and merchant,
Zebulon Baird Vance, a North Carolina mountaineer whose rural Buncombe
County environment was barely postfrontier, was thirty-three. Lee was a distinguished graduate of West Point. Vance's formal education consisted of ab-
breviated study in three neighborhood schools, where his reputation for high
jinks was legend; a few months at Washington College, a college in name
only located near Jonesboro, Tennessee; sporadic schooling in Asheville; and
a year as law student and jester at the University of North Carolina. By com-
parison with Lee, Vance's formal education was meager indeed. Moreover,
while Lee's demeanor, probity, and easy grace exemplified the characteristics
of the proverbial Southern gentleman, Vance was the boisterous source of an
exhaustless flow of humor and wit. Each man was wonderfully charming, but
Vance appeared rough-hewn in contrast to the handsome, refined Lee.[11]

Other apparent impediments to a close Lee-Vance working relationship
were their variant careers and wartime reputations. A professional soldier all
his adult life, the general eschewed politics and deferred to civilian authority;
while politics was the focus of the governor's mature years. Never a careful
legal scholar, Vance viewed the law as an avenue to political preferment. By
1864 Lee symbolized the Confederate war effort; and most Southerners believed that he, with the Army of Northern Virginia, represented the best hope
of achieving independence. Conversely, because of his frequent clashes with
the Davis administration, Vance's loyalty was suspect in some quarters.

---

11. Douglas Southall Freeman, "Robert Edward Lee," *Dictionary of American Biography*, ed.
Allen Johnson, Dumas Malone, et al., 20 vols. (New York: Scribner, 1928): 6:120–29; Russell F.
Weigley, "Robert E. Lee," *American National Biography*, ed. John A. Garraty and Mark C. Carnes,
24 vols. (New York: Oxford University Press, 1999), 13:392–97; Robert D. W. Connor, "Zebulon
Baird Vance," *Dictionary of American Biography*, 10:158–61; Joe A. Mobley, "Zebulon Baird
Vance," *American National Biography*, 22:168–70; Frontis Johnston and Joe A. Mobley, eds., *The
Papers of Zebulon B. Vance* (Raleigh, N.C.: North Carolina Department of Cultural Resources,
Division of Archives and History, 1963), 1:xvii–lxxiv. For an account of Vance's Chapel Hill days,
see Clement Dowd, *Life of Zebulon B. Vance* (Charlotte, N.C.: Observer, 1897), 16–30.

It is apparent that the two men differed notably in age, environment, education, bearing, careers, and wartime reputations. There were, however, several ways in which their experiences prior to March 1864 were similar. Both were influenced by family tradition; both were committed to public service; both were able and successful; and both were determined to act manfully and honorably in the struggle for Southern independence.

A popular military figure, Vance became a candidate for governor in the 1862 state elections. His opponent was William Johnston of Mecklenburg County, a railroad official and an original secessionist. North Carolina was badly divided by the war, and a party of old-line Unionist Whigs chose and elected Vance governor. The campaign was bitterly contested, and the pro-Confederate partisan press accused Vance of disloyalty, calling him the "Yankee" candidate. Apparently this negative description of the veteran colonel convinced the Davis administration that the new North Carolina governor was untrustworthy, though Vance had promised to prosecute the war "at all hazards and to the utmost extremity."[12] Subsequently, in upholding his state's rights within the Confederacy, Vance objected to several Davis administration policies, including conscription, the suspension of habeas corpus, and the impressment of civilian property by the military. Thus, while Southerners held Robert E. Lee in the highest esteem in 1864, some dedicated Confederates considered Zebulon Vance an impediment to gaining independence. Nevertheless, despite their disparate wartime reputations, Lee and Vance, both men of personal integrity, cooperated honorably in pursuit of Confederate victory.

Prior to their 1864 spring meeting, the direct interaction between Lee and Vance had been limited to six communications relating to specific topics involving the Army of Northern Virginia or the defense of North Carolina. Otherwise their exchanges were conducted within appropriate channels, that is, through the Confederate secretary of war. After Vance's visit to the army, though, a substantial, direct correspondence developed. Between July 1864 and March 1865, Lee and Vance exchanged at least thirty-one letters or telegrams, none via the War Department. Lee's confidence in Vance is reflected in a July letter to President Davis. In discussing ways to quell civil unrest in

12. *Fayetteville (N.C.) Observer*, June 16, 1862.

western North Carolina, Lee wrote, "The Governor would be more effica-
cious than anyone else in repressing this spirit of insubordination and in en-
forcing law and order."[13]

In the North Carolina elections of August 1864, Governor Vance won reelection in a landslide victory over William Holden, polling 58,070 votes to
his opponent's 14,491. Vance received 13,209 of 15,033 votes cast by North
Carolina troops in the field. On August 9 Vance informed Lee of his success.
Three days later the general responded in a "private" letter of congratulations. He said that Vance's reelection was "well calculated to cheer and sustain the people of the Confederacy. It dissipates the hopes that our enemies
had cherished, and convinced them that three years of war have in no degree
shaken the resolution of our people to resist, as long as they present them no
alternative but that of a degrading submission." Lee commended Vance for
his patriotism and expressed conviction "that under your administration, the
cause of Southern independence will continue to receive the powerful support of the brave people of North Carolina as fully and efficiently as hereto-
fore." These remarks were a masterful call for Vance's loyalty and support;
moreover they were a balm to a governor frequently at odds with the Davis
administration. This letter reveals Lee's political acumen and suggests the
possibility for close cooperation between the general and the governor.[14]

In the last months of the war, Lee and Vance were preoccupied with the
dangers threatening the Confederacy. Two interrelated issues were particularly pressing: Lee's need for troops to defend the Petersburg-Richmond
nexus, and the protection of North Carolina, especially Wilmington, a vital
port through which supplies still flowed. Desertion was a serious problem
among Lee's troops, especially after the fall of 1863. Following the Overland
Campaign, at which time the Army of Northern Virginia was fixed in trench

13. Robert E. Lee to Jefferson Davis, July 12, 1864, in *Lee's Dispatches: Unpublished Letters of
General Robert E. Lee, C.S.A., to Jefferson Davis and the War Department of the Confederate States of
America, 1862–1865*, rev. ed., ed. Douglas Southall Freeman and Grady McWhiney (New York:
G. P. Putnam's Sons, 1957), 281.

14. John L. Cheney Jr., ed., *North Carolina Government, 1585—1979: A Narrative and Statistical
History* (Raleigh: North Carolina Secretary of State, 1981), 1401; Johnston and Mobley, *Papers of
Zebulon B. Vance*, 1:lxix; Robert E. Lee to Zebulon B. Vance, Aug. 12, 1864, in *The Papers of
Zebulon Vance*, eds. Gordon McKinney and Richard McMurry (microfilm, Frederick, Md., 1987),
Reel 3.

warfare before Petersburg, desertion increased apace with boredom, war-weariness, poignant entreaties from home, and a growing realization that Southern independence was illusory. In the case of North Carolina troops, the peace movement of 1863–64 and Chief Justice R. M. Pearson's rulings suggesting that conscription was illegal combined to exacerbate the problem.[15] The proximity of North Carolina and Virginia made going home easier for those from the Old North State. Going home to help with the spring planting sometimes stretched into several months, even among those soldiers who planned to return to their army duties. The North Carolinians who chose this course were branded "deserters," while Virginians, whose return was typically swifter, were listed as "absent without leave." But regardless of the precise status of those absent, Lee's army was dangerously depopulated.[16]

On August 10, 1864, General Lee issued General Orders No. 54 in an attempt to increase his numbers. The message was clear: those who returned voluntarily would "palliate their offense" and could expect clemency; those arrested for return "shall suffer the extreme penalty of the law." Soldiers were urged to do their duty, civilians to encourage their return, and civil authorities to prosecute those who assisted deserters. Vance issued a proclamation on August 24 that included a guarantee of clemency for thirty days from that date. This promise led to delay by some North Carolinians and occasioned misunderstandings. Otherwise Vance's proclamation was a powerful response to Lee's general order. He urged "most earnestly" that those absent from the army return "to wipe out from their once respected names the foul stain of desertion." He called upon the militia, civilians, and magistrates to assist in returning "misguided men" to their units. To deserters, Vance promised to harry them from the state or to capture and subject them to the full force of the law. He challenged North Carolinians thus: "If every good and loyal citizen would set about to reclaim or capture one deserter by any means in his power, . . . he will have rendered a most valuable and patriotic service to his State and Country." It is apparent that Vance used his

15. For a thorough discussion of this topic, see Memory F. Mitchell, *Legal Aspects of Conscription and Exemption in North Carolina, 1861–1865* (Chapel Hill: University of North Carolina Press, 1965).

16. See Richard Bardolph, "Confederate Dilemma: North Carolina Troops and the Desertion Problem," parts 1 and 2, *North Carolina Historical Review* 66 (Jan. 1989): 61–86; 66 (Apr. 1989): 179–209.

authority to support national policy. Instead of acting like a states' rights obstructionist, he exerted his power and prestige as governor to strengthen Confederate armies. Both he and Lee united their efforts to maximize the South's resources in fighting the war.[17]

Vance explained to Lee his belief that setting a deadline for extending clemency would produce the best results, and their correspondence suggests that the matter was soon forgotten. For example, Lee wrote Vance on August 29 calling upon the governor to exert every effort to protect Wilmington. Since he could send no troops because of Federal movements in Virginia and Georgia, he emphasized that Wilmington's defense would depend on North Carolina reserves and local troops. He urged the governor to induce such men to "come forward freely." Then in the same letter he addressed a state grievance by praising North Carolina troops for their action in the battle of Reams' Station. The North Carolina brigades of Gens. John R. Cooke, William MacRae, and James Lane "advanced through a thick *abattis* of felled trees, under a heavy fire of musketry and artillery, and carried the enemy's works with a steady courage that elicited the warm commendation of their corps and division commanders and the admiration of the army." Lee concluded in a way designed to gain Vance's vigorous assistance in rallying North Carolinians to the defense of Wilmington, by saying, "If the men who remain in North Carolina share the spirit of those they have sent to the field, as I doubt not they do, her defense may securely be trusted to their hands." Not surprisingly, Vance quickly responded, pledging all the aid he could muster for the defense of Wilmington. Lee replied: "I am much gratified at your readiness and ability to render all the aid in your power in the defense of Wilmington. Of the former I never doubted. . . . The prospect of peace and independence depends very much upon the success of this campaign. I need not, therefore, inform Your Excellency of the importance of bringing and maintaining in the field all our available force. The life and safety of the people demand it." How could Vance not cooperate fully with such an appeal from a beloved chieftain?[18]

17. *OR*, 42(2):1169; Vance proclamation, Aug. 24, 1864, in McKinney and McMurry, *Papers of Zebulon Vance*, Reel 13.

18. *OR*, 42(2):1206–7; Robert E. Lee to Zebulon B. Vance, Sept. 5, 1864, in McKinney and McMurry, *Papers of Zebulon Vance*, Reel 13.

Despite the governor's efforts to increase the number of North Carolinians in national or state service, manpower remained a serious problem. As the Federal armies grew in size, Lee's lines became thinner, and his anxiety became palpable. In a "confidential" letter to Vance dated October 8, Lee reported that his position was desperate and that he feared envelopment. He asked that Vance allow four North Carolina regiments in state service be sent to Virginia. The general also wondered whether depleted regiments could be filled if sent to North Carolina. At the same time, Lee wrote Lt. Gen. T. H. Holmes, a member of his West Point class and now commander of North Carolina state troops, noting that he believed Vance "takes as deep an interest in the defense of the whole country, as in any part." Lee hoped that North Carolina would send the regiments in question for Confederate service and wondered if at least "they cannot be assigned to duty with me till the campaign closes."[19]

Vance decided that he could not spare any state troops for Confederate service. His decision was based not so much on a states' rights philosophy as on the fact that manpower was virtually depleted in North Carolina. He did, however, report progress in mobilizing the reserves and home guard. Lee advised that a regiment be sent to western North Carolina to quell civil unrest and round up deserters—Vance must call out all men capable of service. Lee was clearly still concerned about Wilmington. On November 2 the governor regretted that no cavalry could be sent to Virginia; there were only two companies in state service. He did promise that every effort would be made to assist Gen. Braxton Bragg, now charged with the defense of North Carolina, "should it become necessary." By way of suggesting his own manpower problems, Vance reported that he had twice ordered the Sixty-Eighth Regiment of North Carolina Troops from guard duty at Salisbury Prison to Wilmington only to have his orders suspended by the prison commandant, who refused to release the men before new guards could be recruited and trained.[20] Vance's willingness to support Lee was thwarted by Confederate authority, not by some abstract commitment to states' rights. He wanted to help the general, desperate for more troops around Petersburg, but he simply

19. OR, 42(3):1141–42.

20. Robert E. Lee to Zebulon B. Vance, Oct. 29, 1864, in McKinney and McMurry, *Papers of Zebulon Vance*, Reel 13; Zebulon B. Vance to Robert E. Lee, Nov. 2, 1864, in ibid.

lacked the power to send North Carolina units that had been enrolled in national service.

On December 18, 1864, a telegram from Lee reached Raleigh warning Vance that a large force had departed Virginia for a combined land and naval assault on Fort Fisher. Grant had ordered Maj. Gen. Benjamin Butler to reduce Fort Fisher and close the port of Wilmington. Lee reported that eighty-five steamers carrying twenty thousand troops had sailed from Old Point. An additional ten thousand Federals, mostly black soldiers, had left Fortress Monroe for New Bern. Moreover Lee referred to a plan to unite the forces of Grant and Maj. Gen. Philip Sheridan for an attack along the entire length of his Petersburg line. Of this Lee said that it was "exaggerated and improbable but may contain some truth." Although Lee grossly overestimated the size of Butler's expedition, which consisted of sixty-five hundred troops and two batteries, Lee was clearly alarmed. He realized the importance of Wilmington and on December 19 sent Maj. Gen. Robert Hoke's division from Virginia by rail. A terse telegram reached Vance on December 23, saying, "Can you aid Genl Bragg to subsist troops sent to Wilmington?" Because of delays in transportation, the first of Hoke's men did not arrive until the twenty-fifth, but their arrival raised the stakes. Fearing heavy losses in a frontal assault, the Federals withdrew to Hampton Roads.[21]

Lee was greatly concerned by the delay in Hoke's arrival. If it took six days to move troops from Petersburg to Wilmington by rail, interior lines were of little use to the Confederacy. Hoke's division had been routed via Danville, Virginia, along the newly completed Piedmont Railroad to Greensboro, where it transferred to the North Carolina Railroad. Apparently the delays had occurred in Greensboro, where the problem lay in shifting passengers and freight from the Piedmont to the North Carolina line. Lee requested that Vance "ascertain what can be done to facilitate transportation by rail, and give all the assistance in your power." He concluded in a way that must have been painful to the sensitive Vance: "The delay is not only dangerous and injurious, but has given rise to painful suspicions, which in justice to those connected with the management of the roads should be removed." On

21. Robert E. Lee to Zebulon B. Vance, telegram, Dec. 18, 1864; and Robert E. Lee to Zebulon B. Vance, Dec. 23, 1864, in ibid. For a brief and full account of the battle for Fort Fisher, see Rod Gragg, *Confederate Goliath: The Battle of Fort Fisher* (New York: Harper & Row, 1991).

this point Douglas Southall Freeman notes: "At the time this spread suspicion of deliberate treachery, but it should have been accepted as warning that the long-threatened collapse of transportation was imminent."[22]

This implication of treachery must have been devastating to Governor Vance, who was by this time determined to do all in his power to rally North Carolinians to the Confederate cause. The Old North State was seriously threatened in the Wilmington area, and it was anticipated that Maj. Gen. William T. Sherman's army would soon march northward into the state. In a proclamation dated December 20, Vance called upon all loyal citizens "who may be able to stand behind breastworks and fire a musket, of all ages and conditions, to rally at once to the defense of their country and hurry to Wilmington. . . . [E]very man who has the spirit of freedom in his bosom . . . come and come at once." The man who holds back now, whether subject to military service or not, "will find it hard to make us believe that he is not pleading the cause of cowardice and disloyalty. The country needs their help now, and that help must be given in the hour of distress, or they must own that their souls are only fitted to enjoy the freedom purchased with other men's blood." This stirring appeal had little influence on war-weary North Carolinians, but it demonstrates that Vance possessed an overriding commitment to the creation of a Confederate nation. He did not undermine the Southern war effort. His patriotic rhetoric was not empty, for he promptly headed to Wilmington himself to assist in the city's defense.[23]

Fort Fisher and Wilmington enjoyed only a brief respite before a larger and more determined Federal force sailed from Virginia. The new threat consisted of a formidable naval force and Brig. Gen. A. H. Terry's Provisional Corps of eight thousand men. Lee requested that Vance "strengthen Bragg all you can." Anticipating another attack shortly, Col. William Lamb, commandant of Fort Fisher, telegraphed an urgent appeal to Vance for five hundred slaves "with tools and rations" because "no additional labor has been sent to me since the attack & my force is worn out." Warning that "too much precious time is being lost," Lamb concluded that, "Every negro you send me adds to the protection of our soldiers & the safety of our homes." On January

22. *OR*, 42(3):1334–35; Douglas Southall Freeman, *Lee's Lieutenants: A Study in Command*, 3 vols. (New York: Charles Scribner's Sons, 1942–44), 3:618.

23. *OR*, 42(3):1284–85.

13, 1865, a Lee telegram to Vance reported that the enemy fleet had reached the New Inlet, linking the Atlantic Ocean and the Cape Fear River. Bragg "will require all the force you can give him. Please order to him all the troops you can." There was nothing Vance could do, however, and Fort Fisher fell two days later.[24]

Anticipating the loss of Fisher, Lee wrote Vance three curious letters referring to contraband trade across enemy lines in northeastern North Carolina. On January 9, 1865, he requested that the governor use his influence "to prevent any allusion by the papers of Raleigh, or any others in your State to certain commercial transactions which will probably occur on the rivers of eastern N. Carolina, particularly the Chowan." Lee suggested that this trade "may be of such magnitude as to attract attention." Noting the importance of these transactions, he said that any word of them "reaching the enemy may and probably will put an end to them at once, to our great injury." Two days later in a "confidential" letter, Lee reiterated his position by including a portion of Special Orders No. 9, issued January 12, 1865, authorizing the impressment of supplies for the Army of Northern Virginia, which had only two days' rations. Of the trade of contraband, the general emphasized the importance of "keeping it in the hands of government, and maintaining all possible secrecy about its existence and magnitude."[25]

The discussion of the contraband trade in North Carolina continued. On January 16 Lee reported to Secretary of War James Seddon that "traffic is carried on to a large extent without authority, and that the effects are demoralizing in their tendency." Lee noted that he had ordered that no non-Confederate contraband be allowed to pass army lines, but he feared that the private trade could not be suppressed. That same day he wrote Vance, including a report of Capt. E. P. George, who was conducting the Chowan trade. George complained of actions by state agents and recommended impressment of all cotton between the Roanoke and Chowan Rivers. He also suggested that Confederate troops be assigned to crucial junctures by which the

24. Robert E. Lee to Zebulon B. Vance, telegram, Jan. 10, 1865, in McKinney and McMurry, *Papers of Zebulon Vance*, Reel 26; William Lamb to Zebulon B. Vance, telegram, Jan. 10, 1865, ibid.; Robert E. Lee to Zebulon B. Vance, telegram, Jan. 13, 1865, ibid.

25. Robert E. Lee to Zebulon B. Vance, Jan. 9, 1865, in McKinney and McMurry, *Papers of Zebulon Vance*, Reel 4; Robert E. Lee to Zebulon B. Vance, Jan. 11, 1865, ibid. See also Special Orders No. 9, *OR*, 46(2):1041–42.

illicit trade moved so as to interrupt it. Lee begged Vance to halt the transportation of cotton east of the Roanoke and to prevent state agents from authorizing private citizens to move cotton through Confederate lines. With the fall of Fort Fisher, this matter was most urgent. In seeking the governor's aid, Lee said that "if the state authorities would make the illegal traffic a misdemeanor punishable by fine or imprisonment, or both, it would be the most effectual mode of suppressing it."[26] In his desperation he was intruding himself into state affairs, but Vance, facing his own crisis, was receptive to the general's advice.

Given his commitment to states' rights *and* the Confederacy, Governor Vance was conflicted by General Lee's urgent requests that state agents be restricted in the contraband trade; but he was thoroughly in agreement that protecting North Carolina in the wake of Fort Fisher's fall and Sherman's approach was essential. On February 14 Vance issued another proclamation designed to rally popular support. After the failure of the Hampton Roads Conference, he concluded that there was no honorable course except resistance. He implored North Carolinians to fight, reminding them that the Confederacy consisted of its people, not "brick and mortar . . .on particular spots of ground however valuable they may be in a military point of view." Having warned them of the impending dangers to the Confederacy and the state, Vance called upon his fellow citizens, "I now appeal to you by everything held sacred among men, to bear yourselves as becomes your high lineage and future hopes." He urged North Carolinians to set aside partisan bitterness, to restore absentees to the army, to divide their abundance with the poor and suffering, to strengthen the civil and military authorities, and to sustain the soldiers and their leaders in order "to prevent the degradation of your country, and the ruin of its people." He called for local meetings across the state to accomplish these goals and "to let the whole world and especially our enemies know how a free people can meet a proposition for their absolute submission to the will of their conquerors." This was another eloquent appeal to an exhausted populace, and it was vintage Vance. But as William W. Holden's

---

26. *OR*, 46(2):1075; Robert E. Lee to Zebulon B. Vance, July [Jan.] 16, 1865, in McKinney and McMurry, *Papers of Zebulon Vance*, Reel 4.

newspaper noted, "If proclamations could have won the War victory would have come long ago."[27]

Soon Federal armies posed a very real threat to North Carolina. Lee warned Vance that Maj. Gen. John Schofield's corps had landed at Fort Fisher and that more Federals may have reached Morehead City. There was speculation that Sherman would strike Charlotte and move to join Schofield at either Weldon or Raleigh. Vance should "bring out" every able North Carolinian and either move or destroy supplies in the path of the enemy. The governor promised "all assistance in my power" and reported that he had "called out every man liable to duty in the State," but his weakness was revealed by this suggestion of his plight: "I can't destroy provisions without a force of cavalry."[28]

As conditions in the Confederacy deteriorated, General Lee again wrote Vance in late February in an attempt to influence the governor and his state. In pointing out that despondency among civilians was dragging down the army's morale, Lee reported that several hundred men, including many North Carolinians, had deserted from A. P. Hill's corps. He credited this to letters from home claiming that the cause was hopeless and that soldiers "had better provide for themselves." The only response, according to Lee, was the "counsel and exhortation of prominent citizens." He advised that the Federals had concentrated their efforts in Virginia and North Carolina, and if they could be turned back, much territory would lay open to Confederate advances. Contending that the situation was critical for both sides, Lee implored Vance to do all in his power to offset despondency and desertion by encouraging the people to suffer "a little longer" in hopes of regaining the spirit that marked the first two years of the war.[29]

On March 2 Vance replied by referring to his recent proclamation and noting that he had initiated a series of public meetings to offset despondency on the home front. He warned, however, that "the near and triumphant ap-

27. Vance proclamation, Feb. 14, 1865, in McKinney and McMurry, *Papers of Zebulon Vance*, Reel 13; *(Raleigh) North Carolina Standard*, Feb. 22, 1865.

28. Robert E. Lee to Zebulon B. Vance, telegram, Feb. 16, 1865, in McKinney and McMurry, *Papers of Zebulon Vance*, Reel 26; Robert E. Lee to Zebulon B. Vance, Feb. 19, telegram, 1865, ibid.; *OR*, 47(2):1230.

29. *OR*, 47(2):1270–71.

proach of the enemy has so alarmed the timid and so engrossed the loyal in preparation for his coming, that I fear they will hardly have their proper effect." The governor mentioned that his opportunities to speak to the public had been limited by his efforts to rally the militia and "secure my vast private stores." He assured Lee "that I am fully alive to the importance of this crisis, and whatever man can do in my situation shall be done." Then Vance reported a moving response to his appeal to the people for supplies to succor the army. Within two hours of his published plea, a poor widow of his acquaintance had appeared with two pieces of bacon and a barrel of meal. Vance concluded, "Such offerings, on the sacred altar of country, hallow our cause, and I hope will secure God's blessing upon it."[30]

On March 9 Lee penned one of his last substantial letters to Vance. Commending the "widow" for her response to the cause, Lee regretted that he had no cavalry to send to North Carolina. He admonished the governor to use local troops to round up deserters and urged that no quarter be given. Lee praised his proclamation and his addresses to the people and hoped that "you will infuse into your fellow-citizens the spirit of resolution and patriotism which inspires your own actions." He expressed to the governor "my sincere thanks for your zealous efforts in behalf of the army and the cause."[31]

At this time the collaboration of Lee and Vance fell victim to the course of events. By March 1865 they were preoccupied with circumstances thrust upon them by Federal armies, but it is clear that their relationship was unique. An examination of the *Official Records* reinforces this contention. During the last ten months of the war, only two letters by Lee to any other Southern governor are included. Moreover the correspondence between Vance and Lee offers a rare insight into the general's posture toward civil authority, his relationship to those around him, and his political role in the Confederacy. Douglas Southall Freeman's magisterial biography has set the interpretive tone on all these issues. Various statements in his four-volume work assert that Lee accepted the supremacy of civil authority and seldom challenged President Davis on any issue. According to Freeman, Lee "applied literally and loyally his conviction that the President was the commander-in-chief and that the military arm was subordinate to the civil." His respect for

30. Ibid., 1353–54.
31. Ibid.

civil authority "kept him from offering suggestions regarding other armies than his own, except when his views were sought by the President or by the Secretary of War." This view resonates throughout discussions of Lee. Even revisionist Alan T. Nolan agrees that Lee accepted civil authority, with the caveat that the general was very powerful, had tactical control, and had a decisive influence on grand strategy.[32]

The reasons for Lee's great influence lie in his relationship with his superiors and subordinates. A man of great intellect, poise, and character, he inspired those around him by his humility, sense of duty, and devotion to the Confederate nation. Based on handwritten notes found in Lee's military valise after his death, William C. McDonald contends that the key to the general's interpersonal successes lay in his concept of "the true gentleman." Forbearance in the use of power in dealing with subordinates and superiors provide the measure of an individual's character and honor. Lee embraced these qualities, and genuine humility became an integral segment of his character and his style of leadership.[33]

Humility and forbearance were qualities that served Lee well, especially in his relations with Jefferson Davis. It is generally agreed that Davis was a particularly difficult man: excessively proud, sensitive, judgmental, and inflexible. The president's difficulties with Gen. Joseph E. Johnston, Lt. Gen. Daniel Harvey Hill, and Gen. P. G. T. Beauregard are legendary. The fact that Lee enjoyed Davis's confidence and respect is a tribute to the Virginian's personality traits and diplomatic acumen. In a recent biography William C. Davis recites those things one had to do to get along with the Confederate president: "Do not question him unless he invited criticism. Do not challenge him. Keep him fully informed at all times. Do not assail his friends or cronies. Have nothing to do with the press, and eschew public controversy. Avoid politicians, especially those in the growing anti-Davis camp. Most of all remain loyal." These requirements coincided with Lee's ideas of the proper

32. Douglas Southall Freeman, *R. E. Lee: A Biography*, 4 vols. (New York: Charles Scribner's Sons, 1934–35), 3:165, 4:179; Alan T. Nolan, *Lee Considered: General Robert E. Lee and Civil War History* (Chapel Hill: University of North Carolina Press, 1991), 72–73.

33. William C. McDonald, "The True Gentleman: On Robert E. Lee's Definition of the Gentleman," *Civil War History* 32 (1986): 120–21. It should be noted that precisely these qualities have occasioned sharp criticisms of Lee. For example, see J. F. C. Fuller, *Grant and Lee: A Study in Personality and Generalship* (1933; reprint, Bloomington: Indiana University Press, 1957), 113–26.

relationship between himself and his commander in chief, and the two formed "a civil-military team surpassing any other of the war, even Lincoln and Grant."[34] The same qualities demonstrated by Lee in his relationship with Davis explain his treatment of Jeb Stuart after his failure during the Gettysburg Campaign and of A. P. Hill after Bristoe Station. Lee was clearly a masterful diplomat in dealing with superiors and subordinates alike.

One requirement for getting along with President Davis that Lee would have easily met was that he "avoid politicians" and "eschew public controversy." Freeman notes that, though he often "captivated politicians," Lee had little to do with the Confederate Congress and in fact had "an ineradicable distrust of politicians." This assessment is substantiated by Maj. Gen. G. W. Custis Lee, who reported his father's frustration in dealing with politicians. Early in 1865 the elder soldier went to Congress seeking support for his desperate army. Afterward a deeply perturbed Lee complained, "I have been up to see the Congress and they do not seem to be able to do anything except eat peanuts and chew tobacco, while my army is starving."[35]

What then is the accepted interpretation of Lee's attitudes toward civil authority, relationship to others, and political involvement? His correspondence with Governor Vance raises serious doubts about the contention that the general always accepted the supremacy of civil authority, deferred to others, and eschewed politics. Prior to their meeting in 1864, Lee had punctiliously involved the secretary of war as intermediary in important communications with Vance. The fact that he subsequently engaged in frequent correspondence with the governor without reference to civil authority is significant. This is at odds with the traditional Lee posture regarding his obligations to civil authority; the extent of the correspondence makes it so. Likewise the usual deference of Lee to Davis is brought into question. The very fact that he bypassed official channels in dealing with Vance suggests that his "deference" to the president was not complete. It should be noted, however, that Lee's letters to Vance do confirm his tact in dealing with potentially troublesome individuals. He was respectful and professional in his correspondence with the governor.

34. William C. Davis, *Jefferson Davis: The Man and His Hour* (New York: Harper Collins, 1991), 426, 697.

35. Freeman, *R. E. Lee*, 4:181; George Taylor Lee, "Reminiscences of General Robert E. Lee, 1865–68," *South Atlantic Quarterly* 26, 2 (1927): 236.

The last contention suggested above, that Lee eschewed politics, is even more interesting. It would appear that the general was a masterful politician from the way he appealed to Vance for support. He played upon Vance's own military background in seeking to offset the governor's opposition to conscription, impressment, and Confederate affronts to civil rights. He sought to placate North Carolina's disgruntlement at having Virginia officers command North Carolina units, and he tried to redress Tar Heel grievances about the failure of North Carolina troops to get the recognition their services deserved. Lee injected himself into state affairs when he requested that the governor prevent state newspapers from reporting trade across military lines in eastern North Carolina. He also acted politically when he urged Vance to encourage the better class of North Carolinians to rally popular support for the Confederacy. It seems that Lee's deference to civil authority and his distaste for politics must be reconsidered in light of his relationship with Governor Vance.

While the reputation of Robert E. Lee among his contemporaries and historians is almost universally laudatory, Zebulon Vance's reputation has been the subject of controversy. It was well known among his contemporaries that he had opposed secession; and although he quickly raised a company and fought for the Confederacy, he was assailed as the "Northern or Yankee Candidate" when he ran for the governorship in 1862. Original secessionists never forgave him for his Unionism, and their criticism rose apace with the organization of a political party, called the Conservatives, and with Vance's opposition to Davis's policies. As governor he acted upon the premise that the Confederate Constitution guaranteed the rights of member states. He never accepted the idea that, in order to gain independence, the Davis administration had to centralize its control of Southern economic, manpower, and military resources. Vance was frequently at odds with Richmond concerning such issues as conscription, civil liberties, impressment, and control of material resources such as shoes, blankets, and uniforms. North Carolina was the only Rebel state that insisted on providing for its own troops first, with any unneeded surpluses allocated to the Confederacy. This posture became particularly controversial when, late in the war, Wilmington became the principal port open to blockade runners. Since North Carolina conducted a substantial traffic in running the blockade for its own benefit, Vance became irate when Richmond sought to require that a portion of cargo space be allocated to the Confederate government. Somewhat less significant to the outcome of the war were Vance's complaints about the loss of territory in eastern North Carolina to the Federals, the officering of state brigades, and the neglect of North Carolina troops in newspaper reports of battles. The Davis administration found Vance most contrary in regards to these issues. Undoubtedly, as Vance sought to protect what he considered the rights of his state, his reputation as an obstructionist was established early on.[36]

Ironically Vance contributed to his obstructionist reputation even as he attempted to rehabilitate North Carolina's standing among the former Confederate states and to further the war effort. Speaking to the Southern Historical Society at White Sulphur Springs, West Virginia, on August 18, 1875, he sought to emphasize the contributions his state made to the Confederacy. The tone of his remarks is reflected in his contention that "North Carolina is entitled to stand where her troops stood in battle, behind no state, but in the front rank of the Confederation, aligned and abreast with the best, the foremost and bravest." Subsequently he elaborated the ways in which North Carolina had done more than her share in providing manpower, economic resources, and moral support to the common cause. But one statement in this speech haunted Vance in the histories to follow: "At the surrender of General Johnston the State had on hand, ready-made and in cloth, ninety-two thousand suits of uniforms, with great stores of blankets, leather, etc., the greater part of which was distributed among the soldiers and people."[37] This assertion (possibly the boast of a prideful North Carolina partisan) became a standard by which Vance's states' rights beliefs were judged. How could he claim to have been fully committed to the cause if he had horded this wealth of goods, goods so desperately needed by Confederate armies?

Historians have vacillated in their treatment of Vance. Writing in 1907, William E. Dodd suggested that Raleigh was a "centre of disloyalty" to the Richmond government and that Vance "was the most difficult man Davis had

---

36. John G. Barrett, *The Civil War in North Carolina* (Chapel Hill: University of North Carolina Press, 1963), 182. For contemporary attacks on Vance and Holden, see *(Raleigh) State Journal*, July 23, 30, 1862. For a detailed treatment of Vance's positions, see Richard E. Yates, *The Confederacy and Zeb Vance* (Tuscaloosa: University of Alabama Press, 1958).

37. *SHSP*, 14:506, 513. For an analysis of Vance's address, see Gordon B. McKinney, "Zebulon Vance and His Reconstruction of the Civil War in North Carolina," *The North Carolina Historical Review* 75, 1 (Jan. 1998): 68–85.

to deal with." He also characterized the governor as "a shrewd man, in conduct and character, the nearest approach to Lincoln the south had produced." Douglas Southall Freeman described Vance as a "difficult and positive individual." Clement Eaton noted that, next to Georgia's Joe Brown, the North Carolinian was "the most obstreperous war governor opposing the centralizing policies of the Confederacy" while describing Vance as energetic and provincial. E. Merton Coulter called the governor his "state's great war leader" but noted that because of "his excessive desires to see that his state was first served, he tended to lose sight of the paramount needs of the Confederacy."[38]

In 1925 Frank Owsley published the harshest indictment of Governor Vance. Convinced that the Confederacy had "died of state's rights," Owsley laid much of the blame on the North Carolinian. Quotes from *State Rights in the Confederacy* make the author's point. Of Vance he writes, "Governor Vance was a shining example of the governors who neither raised local Confederate troops nor transferred the state troops to the Confederacy." Regarding conscription, "Vance championed the popular discontent and fanned the flames higher. Under his guidance the people began to show distinct signs of unwillingness to leave the state to fight."[39]

Of Vance's vigorous reaction to the 1864 suspension of habeas corpus, Owsley contends that the governor "seemed to lose his self-restraint, and pour forth a torrent of abuse upon the head of the President for his treatment of North Carolinians and his attitude of suspicion toward that state—in fact, he blamed Davis for conscription, impressment, favoritism for appointing to office [Southerners] other than North Carolinians . . . ; he blamed him for everything in such language as only Vance or Brown could command." Owsley also believed that North Carolina was selfish in its hoarding of war supplies. He reported that by the governor's own count the state had warehoused ninety-two thousand uniforms and great stores of other goods and that "his troops in the field were all comfortably clad. At the same time Lee's troops were ragged and without blankets and tents." It should be noted that,

38. William E. Dodd, *Jefferson Davis* (Philadelphia: G. W. Jacobs, 1907), 337; Freeman, *R. E. Lee*, 4:181; Clement Eaton, *A History of the Confederacy* (New York: Macmillan, 1954), 265–66; E. M. Coulter, *The Confederate States of America* (Baton Rouge: Louisiana State University Press, 1950), 398.

39. Frank L. Owsley, *State Rights in the Confederacy* (1925; reprint, Gloucester, Mass.: Peter Smith, 1961), 38, 43.

in his effort to condemn Vance, Owsley had misused the 1875 Southern Historical Society speech. Actually Vance claimed that North Carolina "had on hand, ready made and in cloth, ninety two thousand suits of uniform," without differentiating between completed uniforms and available cloth. Owsley's misuse of this statement is serious; one suspects that the flamboyant Vance was a bit boastful and given to exaggeration.[40]

Governor Vance was beloved by his state for the extraordinary efforts he mounted to provide for needy civilians, especially soldiers' families. Granaries were established to supply the needy, and salt was manufactured and distributed to facilitate the preservation of meat. Each county had a commissioner to distribute the state largess to those desperate for the necessities of life. Many of these supplies arrived by blockade runners; the state-owned *Advance* was among the most successful of these ships. It is true that the governor stockpiled supplies for North Carolina troops and the citizenry. And his people loved him for it. In 1896 historian Stephen Weeks proclaimed Zeb Vance "the War Governor of the South" and contended that because of his executive ability, North Carolina suffered comparatively less than other Southern states.[41]

When Colonel Vance became Governor Vance, his arena became much broader and his responsibilities more complicated. His advocates expected him to safeguard state interests and rights within a confederation engaged in an uncertain struggle for independence from the United States, an established government with vastly greater physical and material resources. Inevitably, as the Confederate government sought to centralize its control of the war, the rights of the states were undermined. Moreover Vance was beholden to those who had nominated and elected him. His most trusted advisers were political chameleon Holden and Old Line Whig leaders, including William A. Graham, David L. Swain, and Jonathan Worth as well as Edward J. Hale, the influential editor of the *Fayetteville Observer*. As the war lengthened and especially after Gettysburg, Vance began to receive contradictory advice from

40. Ibid., 126–27, 178–79. Owsley's influence has been lasting. As recently as 1991 Charles P. Roland published the unadulterated account of ninety-two thousand uniforms in Vance's stockpile at the war's end. See Roland, *An American Iliad: The Story of the Civil War* (Lexington: University Press of Kentucky, 1991), 114.

41. Stephen Weeks, "The University of North Carolina in the Civil War," in *SHSP*, 24:35–36.

those closest to him. Holden had become disenchanted with the Davis administration and predicted that the "Destructives," as he now called the original secessionists, would institute a military despotism and impinge upon the civil liberties of the citizenry. War weariness intensified, and Holden's denunciations as well as desertion by North Carolina troops grew apace. Peace meetings, using the rhetoric of Holden, were held in crossroad communities and towns throughout the state. In the fall elections six of ten men chosen to represent the state in the Confederate Congress favored peace negotiations. Over the summer of 1863, the circulation of Holden's *Standard* increased by 100 percent to about ten thousand subscribers. His stance was well known in the army, in Richmond, and in surrounding states.[42]

A heated political battle with Holden, a man Vance considered a threat to Confederate independence, motivated the governor to visit his soldiers in the Army of Northern Virginia in late March and early April 1864. Vance's strongest backers were in the ranks, and he recognized that a triumphant tour of North Carolina regiments would play well at home and shore up sagging civilian morale. Personally Vance's spirits and rhetoric were uplifted by the reception he received in Virginia. More importantly he was flattered by the attentions he received from Lee and other Confederate generals. His resolve to support the Confederacy to the end was fixed by the Virginia experience; moreover the trust that developed between Lee and Vance at this time became the basis for their special collaboration in the last year of the war.

The Lee-Vance relationship suggests that Lee was willing to act in the political realm, bypassing civil authority as necessary in order to maintain his army in the face of a superior enemy. He dealt very effectively with Vance, capitalizing on the aura of his personage to influence the younger man and even deigned to use flattery in a noble cause. The relationship suggests that Lee's vision was broader than his critics have assumed. He seemed well informed about conditions in North Carolina and offered advice to Vance on numerous subjects. He was particularly involved in efforts to defend Wilmington and in efforts to return deserters to the army. Significantly his letters to Vance bypassed official channels in defiance of the traditional submission of military to civil authority. For his part Vance respected Lee and sought to

42. William C. Harris, *William Woods Holden: Firebrand of North Carolina Politics* (Baton Rouge: Louisiana State University Press, 1978), 134.

respond to the general's suggestions whenever possible. The Lee connection steeled the governor in his decision to keep his state in Confederate harness so long as there was hope of victory and independence. During the last months of the war, Zebulon Vance, under the spell of Lee, subordinated states' rights to the needs of the Confederacy, in contradiction of what Frank Owsley and others have written. Prior to 1864 he was torn between the various factions in North Carolina, feeling that he was particularly indebted to Holden and the Unionist element that had elected him in 1862. In the end Vance, arguably the most popular man in North Carolina history, championed the cause of Southern independence, and one of his strongest backers was the chieftain of the Army of Northern Virginia, Robert E. Lee.

"I Rely upon Your Good Judgment and Skill"

The Command Partnership of Robert E. Lee and
Joseph E. Johnston in 1865

MARK L. BRADLEY

I N EARLY 1865 the Confederacy appeared to be on the brink of final defeat after sustaining three devastating reverses. On December 16, 1864,
the Army of Tennessee—the Confederacy's second-largest field army—was
virtually annihilated at Nashville, Tennessee. Six days later Maj. Gen. William
T. Sherman completed his March to the Sea by occupying Savannah, Georgia,
and presenting the city to Pres. Abraham Lincoln as a Christmas gift. On January 15, 1865, Fort Fisher fell after a desperate fight, closing Wilmington, North
Carolina, the Confederacy's last major blockade-running port. Following a
brief rest at Savannah, Sherman was poised to march northward through the
Carolinas to Richmond, Virginia, the capital of the Confederacy. Sherman's
army would combine with the forces commanded by the Union general in
chief, Lt. Gen. Ulysses S. Grant, and overwhelm the defenders of Richmond,
Gen. Robert E. Lee's Army of Northern Virginia. Hence the Confederacy's
gravest dilemma: how to prevent Sherman from reaching Grant.

An alarmed Confederate Congress relied on Lee to find the solution.
Among its emergency measures was a bill to create the post of general in
chief of the Confederate armies. An amendment to the bill recommended
the appointment of Lee, and it urged the reinstatement of one of the Confederacy's most controversial commanders, Gen. Joseph E. Johnston, who had
languished in semiretirement since his removal from the Army of Tennessee
on July 17, 1864. Although Pres. Jefferson Davis realized that the bill was an
implicit vote of no confidence in his conduct of the war, he signed it in deference to Lee. As for Johnston, Davis had no intention of reinstating a general
whom he had shelved for repeatedly refusing to fight.

On February 6, 1865, Davis appointed Lee general in chief. Three days
later Lee assumed supreme command of a force that the Union army outnumbered by more than three to one; the Confederacy's only substantial concentration of troops was Lee's own Army of Northern Virginia. In the days

GENERAL JOSEPH E. JOHNSTON
Courtesy Library of Congress

following his appointment, Lee sought to improve the desperate odds confronting the Confederacy. The general in chief made public his support of the Confederate Congress's bill to arm the slaves and offered amnesty to the army's deserters. To ameliorate the army's precarious supply situation, Lee secured the replacement of the inept commissary general of subsistence, Col. Lucius B. Northrop, with the capable Brig. Gen. Isaac M. St. John.[1]

The most urgent task Lee faced was in preventing Sherman's 60,000-man army from reaching Richmond and Petersburg and combining with the 115,000 troops commanded by Grant, Lee's Union counterpart. Worse yet, Sherman's army would probably be reinforced by the 25,000 soldiers in eastern North Carolina under Maj. Gen. John M. Schofield. Lee knew that a Federal juggernaut of that size would swiftly crush the 50,000-man Army of Northern Virginia. The general in chief warned Davis that if Grant were reinforced, "I do not see how in our present position he can be prevented from enveloping Richmond." Lee intended to defend Richmond and its remaining supply lines for as long as possible, but he did not want to sacrifice his army in doing so. Although realizing that the loss of the Confederate capital would be a terrible blow to Southern morale, he regarded the preservation of his forces as of the highest priority. "The greatest calamity that can befall us is the destruction of our armies," Lee wrote Davis. "If they can be maintained, we may recover from our reverses, but if lost we have no resource."[2]

1. General Orders No. 3, Feb. 6, 1865, U.S. War Department, *The War of the Rebellion: A Compilation of the Official Records of the Union and Confederate Armies*, 128 vols. (Washington, D.C.: GPO, 1880–1901), 46(2):1205 [hereafter cited as *OR*; all references are to series 1 unless otherwise noted]. See also General Orders No. 1, Feb. 9, 1865, ibid., 1226–27.

On December 31, 1864, the Federal army numbered 495,899 officers and men present for duty, while the Confederate army numbered 154,910. See consolidated abstract from returns of the U.S. Army, Dec. 31, 1864, *OR*, ser. 3, 4:1034; consolidated abstract from returns of the Confederate army, Dec. 31, 1864, *OR*, ser. 4, 3:989.

R. E. Lee to Ethelbert Barksdale, Feb. 18, 1865, quoted in Robert F. Durden, *The Gray and the Black: The Confederate Debate on Emancipation* (Baton Rouge: Louisiana State University, 1972), 206–7; General Orders No. 2, Feb. 11, 1865, *OR*, 46(2): 1229–30; R. E. Lee to Jefferson Davis, Feb. 9, 1865, *OR*, 51(2):1082–83; R. E. Lee to James A. Seddon, Feb. 8, 1865, *OR*, 46(2):381–82. For the principal officials of the War Department and its bureaus from January 1, 1864, to the close of the war, see *OR*, ser. 4, 3:1183.

2. Abstract from returns showing the effective strength of the army in the field under Maj. Gen. William T. Sherman, U.S. Army, Jan. 31, Feb. 28, Mar. 31, 1865, *OR*, 47(1):42–43; abstract

When Lee assumed his duties as Confederate general in chief, Sherman's army was marching northward into South Carolina. Opposing the Federal advance was a motley force under Gen. Pierre G. T. Beauregard, the commander of the Military Division of the West. On February 2, 1865, at a conference near Augusta, Georgia, Beauregard estimated that his force totaled 33,450 effectives, but the general included troops he expected to receive from the Army of Tennessee and the Georgia State Militia. In reality barely more than half that number was available for the defense of South Carolina. Oddly enough Beauregard's estimate of 58,000 soldiers for Sherman's army proved far more accurate. The troop strength figures thus deceived Davis and Lee into assuming that Beauregard faced no more than two-to-one odds in South Carolina—odds that Lee had routinely overcome in the past.[3]

On February 3 Beauregard appealed to Davis for reinforcements from Virginia and eastern North Carolina. "If troops from there . . . could be sent me," the general assured the president, "I would defeat, and might destroy, Sherman's army." Davis relayed Beauregard's request to Lee, who replied that he could spare no more detachments. Lee in turn asked the commander of the Department of North Carolina, Gen. Braxton Bragg, if he could send any troops to Beauregard, but Bragg stated that any reduction of his force would be dangerous. Thus Beauregard's hopes for a massive and devastating concen-

---

from return of the Army of the Potomac, Maj. Gen. George G. Meade, U.S. Army, commanding, Feb. 1865, *OR*, 46(2):737; abstract from the Department of Virginia, Maj. Gen. Edward O. C. Ord, U.S. Army, commanding, Feb. 1865, ibid., 747; abstract from the returns of the Army of Northern Virginia, commanded by Gen. Robert E. Lee, C.S. Army, Feb. 10, 1865, *OR*, 46(1):387; R. E. Lee to Jefferson Davis, Jan. 29, 1865, in *Lee's Dispatches: Unpublished Letters of General Robert E. Lee, C.S.A., to Jefferson Davis and the War Department of the Confederate States of America, 1862–1865*, ed. Douglas Southall Freeman (New York: G. P. Putnam's Sons, 1915), 330; R. E. Lee to Jefferson Davis, Mar. 14, 1865, in *The Wartime Papers of R. E. Lee*, ed. Clifford Dowdey and Louis H. Manarin (Boston: Little, Brown, 1961), 915. The above troop strength figures indicate that about ten thousand troops assigned to Ord's command were actually serving under Maj. Gen. John Schofield in North Carolina.

3. Jefferson Davis to G. T. Beauregard, Feb. 4, 1865, *OR*, 47(2):1090; "Notes of Conference Had on the 2d Day of Feb., A.D. 1865, at Green's Cut Station, Ga.," ibid., 1084–86. It is ironic that Beauregard's accurate estimate of Sherman's total strength was based on erroneous reports that Sherman had been reinforced by the Nineteenth Corps from Virginia and the Twenty-Third Corps from Tennessee.

tration against Sherman collided with the sobering reality that the Confederate army was hard-pressed on all fronts.[4]

The troops Lee had transferred to the Carolinas were veterans who would be missed in Virginia. In December 1864 he sent Maj. Gen. Robert Hoke's division to North Carolina to bolster the defense of Wilmington. The next month Davis yielded to the entreaties of Gov. Andrew G. Magrath of South Carolina and ordered Lee to transfer Conner's Brigade to the Palmetto State. Under its former commander, Brig. Gen. Joseph B. Kershaw, this brigade of South Carolinians had earned a reputation as one of the finest in the Army of Northern Virginia. A few weeks later Lee sent Maj. Gen. Matthew Butler's division of cavalry to South Carolina along with the army's cavalry commander, the newly promoted Lt. Gen. Wade Hampton. Both Hampton and Butler were native sons, and one of Butler's two brigades consisted of South Carolina regiments. Lee hoped that the infusion of veteran troops fighting to defend their homeland would improve Bragg and Beauregard's prospects. Although Lee regarded the troop transfers as loans, he would not see these units again.[5]

From the start, Beauregard made poor use of the troops at his disposal, thereby dooming his strategy for the defense of South Carolina. Believing that "the pending negotiations for peace" impelled him to hold the cities of Augusta, Georgia, and Charleston for "as long as it was humanly possible," Beauregard divided his meager force to defend the two distant points. He thus rendered himself vulnerable to defeat in detail, for Sherman effectively isolated Beauregard's forces by advancing through the heart of the Palmetto

4. G. T. Beauregard to Jefferson Davis, Feb. 3, 1865, *OR*, 47(2):1084; R. E. Lee to Jefferson Davis, Feb. 4, 1865, Robert E. Lee Papers, Perkins Library, Duke University, Durham, N.C.; R. E. Lee to Braxton Bragg, Feb. 4, 1865, ibid., 1098; Braxton Bragg to Robert E. Lee, Feb. 5, 1865, ibid., 1103.

5. James Longstreet to R. E. Lee, Dec. 19, 1864, *OR*, 42(3):1280; Osmun Latrobe to Robert F. Hoke, Dec. 19, 1864, ibid., 1280–81; Osmun Latrobe to Joseph B. Kershaw, Jan. 3, 1865, *OR*, 46(2):1008–9; Jefferson Davis to Andrew G. Magrath, Jan. 5, 1865, *OR*, 47(2):991; Jefferson Davis to William J. Hardee, Jan. 7, 1865, ibid., 997; R. E. Lee to Jefferson Davis, Jan. 15, 1865, in *Wartime Papers of R. E. Lee*, 881–82; Douglas Southall Freeman, *Lee's Lieutenants: A Study in Command*, 3 vols. (New York: Charles Scribner's Sons, 1942–44), 3:639. On Hampton's promotion, see Jefferson Davis to Wade Hampton, Feb. 16, 1865, *OR*, 47(2):1207.

State. Beauregard's strategy would have been justified had it coincided with President Davis's objective for the so-called Hampton Roads Peace Conference of February 3, 1865. Unknown to Beauregard, however, Davis hoped to sabotage the negotiations by countering President Lincoln's stated intention of "securing peace to our one common country" with his own desire "to secure peace to the two countries." Given that Davis planned to rekindle Southern patriotic zeal by denouncing the Lincoln government's demand of "unconditional surrender," Beauregard based his defensive strategy on a peace conference whose failure was already assured.[6]

By dividing his force at the outset of the Carolinas Campaign, Beauregard squandered his best opportunity to block Sherman's northward march. Had the Confederate general concentrated his available force on one isolated Federal column—particularly along the Salkehatchie River line—he would have enjoyed respectable numerical odds and the advantage of defending swampy terrain strewn with natural and manmade obstructions. The defeat or even the delay of one Union column in the South Carolina lowlands might have compelled Sherman to withdraw to the coast. Despite Lee's opinion to the contrary, Beauregard decided that such a concentration was impractical.[7]

Perhaps Beauregard relied too heavily on impassable swamps and inclement weather to defeat Sherman's army: he would not have been the only Confederate general to do so. The commander at Charleston, Lt. Gen. William J. Hardee, assured Joe Johnston, who was living in Columbia, South Carolina, that Sherman could not possibly cross the swamps bordering the Salkehatchie River. But Hardee was mistaken. "[W]hen I learned that Sherman's army was marching through the Salkehatchie swamps, making its own corduroy road at the rate of a dozen miles a day or more, and bringing its artillery

6. "Notes of Conference Had on the 2d Day of Feb., A.D. 1865," 1085. Lincoln and Secretary of State William H. Seward were the Federal commissioners at the conference, and Vice Pres. Alexander H. Stephens, Sen. Robert M. T. Hunter of Virginia, and Assistant Secretary of War John A. Campbell were the Confederate commissioners. For an excellent account of the Hampton Roads meeting, see James M. McPherson, *Battle Cry of Freedom: The Civil War Era* (New York: Oxford University Press, 1988), 822–24.

7. "Notes of Conference Had on the 2d Day of Feb., A.D. 1865," 1084–85; R. E. Lee to Jefferson Davis, Feb. 4, 1865, Lee Papers.

and wagons with it," Johnston later confessed, "I made up my mind that there had been no such army in existence since the days of Julius Caesar."[8]

Beauregard's strategy had provided for a concentration at Columbia, the state capital, but when Sherman reached the outskirts on February 16, the city was defended by only a scratch force consisting of cavalry commanded by Maj. Gen. Joseph Wheeler, elements of Stephen D. Lee's corps from the Army of Tennessee, and Butler's cavalry division. After offering token opposition, Beauregard withdrew his troops from Columbia and ordered Hardee to evacuate Charleston. Among the refugees from Columbia was Johnston, who joined the exodus fleeing toward Lincolnton, North Carolina.[9]

Whereas the aggressive Hampton maintained that Sherman's widely dispersed columns might enable the Confederates to "concentrate on one of his corps and destroy it," Beauregard had already conceded South Carolina to the Federals. On February 19 Beauregard reported to Lee that Sherman appeared to be heading toward Petersburg via Charlotte and Greensboro, North Carolina, with a possible detour to Raleigh, the capital of the Tar Heel State, for supplies and a junction with Schofield. (In truth Sherman's destination was Goldsboro, North Carolina, 130 miles southeast of Greensboro.) Later that night he informed Lee that Greensboro was the nearest point at which the Army of Tennessee contingent and Hardee's corps could combine with the force retreating from Columbia. Oblivious to the fact that Wilmington was about to fall to Schofield, Beauregard intended to transport Hardee's and the Army of Tennessee's troops to Greensboro by rail via Wilmington. But he had to abandon this plan when Bragg informed him that Schofield had cut the railroad.[10]

The reports from South Carolina so alarmed Davis that he asked Lee to

8. Johnston quoted in "General Cox's Speech," in *Report of the Proceedings of the Society of the Army of the Tennessee at the Fourteenth Annual Meeting, Held at Cincinnati, Ohio, April 6th and 7th, 1881* (Cincinnati: published by the Society, 1885), 116.

9. "Notes of Conference Had on the 2d Day of Feb., A.D. 1865," 1085; Mark L. Bradley, *This Astounding Close: The Road to Bennett Place* (Chapel Hill: University of North Carolina Press, 2000), 6.

10. Wade Hampton to G. T. Beauregard, Feb. 18, 1865, *OR*, 47(2):1218–19; G. T. Beauregard to R. E. Lee, Feb. 19, 1865 (12:45 P.M.), ibid., 1222; G. T. Beauregard to R. E. Lee, Feb. 19, 1865 (10:00 P.M.), ibid., 1222–23; Braxton Bragg to G. T. Beauregard, Feb. 21, 1865, ibid., 1242.

travel to Beauregard's headquarters for a conference and a personal inspection. Believing that he could ill afford to leave Virginia for even a few days, Lee dodged Davis's request and instead warned the president that he could not hold Richmond unless Sherman were defeated. When the Confederate War Department ordered Beauregard to remove or destroy all supplies in Sherman's path, the general complained to Lee that he lacked the troops to make a clean sweep of the region. "Genl Beauregard makes no mention of what he proposes or what he can do, or where his troops are," a frustrated Lee wrote Davis. "He does not appear from his despatches to be able to do much." Lee concluded that the ineffectual Beauregard had to be replaced.[11]

On February 21 Beauregard submitted a grandiose plan to Davis that underscored his failure to come to grips with military reality. Still convinced that Sherman was advancing along a western route via Charlotte and Salisbury, Beauregard urged a concentration "of at least 35,000 infantry and artillery at latter point, if possible, to give him battle there, and crush him, then to concentrate all forces against Grant, and then to march on Washington to dictate a peace." He indicated that he could provide fifteen thousand troops for the operation and requested that Bragg and Lee contribute an additional twenty thousand. Davis forwarded this "startling" telegram to Lee, who damned the proposal with faint praise: "The idea is good but the means are lacking."[12]

Lee in fact had already decided to replace Beauregard with Johnston, citing Beauregard's rumored ill health as the reason. Only the week before, Lee had refused to accede to a petition from Vice Pres. Alexander H. Stephens and seventeen Confederate senators urging him to restore Johnston to the command of the Army of Tennessee. He justified his refusal by stating that a continual change of commanders would demoralize the troops (as if their morale could get much worse) and that as general in chief he could "only

11. Jefferson Davis to R. E. Lee, Feb. 19, 1865, OR, 47(2):1222; R. E. Lee to Jefferson Davis, Feb. 19, 1865, in Wartime Papers of R. E. Lee, 905–6; Samuel Cooper to G. T. Beauregard, Feb. 20, 1865, OR, 47(2):1228; G. T. Beauregard to R. E. Lee, Feb. 20, 1865, ibid., 1229. When Lee balked at traveling to Beauregard's headquarters, Davis ordered Maj. Gen. Jeremy F. Gilmer, the chief of the Engineer Bureau, to go instead. See Jefferson Davis to J. F. Gilmer, Feb. 20, 1865, ibid., 1229.

12. G. T. Beauregard to Jefferson Davis, Feb. 21, 1865, OR, 47(2):1238; Jefferson Davis to R. E. Lee, Feb. 21, 1865, ibid., 1237; R. E. Lee to Jefferson Davis, Feb. 23, 1865, in Wartime Papers of R. E. Lee, 909.

employ such troops & officers as may be placed at my disposal by the War Department." Above all Lee realized that Davis was determined to prevent Johnston's return to command: "Those withheld or relieved from service are not at my disposal."[13]

In the meantime Beauregard's apparent breakdown compelled Lee to adopt drastic measures. On February 19 he informed the new secretary of war, John C. Breckinridge, that should Beauregard's "strength give way, there is no one on duty in the department who could replace him, nor have I any one to send there. Genl J. E. Johnston is the only officer whom I know who has the confidence of the army & the people, & if he was ordered to report to me I would place him there on duty." Puzzled by the oblique nature of Lee's request, Breckinridge asked the general in chief if he wished to assign Johnston to duty. Lee repeated his request in more positive terms, thereby securing the secretary of war's cooperation—and Davis's grudging consent. On February 22 Lee sent the following telegram to Johnston: "Assume command of the Army of Tennessee and all troops in Department of South Carolina, Georgia, and Florida. Assign General Beauregard to duty under you, as you may select. Concentrate all available forces and drive back Sherman." Seven months after his removal as commander of the Army of Tennessee, Johnston was recalled to duty.[14]

Thanks to Beauregard's inflated troop estimates, Lee believed that Johnston possessed the resources to defeat Sherman, but Johnston hastened to disabuse the general in chief of this notion. "It is too late to expect me to concentrate troops capable of driving back Sherman," he replied from his refuge in Lincolnton. "The remnant of the Army of Tennessee is much divided. So are other troops." According to his memoirs, Johnston assumed command believing that the Confederacy's sole objective for prolonging the war was "to obtain fair terms of peace."[15]

The general also believed that Jefferson Davis had restored him to com-

13. R. E. Lee to Alexander H. Stephens et al., Feb. 13, 1865, in *Wartime Papers of R. E. Lee,* 894.

14. R. E. Lee to J. C. Breckinridge, Feb. 19, 1865, in ibid., 904; J. C. Breckinridge to R. E. Lee, Feb. 20, 1865, *OR,* 46(2):1242; R. E. Lee to J. C. Breckinridge, Feb. 21, 1865, in *Wartime Papers of R. E. Lee,* 906; R. E. Lee to J. E. Johnston, Feb. 22, 1865, *OR,* 47(2):1247.

15. J. E. Johnston to R. E. Lee, Feb. 22, 1865, *OR,* 47(2):1247; Joseph E. Johnston, *Narrative of Military Operations during the Civil War* (New York: Da Capo, 1990 reprint), 372.

mand so that he would have to endure the humiliation of surrender, unaware that the president had recently penned a forty-five-hundred-word diatribe justifying his adamant refusal to reinstate Johnston. Davis had planned to submit the document to the Confederate Congress in response to a joint resolution urging Johnston's reinstatement, but he decided against it. Less than a week later, Lee made his request. Against his better judgment, Davis gave his assent "in the hope that General Johnston's soldierly qualities may be made serviceable to his country when acting under General Lee's orders."[16]

Prospects for the new command partnership were less than auspicious, for Johnston resented the phenomenal success Lee had enjoyed at the head of his former command, the Army of Northern Virginia. In response to Lee's defensive victory at Fredericksburg in December 1862, Johnston had complained: "What luck some people have. Nobody will ever come to attack me in such a place." During a walk with the diarist Mary Chesnut at Lincolnton, Johnston analyzed "all of Lee and Stonewall Jackson's mistakes. He was radiant and joyful," Chesnut reported. Aggravating his resentment was a suspicion that Lee had advised his removal from command the previous July.[17]

Johnston, however, never forgot that the Lee-Johnston family destinies were joined since the Revolutionary War: Johnston's father, Peter, had served as a lieutenant in the cavalry legion commanded by Lee's father, Col. Henry "Light Horse Harry" Lee. Nor had he forgotten his close friendship with Lee during their four years as West Point cadets. After graduation, duty separated them for long stretches, and Johnston regretted that the easy familiarity of their West Point days gradually gave way to a cold formality. He therefore assumed that Lee had long forgotten their old friendship.[18]

Despite his misgivings, Johnston wasted no time in returning to the army. Arriving at Charlotte on February 23, he conferred with Beauregard and ap-

16. Lydia Johnston quoted in *Mary Chesnut's Civil War*, ed. C. Vann Woodward (New Haven: Yale University Press, 1990), 729; Jefferson Davis to James Phelan, Mar. 1, 1865, *OR*, 47(2):1303–11.

17. J. E. Johnston to L. T. Wigfall, Dec. 15, 1862, Wigfall Family Papers, Library of Congress, Washington, D.C.; Woodward, *Mary Chesnut's Civil War*, 725; Craig L. Symonds, *Joseph E. Johnston: A Civil War Biography* (New York: W. W. Norton, 1992), 343.

18. J. E. Johnston to B. T. Johnson, Aug. 2, 1887, Bradley T. Johnson Papers, Perkins Library, Duke University, Durham, N.C.; J. E. Johnston to L. T. Wigfall, Mar. 14, 1865, Wigfall Family Papers.

pointed him second in command, then for the next two days, the new commanding general reviewed the remnant of his old Army of Tennessee. The veterans greeted "Old Joe" with three cheers, "given in a very joyful tone and manner expressive of great satisfaction," reported an Alabama soldier. "He is as well loved in this army among the men, as an officer can be. They have every confidence in him, and that alone will benefit the army and the service." Although Johnston appreciated the soldiers' enthusiastic welcome, the reviews and his conference with Beauregard confirmed what he had suspected about his army's condition.[19]

On February 25 Johnston officially assumed command. He informed Lee that his small force was "too weak to cope with Sherman," whose strength he nevertheless underestimated at forty thousand troops—a shortage of almost twenty thousand. Johnston reported that his own force was badly dispersed and numbered about twenty-five thousand men, but the actual figure was closer to eighteen thousand. These inaccurate figures led Lee to believe that Sherman's numerical advantage amounted to less than two to one, suggesting that Johnston could defeat the Federals once he concentrated his army.[20]

Indeed Johnston's first priority was to build an army from the scattered debris inherited from Beauregard. Sherman's columns advanced through the center of the Palmetto State and thus separated the three main components of Johnston's force. To the east Hardee's corps raced Sherman's right wing to Cheraw, South Carolina; to the north the cavalry under Hampton harried Sherman's advance across a broad front; to the west the Army of Tennessee formed a straggling column that stretched nearly the length of the state. "[I]t would scarcely have been possible to disperse a force more effectually," Hampton later recalled.[21]

Fortunately for Johnston, the incessant winter rains flooded the Catawba River and Lynch's Creek, stalling the Federals' march for almost a week. The

19. J. E. Johnston to R. E. Lee, Feb. 23, 1865, *OR*, 47(2):1257; George to Father, Feb. 24, 1865, Civil War Soldiers' Letters: M. J. Blackwell, Alabama Department of Archives and History, Montgomery; J. E. Johnston to R. E. Lee, Feb. 25, 1865, *OR*, 47(2):1271.

20. General Orders No. 1, Feb. 25, 1865, *OR*, 47(2):1274; J. E. Johnston to R. E. Lee, Feb. 25, 1865, ibid., 1271.

21. J. E. Johnston to R. E. Lee, Feb. 25, 1865, *OR*, 47(2):1271; Wade Hampton, "The Battle of Bentonville," in *Battles and Leaders of the Civil War*, ed. Robert U. Johnson and Clarence C. Buel, 4 vols. (New York: Century, 1887–88), 4:701.

delay bought Johnston invaluable time to concentrate his forces and encouraged him to believe that Sherman could be stopped. On the evening of February 28, Johnston received a dispatch from Lee that further lifted his spirits, for it indicated that the general in chief appreciated the difficulty of stopping Sherman. The letter also revealed that Lee had a better understanding of the Federals' intentions than Beauregard. Lee believed that Sherman "would turn toward the coast and reopen his communications and endeavor to unite with the army of General Schofield." The general in chief told Johnston that if he could concentrate his forces "in time to strike General Sherman before he reaches the coast or unites with Schofield, I hope for favorable results. His progress can be embarrassed and retarded by removing or destroying all kinds of supplies on his route, and I hope you will spare no effort to accomplish this object." Lee stated that he could send no reinforcements at present, but he informed Johnston that Bragg's troops would be subject to his orders. He also mentioned the contingency of combining with Johnston should Sherman reach the Roanoke River near the Virginia border.[22]

On March 1 Johnston replied, "The general views you express strengthen my hopes greatly." He agreed with Lee's supposition that Sherman was heading in an easterly direction toward Schofield, but he doubted the feasibility of a scorched-earth policy. "We are compelled to leave in the houses of the inhabitants the food necessary for their subsistence," Johnston explained, "but the U.S. officers feel no such obligation." Yet Johnston was confident that the junction of Hardee's corps and the Army of Tennessee would enable him to "impede the march of the Federal army, and even find opportunities to strike heavy blows, or at least prevent it from gathering food." If this optimism gave Lee a flicker of hope, the next two sentences probably extinguished it: "Would it be possible to hold Richmond with half your army, while the other half joined us near [the] Roanoke to crush Sherman? We might then turn upon Grant." Johnston's proposal no doubt reminded Lee of Beauregard's fantastic schemes.[23]

By mid-February Lee had resigned himself to the likelihood of evacuating Richmond and Petersburg. On the nineteenth he warned Breckinridge that "it

22. Bradley, *This Astounding Close*, 11; R. E. Lee to J. E. Johnston, Feb. 23, 1865, *OR*, 47(2):1256–57.

23. J. E. Johnston to R. E. Lee, Mar. 1, 1865, *OR*, 47(2):1297–98.

may be necessary to abandon all our cities, & preparation should be made for this contingency." Two days later Lee asked his wife, Mary: "Should it be necessary to abandon our position to prevent being surrounded, what will you do? Will you remain or leave the city?" On February 22 he informed his senior corps commander, Lt. Gen. James Longstreet, that should Sherman and Schofield join Grant outside Richmond, "we shall have to abandon our position on the James River, as lamentable as it is on every account." On the twenty-third Lee gave Davis the same bleak assessment, warning that "every preparation" should be made for the evacuation of the Confederate capital. But the general in chief stopped short of predicting final defeat for his army.[24]

Lee nevertheless believed that a negotiated settlement might avert further bloodshed. Although the failure of the Hampton Roads conference left scant room for hope, Lee explored the possibility of reopening negotiations with the Federal government, if only to buy time. The general in chief stepped into the political arena and attempted to persuade one of the Hampton Roads commissioners, Sen. Robert M. T. Hunter of Virginia, to introduce a resolution in the Senate calling for peace talks. Lee told him that if he could propose a solution better than surrender at the enemy's discretion, then it was his duty to speak out. The senator replied that he had already spoken to the president privately about reopening negotiations, only to learn afterward that Davis's aides had branded him a defeatist. Until that matter was resolved, Hunter said, he would have no further dealings with the president. Unimpressed with this flimsy excuse, Lee told the senator to keep trying. As for himself, the general stated that he could not publicly advocate peace negotiations, for it would be "almost equivalent to surrender." Hunter agreed and then turned the tables on Lee, suggesting that *he* broach the subject of negotiations with Davis. But Lee made no reply. Although the general in chief did not admit that he believed the cause was lost, Hunter thought "the tone and temper of his remarks" suggested as much.[25]

Following Hunter's rejection of his proposal, Lee continued to seek op-

24. R. E. Lee to J. C. Breckinridge, Feb. 19, 1865; R. E. Lee to Mary Lee, Feb. 21, 1865; R. E. Lee to James Longstreet, Feb. 22, 1865; and R. E. Lee to Jefferson Davis, Feb. 23, 1865, in *Wartime Papers of R. E. Lee*, 905–10.

25. R. M. T. Hunter to William Jones, n.d. [ca. Nov. 1877], in *Jefferson Davis, Constitutionalist: His Letters, Papers, and Speeches*, ed. Dunbar Rowland, 10 vols. (Jackson: Mississippi Department of Archives and History, 1923), 7:576–77.

portunities for negotiations. When Longstreet returned from a parley with Union major general Edward O. C. Ord reporting that Grant would agree to a conference with Lee, the general in chief secured Davis's permission to communicate with Grant. Lee assured the Federal commander that he possessed the authority "to do whatever the result of the interview may render necessary or advisable." In a March 2 letter to Davis, however, Lee confessed that he was "not sanguine" as to the outcome, for he believed that Grant would "consent to no terms, unless coupled with the condition of our return to the Union. Whether this will be acceptable to the people yet awhile I cannot say." In his use of "yet awhile," Lee suggested that "the people" did not share the president's determination to fight on in the face of certain defeat. In any event Lee requested a meeting with Davis to discuss their options.[26]

The night before his conference with Davis, Lee summoned his youngest corps commander, Maj. Gen. John B. Gordon, to his headquarters. Lee asked him to read the reports of his various commands "and to carefully note every important fact contained in them," Gordon recalled. "The revelation was startling." The reports described an army on the verge of collapse: the soldiers were woefully underfed, and they lacked shoes, hats, blankets, and overcoats. Prolonged hardship, fatigue, and malnutrition had rendered many of the men insensible to discipline.

Lee then informed Gordon of the overwhelming odds they faced: the Army of Northern Virginia totaled 50,000 men—though only 35,000 were fit for duty—while Grant's forces numbered about 200,000 (the actual figure was closer to 120,000). He reported that the Union Army of the Shenandoah under Maj. Gen. Philip H. Sheridan had just routed Lt. Gen. Jubal A. Early's Confederate force at Waynesboro, enabling Sheridan to transfer his 20,000 troops to the Richmond-Petersburg front. In the Carolinas Johnston could muster only 15,000 soldiers against 80,000 Federals under Sherman and Schofield. Lee estimated that the combined Union forces outnumbered his by more than four to one.

After his briefing, Lee asked Gordon to "state frankly" what he thought their options were. The Georgian replied that he believed they had three courses: "First, make terms with the enemy, the best we can get. Second, if

26. R. E. Lee to Ulysses S. Grant, Mar. 2, 1865, in *Wartime Papers of R. E. Lee*, 911; Douglas Southall Freeman, *R. E. Lee: A Biography*, 4 vols. (New York: Charles Scribner's Sons, 1934–35), 4:6; R. E. Lee to Jefferson Davis, Mar. 2, 1865, in *Wartime Papers of R. E. Lee*, 911.

that is not practicable, the best thing to do is retreat—abandon Richmond and Petersburg, unite by rapid marches with General Johnston in North Carolina, and strike Sherman before Grant can join him. . . . Lastly, we must fight, and without delay." After a brief silence, Lee asked his nervous subordinate, "Is that your opinion?" Gordon bristled at Lee's sarcastic tone and asserted that he in turn "had the right to ask" his superior's opinion. "Certainly, general," Lee replied, "you have the right to ask my opinion. I agree with you fully." Gordon then asked Lee if he had made his views known to the president or Congress, and Lee—keeping his overture to Grant confidential—said that he had not. According to Gordon, the Virginian maintained that as a military officer, "he scarcely felt authorized to suggest to the civil authorities the advisability of making terms" with the Federal government. Yet Lee's scruples did not prevent him from urging Senator Hunter to initiate a peace resolution in Congress.[27]

Lee met with Davis on March 4, only hours after his conference with Gordon. The general in chief informed the president that the evacuation of Richmond and Petersburg was simply a matter of time. Davis accepted the news calmly and asked Lee if they should evacuate at once. Lee replied that because his famished artillery and draft horses were too weak to haul wagons, ambulances, and artillery on muddy roads, he must wait for the winter rains to cease so the roads could dry. Yet he knew that the Federals were waiting for the same reason—Grant's army was gathering strength, while Lee's diminished daily—suggesting that the Confederates should move before the enemy could pursue. The substandard draft animals could be replaced by impressments collected on the retreat, and the army could live off the land. For a demonstration of this, Lee had to look no further than Sherman, who had thus far managed quite well marching through a sparsely settled region in midwinter.[28]

Lee stated that the line of retreat should be southwest to Danville, through country that provided much of the army's manpower and supplies. At Danville he would unite with Johnston and then attack and defeat Sher-

27. John B. Gordon, *Reminiscences of the Civil War* (New York: Charles Scribner's Sons, 1904), 385–90. Gordon's book is notoriously unreliable, but the general's account of his conference with Lee rings true. Lee's decision to entrust the March 25 assault on Fort Stedman to Gordon indicates the confidence he had in the thirty-three-year-old corps commander.

28. Freeman, *R. E. Lee,* 4:9; Jefferson Davis, *The Rise and Fall of the Confederate Government,* 2 vols. (1881; reprint, New York: Da Capo, 1990), 2:550–51.

man before Grant could come to his aid. Buoyed by the news of victory, the "liberated" states of the Deep South would then send reinforcements northward, enabling Lee to defeat Grant and drive him from Virginia. Such was the Davis-Lee plan, as Davis recalled it, and in sheer unblinking self-delusion, it rivaled even Beauregard's most extravagant schemes.[29]

Meanwhile reality crashed down with the arrival of Grant's reply to Lee's March 2 peace overture: "I have no authority to accede to your proposition for a conference on the subject proposed. Such authority is vested in the President of the United States alone."[30] Time was running out for the Confederacy, and Lee had to act quickly and decisively. Instead he kept his army huddled inside its trenches as Grant prepared to deliver the killing blow. Nor would he assume the responsibility of telling Davis that the war was lost. Lee knew his options—negotiate, fight, or flight—but he could not bring himself to act on them.

In his ongoing effort to prod the president into conceding defeat, Lee found a capable ally in Secretary of War Breckinridge, who had aided Lee's futile effort to persuade Hunter to urge peace negotiations and had helped the general in chief convince Davis of the need to evacuate Richmond. Almost from the moment he assumed office, Breckinridge had realized that the Confederacy was doomed. Reports from the War Department's bureau chiefs confirmed his suspicion that the Confederate army was on the brink of disintegration. In a lengthy letter to Breckinridge, the assistant secretary of war, John A. Campbell, enumerated the problems besetting the Confederacy: no public funds or credit, a skyrocketing national debt, wholesale desertion, an exhausted manpower pool, insufficient ordnance and other supplies, failing morale, and widespread dissension. Having served as a commissioner in the ill-fated Hampton Roads conference, Campbell maintained that a negotiated peace based on reconstruction was preferable to the South's annihilation. The assistant secretary regretted that few men of influence in Richmond "are willing to give counsel. Still fewer are willing to incur the responsibility of taking or advising action." Campbell therefore suggested that Breckinridge solicit Lee's opinion for the benefit of Davis and the Confederate Congress.[31]

29. Davis, *Rise and Fall*, 2:551.

30. U. S. Grant to R. E. Lee, Mar. 4, 1865, *OR*, 46(2):825.

31. J. A. Campbell to J. C. Breckinridge, Mar. 5, 1865, *OR*, 51(2):1064–67; Michael B. Ballard, *A Long Shadow: Jefferson Davis and the Final Days of the Confederacy* (Jackson: University Press of Mississippi, 1986), 22.

The secretary of war heeded Campbell's advice. On March 8 he requested that Lee submit a report describing the "present posture of affairs" to determine what action was necessary "to rescue the Confederacy from its present danger." Breckinridge intended to submit Lee's report and his own comments to Davis for transmittal to Congress. The secretary had provided the general in chief an opportunity to state his case to the civil authorities.[32]

Lee began by rehashing the obvious: the "military condition of the country" was "full of peril" and required "prompt action." He warned that the present supply system was inadequate to meet the needs of the army. "Unless the men and animals can be subsisted," Lee wrote, "the army cannot be kept together, and our present lines must be abandoned. Nor can it be moved to any other position where it can operate to advantage without provisions to enable it to move in a body."

Once again, however, Lee stopped short of admitting defeat. "If the army can be maintained," he continued, "I do not regard the abandonment of our present position as necessarily fatal to our success." Rather than urge peace negotiations, Lee instead noted the Confederacy's ability to survive against overwhelming odds: "While the military situation is not favorable, it is not worse than the superior numbers and resources of the enemy justified us in expecting from the beginning. Indeed, the legitimate military consequences of that superiority have been postponed longer than we had reason to anticipate." He then shifted the responsibility for determining the Confederacy's fate onto the shoulders of the politicians, for they could "best decide" how the people "will bear the difficulties and sufferings of their condition and how they will respond to the demands which the public safety requires." Despite all the evidence confronting him, Lee proved as incapable of conceding defeat as Davis.[33]

32. J. C. Breckinridge to R. E. Lee, Mar. 8, 1865, OR, 46(2):1292.

33. R. E. Lee to J. C. Breckinridge, Mar. 9, 1865, in Wartime Papers of R. E. Lee, 912–13. Alan T. Nolan holds Lee accountable for failing to recommend an end to the fighting by the winter of 1865, given the general's belief in the futility of further resistance. Prior to his surrender at Appomattox, however, Lee never expressed an outright admission of defeat, even if Hunter and several others inferred as much. Although Lee favored peace negotiations, this does not mean that he regarded Confederate defeat as inevitable. His March 9 report indicates that he believed that even if Richmond and Petersburg had to be abandoned, the war was not lost so long as the Confederate army remained intact. Rather, Lee's culpability rests in his apparent paralysis dur-

A disappointed Breckinridge collected Lee's report and those of his bureau chiefs and submitted them to Davis. But he attached no recommendation to open peace negotiations, probably because he lacked a clear concession of defeat from Lee. The secretary of war hoped that Congress would act once it saw the evidence, but instead the legislators spent the final days of the session drafting messages that blamed Davis for the Confederacy's present woes.[34]

Upon adjournment, a group of congressmen sent Sen. William A. Graham of North Carolina on a mission to persuade that state's governor, Zebulon B. Vance, to convene the general assembly for the purpose of considering peace negotiations. Vance seemed to be an excellent choice, for he was a frequent and pugnacious opponent of Davis's policies. But he refused to take the first step and thus render himself and the Old North State culpable for final defeat. The South appeared to contain no one who would tell Davis that the Confederacy was defeated and the time had come to obtain the best terms possible.[35]

Thwarted in their peacemaking efforts, Breckinridge and Lee prepared for the army's withdrawal from Richmond and Petersburg by stockpiling provisions along the projected line of retreat and by widening the North Carolina Railroad to facilitate the movement of locomotives and rolling stock from Virginia. When Vance got wind of the railroad-widening project, he protested to Breckinridge so forcefully that work was halted. Johnston likewise was chagrined to learn that the supplies in the North Carolina Railroad depots were reserved for the Army of Northern Virginia (the general later discovered that

---

ing this crucial period while admitting the necessity of either negotiating, attacking, or abandoning the Confederate capital and combining with Johnston's army. See Nolan, *Lee Considered: Robert E. Lee and Civil War History* (Chapel Hill: University of North Carolina Press, 1991), 129–31.

34. For an excellent account of Breckinridge's peacemaking efforts, see William C. Davis, *An Honorable Defeat: The Last Days of the Confederate Government* (New York: Harcourt, 2001), 38–48.

35. William A. Graham to David L. Swain, Apr. 8, 1865, in *The Papers of William Alexander Graham*, ed. J. G. de Roulhac Hamilton, Max R. Williams, and Mary Reynolds Peacock, 8 vols. (Raleigh: Division of Archives and History, Department of Cultural Resources, 1957–92), 6:294–95; Zebulon B. Vance quoted in Clement Dowd, *Life of Zebulon B. Vance* (Charlotte, N.C.: Observer, 1897), 460.

the depots held enough rations to feed an army of sixty thousand for four months). Lee told Johnston that his army must forage for subsistence. Using impressed wagons and teams, Johnston's troops collected provisions in the path of Sherman's army, thus fulfilling Lee's orders to deny them to the enemy. Johnston was further disappointed in his efforts to obtain pay for his men (the Confederate Treasury was broke) and to secure supplies from the landlocked Confederate naval yard at Charlotte (Secretary of the Navy Stephen R. Mallory refused to part with them). On March 4, however, Lee granted Johnston's request to place Bragg's Department of North Carolina troops under his command—much to Bragg's mortification, for as Davis's chief of staff, he had recommended Johnston's dismissal the previous year. Rather than offer advice on how his lieutenant should utilize Bragg's troops, Lee simply told him: "I wish you to act as you think best." Johnston no doubt appreciated the general in chief's willingness to trust his judgment.[36]

On March 4 Johnston traveled to Fayetteville to be nearer Sherman's line of march, leaving Beauregard at Charlotte to supervise the transfer of the Army of Tennessee contingent to Smithfield; from there the troops would march southwest about forty miles to Fayetteville for a junction with Hardee's corps. Encouraged by the Federals' difficult crossing of the Catawba River and Lynch's Creek, Johnston hoped to strike Sherman's army in detail as it crossed the Cape Fear River.[37]

Meanwhile Bragg's force was concentrating near Kinston after its withdrawal from Wilmington. The general saw an excellent opportunity to defeat

36. S. B. French to I. M. St. John, Mar. 10, 1865, OR, 46(2):1297; T. G. Williams to I. M. St. John, Mar. 10, 1865, ibid., 1298; J. H. Claiborne to I. M. St. John, Mar. 10, 1865, ibid. 1298–99; J. E. Johnston to J. C. Breckinridge, Mar. 2, 1865, OR, 47(2):1311; J. E. Johnston to Z. B. Vance, Mar. 2, 1865, ibid., 1313; R. E. Lee to J. E. Johnston, Mar. 2, 1865, ibid.; Z. B. Vance to J. C. Breckinridge, Mar. 18, 1865, ibid., 1425; R. E. Lee to J. E. Johnston, Mar. 5, 1865, ibid., 1324; J. E. Johnston to J. C. Breckinridge, Feb. 28, 1865 (two letters), ibid., 1290; J. C. Breckinridge to J. E. Johnston, Mar. 6, 1865, ibid., 1297; A. H. Cole to J. E. Johnston, Mar. 2, 1865, ibid., 1313; J. E. Johnston to Z. B. Vance, Mar. 3, 1865, ibid., 1316; Z. B. Vance to J. E. Johnston, Mar. 4, 1865, ibid., 1320; A. H. Cole to J. E. Johnston, Mar. 6, 1865 (two letters), ibid., 1332; Johnston, *Narrative*, 374–76, 378; J. E. Johnston to R. E. Lee, Mar. 3, 1865, OR, 47(2):1316; R. E. Lee to J. E. Johnston, Mar. 4, 1865, ibid., 1320; Braxton Bragg to Jefferson Davis, Mar. 5, 1865, ibid., 1328; R. E. Lee to J. E. Johnston, Mar. 5, 1865, ibid., 1325; Archer Anderson to Braxton Bragg, Mar. 6, 1865, ibid., 1334.

37. J. E. Johnston to R. E. Lee, Mar. 4, 1865, OR, 47(2):1319; Johnston, *Narrative*, 377–78.

the Federals on his front and asked Johnston to send him the Army of Tennessee troops en route to Smithfield. Realizing that Sherman would probably reach Fayetteville before he could combine against him, Johnston granted Bragg's request with the proviso that he return the Army of Tennessee contingent to Smithfield immediately after the battle. Advancing against Bragg from New Bern was one of Schofield's two corps commanded by Maj. Gen. Jacob D. Cox. Bragg intended to prevent Cox from forming a junction with Sherman. On March 8 the battle of Wise's Forks began impressively for the Confederates, who overran a portion of Cox's line, capturing eight hundred Federals and one cannon. Despite this setback, Cox held his ground, and his troops dug in that night. March 9 saw only scattered skirmishing, but on the tenth Bragg resumed the offensive. Fighting behind strong entrenchments, the Federals easily repulsed the Confederates' assaults. Informed that Cox was receiving reinforcements, Bragg ordered his command to retreat toward Goldsboro and an eventual junction with Johnston.[38]

Johnston's decision to augment Bragg's force with the Army of Tennessee troops was sound, but Bragg nullified the Confederates' advantage of interior lines by monopolizing the rolling stock of the North Carolina Railroad, which formed a 220-mile arc from Goldsboro to Charlotte. While he held the cars on one end of the rail line, a massive backlog of soldiers and supplies accumulated on the other. Johnston failed to ensure that the railroad was properly managed, and as a result much of his force remained stranded at Charlotte and Salisbury as he prepared to strike Sherman.

While Bragg battled Cox, a second Confederate offensive occurred at Monroe's Crossroads near Fayetteville. At dawn on March 10, Johnston's ablest subordinate, Wade Hampton, launched a surprise attack on Union cavalry commander Judson Kilpatrick's camp, which blocked the road to Fayetteville. The Confederate riders briefly overran Kilpatrick's position, but the veteran Federal horsemen managed to drive them off after a fierce struggle. The Southerners nevertheless succeeded in opening the Fayetteville road. Telegrams announcing Bragg's and Hampton's successes reached Lee at his Petersburg headquarters, only to be followed by messages stating the neces-

---

38. Braxton Bragg to J. E. Johnston, Mar. 6, 1865, OR, 47(2):1334; J. E. Johnston to Braxton Bragg, Mar. 6, 1865, ibid.; J. E. Johnston to W. J. Hardee, Mar. 6, 1865, ibid., 1333; Johnston, *Narrative*, 378–80; Bradley, *This Astounding Close*, 12–13.

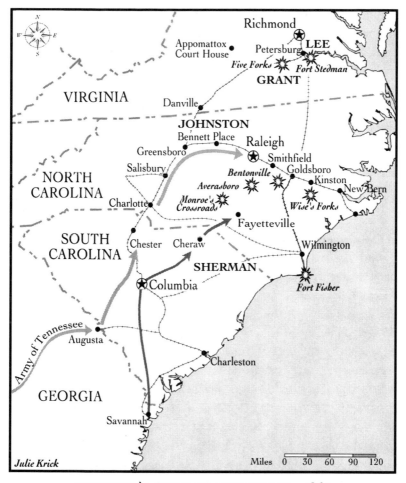

JOHNSTON'S FIELD OF OPERATIONS, 1865

sity for retreat, suggesting that the attackers lacked sufficient numbers to exploit their initial gains. Yet Lee was pleased with the aggressive spirit
displayed by Johnston's command.[39]

On March 11 Johnston wrote the general in chief from his new headquarters at Raleigh: "In a battle with Sherman on equal ground the chances would

39. R. E. Lee to J. C. Breckinridge, Mar. 9, 1865, OR, 47(1):1045; R. E. Lee to J. C. Breckinridge, Mar. 10, 1865, ibid.; R. E. Lee to J. C. Breckinridge, Mar. 11, 1865, ibid.; Bradley, *This
Astounding Close*, 13–15.

be decidedly against us." He estimated his force at twenty-five thousand troops of uneven quality and Sherman's at forty-five thousand (exclusive of Schofield's force), once again indicating no more than a two-to-one advantage. But Johnston warned that should Sherman and Schofield form a junction, he could not prevent them from joining Grant in Virginia. If Sherman's destination were Goldsboro, then Johnston planned to strike Schofield before Sherman could reach him; if Raleigh, then he hoped to attack Sherman while his army was divided. Johnston again proposed that Lee hold the inner lines of Richmond with part of his army while the remainder joined Johnston in North Carolina. "If the possession of the [rail]road by Raleigh is necessary for the subsistence of your army," he wrote, "I should be glad to be informed."[40]

Alarmed by Johnston's query, Lee replied, "I fear I cannot hold my position if road to Raleigh is interrupted. Should you be forced back in this direction both armies would certainly starve." In a subsequent dispatch the general in chief conceded that he did not expect Johnston to risk "a general battle without a reasonable prospect of success . . . [but] an opportunity may occur for you and Bragg to unite upon one of their columns and crush it." Lee rejected the request to detach part of the Army of Northern Virginia and send it south: "I do not think I could maintain my position were I further to reduce my force." He intended to hold his position for as long as possible, but if compelled to abandon Richmond, he would withdraw toward Danville. In that event, Lee wrote, "the sooner we strike the enemy the better, but on which side of the Roanoke must depend on circumstances." Lee knew that all depended on Johnston's ability to halt or delay Sherman. "You must judge what the probability will be of arresting Sherman by a battle," he told Johnston. "If there is a reasonable probability I would recommend it. A bold & unexpected attack might relieve us."[41]

On March 11 Sherman occupied Fayetteville and rested his army there for four days. In the meantime Johnston ordered his forces to concentrate at Smithfield, midway between Goldsboro and Raleigh, Sherman's two most likely objectives. On the fourteenth Beauregard told Johnston that he believed Sherman was "moving doubtless to form junction with Schofield's

40. J. E. Johnston to R. E. Lee, Mar. 11, 1865, OR, 47(2):1372–73.

41. R. E. Lee to J. E. Johnston, Mar. 11, 1865, ibid., 1372; R. E. Lee to J. E. Johnston, Mar. 15, 1865, ibid., 1395–96.

forces about Goldsborough." Since Johnston lacked the numbers to defeat Sherman, Beauregard wrote, he should concentrate against Schofield instead and "crush him." Mindful of Lee's warning, Johnston decided against uncovering Raleigh to attack Schofield and clung to his plan of striking an isolated column of Sherman's army.[42]

That same day Johnston received heartening news from his friend and political ally Sen. Louis T. Wigfall of Texas. "You are mistaken as to the motive which induced your being ordered to command," Wigfall wrote from Richmond. "It was out of confidence & kindness & a real desire to obtain the benefit of your ability in this crisis." Wigfall then named the man responsible for Johnston's reinstatement: "It was Lee & not Davis. . . . For God's sake communicate with Lee fully & freely & with kindness & confidence & give him the full benefit of your judgment in this hour of peril."[43]

"What you write me of Lee gratifies me beyond measure," Johnston replied. "In youth & early manhood I loved and admired him more than any man in the world," the general confessed, recalling his friendship with Lee at West Point. "I have long thought that he had forgotten our early friendship. To be mistaken in so thinking would give me inexpressible pleasure. Be assured however, that knight of old never fought under his King more loyally than I'll serve under General Lee." Thanks to Wigfall's letter, Johnston redoubled his efforts to assist Lee. His renewed commitment was all the more remarkable in light of his belief that his reinstatement had come too late to offer any hope of stopping Sherman.[44]

On the heels of the Wigfall letter came a dispatch from Lee that Johnston regarded as a vote of confidence. "I have not pretended to lay down fixed rules which at this distance and this time cannot be safely done," Lee wrote, "but rely upon your good judgment and skill to accomplish everything that is possible to attain our common end—the greatest success. Unity of purpose and harmony of action between the two armies, with the blessing of God, I trust will relieve us from the difficulties that now beset us." Johnston accepted Lee's letter as irrefutable evidence that his old friend still believed in him.[45]

42. G. T. Beauregard to J. E. Johnston, Mar. 14, 1865, ibid., 1392; Johnston, *Narrative*, 382; Bradley, *This Astounding Close*, 15.

43. L. T. Wigfall to J. E. Johnston, Mar. 3, 1865, JO 305, Joseph E. Johnston Papers, Henry E. Huntington Library, San Marino, Calif.

44. J. E. Johnston to L. T. Wigfall, Mar. 14, 1865, Wigfall Family Papers.

45. R. E. Lee to J. E. Johnston, Mar. 15, 1865, OR, 47(2):1396.

On March 15 Johnston traveled to Smithfield to oversee the concentration of his forces: Hardee's corps, the Army of Tennessee contingent, Bragg's command (consisting mainly of Hoke's Division), and Hampton's cavalry. Meanwhile, acting on Johnston's discretionary orders to delay Sherman, Hardee established a three-line defensive position five miles south of Averasboro and awaited Sherman's northward advance from Fayetteville. The next day Sherman's left wing drove back Hardee's first two lines, but the third and main line held until nightfall. Hardee then ordered his command to withdraw toward Smithfield, having bought Johnston an extra day to concentrate his army. On March 17 he reported that Sherman had turned east and appeared to be heading toward Goldsboro rather than Raleigh.[46]

That night Johnston sought more specific information from Hampton, whose cavalry had been shadowing Sherman's army since its departure from Fayetteville. He instructed Hampton to report the location of Sherman's army, the direction it was headed, its distance from Goldsboro, the number of its columns, and the distance separating them. Most importantly, Johnston asked him if he believed the Confederates at Smithfield could intercept the Federals before they reached Goldsboro. Hampton replied that Sherman's army was moving in two widely separated columns and that the location of his headquarters two miles south of Bentonville was an excellent site for a surprise attack on the column marching from Averasboro. The cavalry commander assured Johnston that, if necessary, he could delay the Union advance and enable the Confederate army to arrive from Smithfield. Johnston's state map indicated that the two Federal columns were more than a day's march apart: here was the opportunity he had sought since assuming command. On the morning of the eighteenth, the general ordered his forces to march for Bentonville, informing Hampton that the army was on its way. He also notified Lee of the impending offensive.[47]

Johnston decided to attack Sherman at Bentonville for three reasons. First, he wanted to strike Sherman before any junction with Schofield; once

---

46. Bradley, *This Astounding Close*, 16–18.

47. J. E. Johnston to Wade Hampton, Mar. 17, 1865, *OR*, 47(2):1415; J. E. Johnston to R. E. Lee, Mar. 27, 1865, *OR*, 47(1):1055–56; J. E. Johnston to R. E. Lee, Mar. 18, 1865, *OR*, 47(2):1426; J. E. Johnston to Wade Hampton, Mar. 18, 1865, ibid., 1429; Johnston, *Narrative*, 384–85; Hampton, "Battle of Bentonville," 701.

that occurred, Johnston believed, the Confederates would be overwhelmingly outnumbered. Second, he hoped that a stunning blow to Sherman's army would ensure the South leverage at the bargaining table by demonstrating the still-dangerous offensive power of the Confederate army. Third, Lee had urged him "to neglect no opportunity of delivering the enemy a successful blow," and this, Johnston realized, might well be his last chance to do so.[48]

In truth the battle of Bentonville merely proved that Johnston lacked the manpower to defeat even one wing of Sherman's army. On March 19 the battle began auspiciously for the attacking Confederates, who routed one Union division and elements of two others, but the rest of the Federal left wing dug in and managed to hurl back several determined Southern attacks. The first day's fighting thus ended in a draw. "I concentrated our troops here yesterday and attacked the enemy about 3 P.M.," Johnston informed Lee on the twentieth. "[We] routed him, capturing three guns, but [a] mile in rear he rallied upon fresh troops." The Federals remained on the field behind strong entrenchments. "Our loss was small," Johnston reported. "The troops behaved extremely well."[49]

On March 20 the right wing of Sherman's army arrived at Bentonville, giving the Federals an overwhelming three-to-one numerical advantage. Johnston now found himself surrounded on three sides, his only avenue of retreat a wooden bridge that spanned a flooded creek. But rather than withdraw before dawn on the twenty-first, as Sherman expected, Johnston chose to hold his ground. He later reported that he did so to cover the removal of his wounded and to induce the overconfident Federals to launch a frontal assault. Implicit in Johnston's rationale was a third reason: his army's morale. He believed that a hasty retreat would have been tantamount to conceding defeat, given that his army had come so close to defeating the Federals on the nineteenth (or so the Confederates thought). Worse yet, a retreat meant that the soldiers would be abandoning their wounded comrades to the enemy—not even the Union army's superior medical facilities could remove that stigma.

48. R. E. Lee to J. E. Johnston, Mar. 15, 1865, *OR*, 47(2):1395; Bradley, *This Astounding Close*, 18–19. For a comprehensive discussion of Johnston's reasons for fighting at Bentonville, see Mark Grimsley, "Learning to Say 'Enough': Southern Generals and the Final Weeks of the Confederacy," in *The Collapse of the Confederacy*, ed. Mark Grimsley and Brooks D. Simpson (Lincoln: University of Nebraska Press, 2001), 57–59, 77–78 n. 41.

49. J. E. Johnston to R. E. Lee, Mar. 20, 1865, *OR*, 47(1):1054.

Looking ahead to his junction with Lee's army and an impending campaign against Grant and Sherman's combined forces, Johnston believed that bolstering his army's morale justified the risk of remaining at Bentonville.[50]

Johnston's decision nearly proved disastrous, for on the afternoon of March 21, a Union division launched an unauthorized assault on Johnston's left flank at Bentonville that threatened his sole line of retreat. Only a desperate counterattack succeeded in halting the Union breakthrough. That night Johnston ordered his army to withdraw to Smithfield, having learned that Sherman was preparing to combine with Schofield at Goldsboro. But Johnston believed that he had done his part—it was now Lee's move. "Sherman's course cannot be hindered by the small force I have," he wrote Lee on March 23. "I can do no more than annoy him. I respectfully suggest that it is no longer a question whether you leave [your] present position; you have only to decide where to meet Sherman. I will be near him." Johnston gathered his army at Smithfield because it stood midway between Raleigh and the direct route to Richmond along the Wilmington and Weldon Railroad.[51]

On the twenty-fourth Johnston again wrote Lee, stating that Sherman, whose army was resting and refitting around Goldsboro, would probably cross the Roanoke River at Weldon. "It would be best," he suggested, "to fight on this side" of the river. The general promised to delay Sherman's march "if possible and keep to his front to join you should you wish to fight Grant first." Lee, however, brought Johnston back to reality with his reply: "We cannot fight Grant to advantage as long as he holds his intrenchments." Although convinced of Sherman's overwhelming numerical superiority, Johnston underestimated his total strength as sixty thousand (it was closer to eighty thousand). Along with his dispatch, Johnston sent a mutual friend and West Point classmate, Lt. Gen. Theophilus H. Holmes, to discuss his plans for the junction with Lee.[52]

In reply to Johnston's telegram describing his March 19 attack at Bentonville, Lee sent his subordinate a complimentary message. "I can but express

---

50. Ibid., 1055; J. E. Johnston to R. E. Lee, Mar. 27, 1865, *OR*, 47(1):1056; Bradley, *This Astounding Close*, 22–23; Grimsley, "Learning to Say 'Enough,'" 58–59.

51. J. E. Johnston to R. E. Lee, Mar. 23, 1865, *OR*, 47(1):1055; Johnston, *Narrative*, 394.

52. J. E. Johnston to R. E. Lee, Mar. 24, 1865, *OR*, 47(3):682; R. E. Lee to J. E. Johnston, Mar. 24, 1865, ibid.; Johnston, *Narrative*, 395.

my hearty congratulations at your victory of the 19th," he wrote. "It was skillfully planned and boldly executed. The gratification it will give to the country will be equaled by the gratification which will be felt for yourself and the bold army that achieved it." Noting that Lee seemed to have "an exaggerated idea" of his success at Bentonville, Johnston nevertheless sent the general in chief a report that indicated he had won a moral victory. "The spirit of the army is greatly improved and is now excellent," he stated. "I am informed by persons of high standing that a similar effect is felt in the country."[53]

No sooner had Johnston withdrawn to Smithfield than Lee prepared to launch his own surprise attack against Grant's force at Petersburg. He planned to punch a hole in a vulnerable part of the Union line and sweep southward, seizing the enemy's fortifications and compelling Grant to contract his lines. (In short, Lee hoped that the aggressive Grant would step out of character and react timidly, á la George B. McClellan or Joseph Hooker.) Holding Richmond and Petersburg with a reduced force, Lee would then reinforce Johnston with the remainder of his army for an offensive against Sherman. Although he had rejected similar proposals from Beauregard and Johnston on the grounds that he lacked the requisite manpower, the general in chief now believed that the plan was preferable to abandoning Richmond and Petersburg.[54]

Lee entrusted the planning and execution of the attack to General Gordon, his junior corps commander. Gordon's main objective was Fort Stedman east of Petersburg, where the Union position converged to within two hundred yards of the Confederate line. His assault force was substantial, consisting of half the army's infantry and one cavalry division. Gordon launched the attack before dawn on March 25. After achieving a limited breakthrough, the force proved insufficient to resist a Union counterattack that quickly sealed the breach. The battle of Fort Stedman was a Confederate disaster, resulting in the irreplaceable loss of at least twenty-seven hundred veteran troops and gaining none of the objectives. Worse yet, Lee now deemed it necessary to rest Gordon's troops for several days before evacuating Richmond and Petersburg.[55]

53. R. E. Lee to J. E. Johnston, Mar. 20, 1865, *OR*, 47(2):1441; J. E. Johnston to R. E. Lee, Mar. 27, 1865, *OR*, 47(1):1055–57.

54. R. E. Lee to Jefferson Davis, Mar. 26, 1865, in *Wartime Papers of R. E. Lee*, 917.

55. A. Wilson Greene, *Breaking the Backbone of the Rebellion: The Final Battles of the Petersburg Campaign* (Mason City, Iowa: Savas, 2000), 156–60.

The opportunity to escape southward and join Johnston was rapidly slipping away from Lee. For almost a month the general in chief had delayed the evacuation because of muddy winter roads while Sherman and Sheridan approached ever nearer. Meanwhile Grant had awakened each morning dreading to hear that the Rebels had evacuated their lines during the night and slipped away to combine with Johnston. But after Sheridan's arrival in late March, Grant began to breathe easier, for he was confident that the Union cavalryman would soon close Lee's remaining escape route to Danville.[56]

After the Fort Stedman fiasco, Lee realized that the momentum had shifted to the Union army. "I fear now it will be impossible to prevent a junction between Grant and Sherman," he warned Davis on March 26, "nor do I deem it prudent that this army should maintain its position until the latter shall approach too near." Lee estimated that Grant and Sherman's forces now outnumbered his and Johnston's by about one hundred thousand—a surprisingly accurate figure. "I have thought it proper to make the above statement to your Excellency of the condition of affairs," he wrote, "knowing that you will do whatever may be in your power to give relief." Once again Lee hoped that Davis would take the hint, but the president stubbornly refused to admit defeat.[57]

In any event time had almost run out for Lee and the Army of Northern Virginia. On April 1 Johnston wired the general in chief, "Do you think that conference between us would be advantageous?" Later that day Lee replied, "I think what you propose advisable if you can come on." The proposed meeting never took place, for even as the generals' messages traveled over the wires, Sheridan was routing the Confederates at Five Forks, rendering Richmond and Petersburg untenable. For four days Johnston knew nothing of Lee's predicament, only learning of the evacuation through a press dispatch. Even then he assumed that Lee had broken out of Richmond and was en route to North Carolina, for no Confederate official had told him otherwise. From Danville President Davis informed Johnston that he had received no word from Lee, "only rumors of hard fighting." Davis stated that he had sent

56. Ulysses S. Grant, *Personal Memoirs of U. S. Grant* (1885–86; reprint, 2 vols. in 1, New York: Da Capo, 1982), 524–25.

57. R. E. Lee to Jefferson Davis, Mar. 26, 1865, in *Wartime Papers of R. E. Lee*, 917–18.

a courier to Lee and was awaiting the general's reply. In the meantime, he suggested, Johnston should govern his movements according to his knowledge of Lee's plans. Of course the general was as much in the dark as Davis was, nor could he afford to disregard Sherman's intentions.[58]

On April 8 an anxious Johnston wrote the general commanding at Danville: "What are General Lee's position and condition? I hear nothing of him." On the same day he received a telegram from presidential aide Col. John Taylor Wood indicating that Lee's army was holding its own. But a message from Secretary of War Breckinridge, who had been with Lee until the morning of April 7, was less optimistic: "Straggling has been great and the situation is not favorable." Lee's army had "met a serious reverse" on the sixth, Breckinridge reported, but it apparently was not being pressed, for he had heard "very little firing" since then. He further stated that Lee was still trying "to move around toward North Carolina," but the general in chief "did not know what route circumstances would permit him to take."[59]

On the morning of April 10, Johnston received word from Hampton that Sherman was marching from Goldsboro and appeared to be heading toward Raleigh. Johnston ordered his army to retreat in front of Sherman. That night the Confederate commander camped fourteen miles southeast of Raleigh. About 1:30 A.M. on April 11, he received a telegram from Davis stating that a scout had brought unofficial word of Lee's surrender at Appomattox Court House on April 9. That afternoon Davis summoned Johnston to Greensboro for a conference. Before Johnston left Raleigh, Governor Vance asked his advice, for he had just received a vague message from Davis indicating that Lee's army had met with "extreme" disaster. Observing that Sherman was only a few days' march from the state capital, Johnston suggested that the governor obtain the best terms for his state that he could. Like Vance, Johnston believed that Lee's surrender meant the end of the war. To ensure a strong bargaining position, the general intended to conceal the news of Lee's

58. J. E. Johnston to R. E. Lee, Apr. 1, 1865, OR, 47(3):737; R. E. Lee to J. E. Johnston, Apr. 1, 1865, ibid.; Jefferson Davis to J. E. Johnston, Apr. 5, 1865, ibid., 755; J. E. Johnston to G. T. Beauregard, Apr. 5, 1865, ibid.; Johnston, Narrative, 395.

59. J. E. Johnston to H. H. Walker, Apr. 7, 1865, OR, 47(3):765; J. Taylor Wood to J. E. Johnston, Apr. 8, 1865, ibid., 767–68; J. C. Breckinridge to J. E. Johnston, Apr. 8, 1865, ibid., 767.

surrender from his men for as long as possible and to keep his army well beyond Sherman's reach. In the meantime he would advise the president to open peace negotiations with the Federals.[60]

Johnston reached Greensboro on the morning of April 12 and was met at the depot by Beauregard, who probably recounted his futile briefing of the president the previous day. A lengthy recital of recent Union victories and Confederate setbacks had left Davis unperturbed, and Beauregard wondered how much evidence the president required to realize that the Confederacy was beaten. The two generals assumed that Davis sought Johnston's advice on whether to continue the war or surrender; they also agreed that it was pointless to discuss the military situation with the president until they had official word on the fate of Lee's army. In any event Davis sent for Johnston and Beauregard at noon on the twelfth. When they arrived, the president was already conferring with several members of his cabinet. Rather than seek the advice of generals whose judgment he had long ceased to respect, Davis instead outlined a quixotic scheme to raise a large field army by recalling the army's deserters and draft dodgers. Johnston argued that it would be impossible to persuade such men to enter the ranks when the cause appeared lost. At that point Davis adjourned the meeting with the announcement that Breckinridge was expected to arrive that night with news of Lee's army.

The secretary of war arrived as scheduled, reporting that Lee had indeed surrendered at Appomattox Court House on April 9. Believing that Lee's surrender spelled the end of the Confederacy, Johnston told Breckinridge, "the only power of government left in the President's hands was that of terminating the war" and that Davis should exercise that power without delay. The secretary of war promised to secure Johnston an opportunity to so advise the president. Soon afterward Secretary of the Navy Stephen R. Mallory told Johnston—now the Confederacy's ranking field commander—that he was best qualified to urge upon Davis the necessity for peace negotiations. The general replied that such a suggestion should come from one of Davis's "constitutional advisors" but added that he had already agreed to perform the task.[61]

60. Jefferson Davis to J. E. Johnston, Apr. 10, 1865, OR, 47(3):777; Jefferson Davis to J. E. Johnston, Apr. 11, 1865 (4:30 P.M.), ibid., 788; Johnston, *Narrative*, 396; Bradley, *This Astounding Close*, 94.

61. Johnston, *Narrative*, 396–98; Bradley, *This Astounding Close*, 137–39, 140–41.

On the morning of April 13, Johnston and Beauregard were summoned to the president's quarters. After a lengthy and rambling introduction, Davis at last gave Johnston his opportunity to speak. In his briefing the general described an exhausted and overwhelmed Confederacy and then urged the president to "open negotiations for peace." When Johnston finished, Davis polled Beauregard and his cabinet and found that, with one exception, they too favored negotiations. Yielding to his advisors, Davis dictated a letter to Sherman that proposed an armistice "to permit the civil authorities to enter into the needful arrangements to terminate the existing war."[62]

Davis, however, had no intention of negotiating with Lincoln and had resumed his southward flight even before the arrival of Sherman's reply. Assisted by Breckinridge and Postmaster General John H. Reagan, Johnston conducted the Bennett Place negotiations with Sherman—who meanwhile informed his counterpart of Lincoln's assassination. The surrender terms offered the Confederates closely resembled those drafted by Reagan and submitted by Johnston to the Federal commander. Sherman's terms were generous: the former Confederates could keep their arms and deposit them in their state arsenals; the Southern state governments and their officials would be retained; the Southerners' personal, political, and property rights would be preserved; and the Southern people would receive universal amnesty. Regarding the last point, Johnston and Breckinridge could not believe their good fortune, for Sherman initially had refused to offer amnesty to Davis and his cabinet—yet the agreement contradicted Sherman's original intentions.[63]

62. Stephen R. Mallory Recollections, 2:336, Southern Historical Collection, Wilson Library, University of North Carolina at Chapel Hill; J. E. Johnston to W. T. Sherman, Apr. 14, 1865, OR, 47(3):206–7. The primary sources for the April 13 conference are J. E. Johnston to P. G. T. Beauregard, Dec. 26, 1867, JO 187, Johnston Papers; Johnston, Narrative, 398–400; Johnston, "My Negotiations with General Sherman," North American Review 143 (Aug. 1886): 187–88; Alfred Roman, The Military Operations of General Beauregard in the War between the States, 1861–1865, 2 vols. (New York: Harper & Brothers, 1884), 2:395, 665–66; Davis, Rise and Fall, 2:679–81; Mallory Recollections, 2:334–36; Stephen R. Mallory, "Last Days of the Confederate Government," McClure's Magazine 16 (1901): 240–42; John H. Reagan, Memoirs, with Special Reference to Secession and the Civil War (New York: Neale, 1906), 199; and John H. Reagan to Jefferson Davis, Dec. 12, 1880, in Rowland, Jefferson Davis, 8:535–39.

63. John H. Reagan, untitled document, Apr. 17, 1865, ibid., 244–45, 806–7 (two copies); William T. Sherman, "Memorandum or Basis of Agreement," Apr. 18, 1865, ibid., 243–44; Bradley, This Astounding Close, 174–76.

On April 24, shortly after Davis's approval of the terms had arrived, Johnston received a message from Sherman stating that the Federal authorities
had rejected the agreement and demanding Johnston's surrender in accordance with the Appomattox terms. According to the cease-fire, Johnston had
until noon on April 26—less than forty-eight hours—before the resumption
of hostilities. Johnston wired Breckinridge for instructions, but the general
also suggested, "We had better disband this small force to prevent devastation
to the country." Breckinridge sent him discretionary orders to disband the
infantry and artillery, instructing them to rendezvous at a later time, and to
send out all cavalry and other mounted troops.[64]

"We have to save the people, spare the blood of the army, and save the
high civil functionaries," Johnston replied on the twenty-fifth. "Your plan, I
think, can only do the last. We ought to prevent invasion, make terms for
our troops, and give an escort of cavalry to the President, who ought to move
without loss of a moment." He further stated that his subordinates believed
their men would no longer fight. In a second message the general informed
Breckinridge that he had proposed resuming negotiations with Sherman.
Breckinridge responded with a dispatch instructing Johnston to allow volunteers from the infantry and artillery to join Hampton's cavalry.[65]

At 7:00 A.M. on April 26, Johnston telegraphed the secretary of war that
he would meet Sherman that day. Breckinridge made no reply—probably because he saw no point in doing so—thus leaving Johnston free to act on his
own responsibility. That afternoon Johnston surrendered in accordance with
terms virtually identical to those of the Appomattox agreement, though he
obtained several additional concessions in a supplementary agreement
drafted a few days later. In surrendering as he did, Johnston had secured
"fair terms of peace" for his army and for the civilians within his sphere of
command.[66]

Johnston has been accused of violating the American tradition of civil-
military relations by advising Davis to surrender and then by surrendering in

64. J. E. Johnston to J. C. Breckinridge, Apr. 24, 1865, OR, 47(3):835; J. C. Breckinridge to
J. E. Johnston, Apr. 24, 1865, ibid.

65. J. E. Johnston to J. C. Breckinridge, Apr. 25, 1865 (two letters), ibid., 836; J. C. Breckinridge to J. E. Johnston, Apr. 25, 1865, ibid., 837.

66. J. E. Johnston to J. C. Breckinridge, Apr. 26, 1865, ibid., 839; "Terms of a Military Convention," Apr. 26, 1865, ibid., 313; "Military Convention of 1865—Supplemental Terms," ibid., 482.

defiance of his civilian superiors. Both accusations are misguided, for they wrongly assume that the general exceeded his military authority. In urging Davis to open negotiations with the Federal government, Johnston was merely performing his duty as the Confederacy's ranking field commander by advising his commander in chief of the military situation and the course of action to take. Davis was then free to heed that advice or reject it. After polling his cabinet, Davis yielded to the majority and followed Johnston's advice. When Federal authorities rejected the original surrender terms, Johnston requested instructions from Breckinridge and also recommended that his army capitulate. Breckinridge's orders to escape were discretionary and rightly so, for Johnston was the best judge of the situation in his theater of operations. The general knew that continuing the war would lead only to widespread death and devastation, for his army was rapidly disintegrating and Sherman's forces were bent on avenging Lincoln's assassination. He also believed that he faced his final opportunity to obtain generous terms.[67]

Furthermore Johnston was compelled to advise the president to open peace negotiations because no one else—neither Lee, Breckinridge, Beauregard, Mallory, Reagan, Hunter, nor Vance—would flatly tell the president that the Confederacy was beaten. For all his hatred of Davis, Johnston was only too eager to turn over that onerous task to one of the president's "constitutional advisors." By virtue of his prestige and position, Lee was best qualified to advise Davis to open peace negotiations, but he proved no more able than the president to admit defeat.[68]

67. For the argument that Johnston violated the American tradition of civil-military relations, see Grimsley, "Learning to Say 'Enough,'" 64, 68, 74. Grimsley maintains that "Johnston thus did what no American commander has ever done, before or since: he exercised the full weight of his military position to tell his government how to conclude a war." In truth it was Johnston's situation that was unprecedented: as the ranking field commander of the Confederate army after Lee's surrender, Johnston faced a dilemma that no other American commander has confronted before or since—what to do after the loss of the government's principal field army. Had he attempted to escort the president and his party to the Trans-Mississippi (as Grimsley suggests was his proper course), the war probably would have assumed a far more ruthless and vindictive character, and Johnston's conduct might have provided historians with a cautionary tale against military officers blindly obeying orders in defiance of logic and humanity.

68. Alan T. Nolan quotes Clifford Dowdey on the subject of the failure of Lee and several other high-ranking Confederates to assume the responsibility of trying to convince Davis that the war was lost. "Considering Dowdey's unflinching admiration for Lee," he writes, "his attrib-

Nevertheless, as general in chief, Lee succeeded where Davis utterly failed: he motivated Johnston to fight. Lee managed this by handling the hypersensitive general with the same consummate diplomacy that he had employed in his dealings with the equally touchy president. As a result, in March 1865, Johnston and his subordinates conducted an aggressive campaign in North Carolina that included assaults at Wise's Forks, Monroe's Crossroads, and Bentonville as well as a skillful delaying action at Averasboro. Contrary to the inveterate micromanager Davis, Lee allowed Johnston to conduct operations as he saw fit, and no other Confederate could have accomplished more in the Old North State in such a short span and with so few resources. Although it is tempting to dismiss Johnston's achievement as a dubious success at the close of a lost war, it is also indicative of how Johnston might have conducted operations had he served under Lee a year or two earlier. The Joe Johnston of March 1865 was neither timid nor indecisive but was prudently aggressive in the face of overwhelming odds. Lee's role in Johnston's improbable transformation was his outstanding contribution as the Confederacy's general in chief.

---

uting Lee's position and that of the others mentioned to an unwillingness to take responsibility is surely an unintended indictment." But Nolan fails to note that someone did in fact assume that responsibility—Joseph E. Johnston. See Nolan, *Lee Considered*, 123–24.

CONTRIBUTORS

MARK L. BRADLEY is the author of *This Astounding Close: The Road to Bennett Place* and *Last Stand in the Carolinas: The Battle of Bentonville*. He is a doctoral candidate in history at the University of North Carolina at Chapel Hill.

PETER S. CARMICHAEL is a member of the Department of History at the University of North Carolina at Greensboro. The author of *Lee's Young Artillerist: William R. J. Pegram* as well as several essays and articles in popular and scholarly journals, he is completing a study of Virginia slaveholders' sons and the formation of Southern identity in the late antebellum years.

ROBERT E. L. KRICK, a Richmond-based historian, is the author of *The Fortieth Virginia Infantry* and a number of essays and articles. He has also published a complete biographical register of the staff officers of the Army of Northern Virginia. He is currently researching a study of the battle of Gaines's Mill.

WILLIAM J. MILLER is the author of *The Training of an Army: Camp Curtin and the North's Civil War* and *Mapping for Stonewall: The Civil War Service of Jed Hotchkiss*, editor and coauthor of the three-volume *The Peninsula Campaign: Yorktown to the Seven Days*, and editor of a forthcoming volume of Jed Hotchkiss's Civil War letters. He resides in Hotchkiss's wartime home in Churchville, Virginia.

GORDON C. RHEA is the author of *The Battle of the Wilderness, May 5–6, 1864; The Battles for Spotsylvania Court House and the Road to Yellow Tavern, May 7–12, 1864;* and *To the North Anna River: Grant and Lee, May 13–25, 1864.* He received his master's degree in history from Harvard University and his juris doctorate from Stanford University Law School. He lives in St. Croix, U.S. Virgin Islands, and in Mount Pleasant, South Carolina.

MAX R. WILLIAMS is professor of history emeritus at Western Carolina University. Among his many publications are four edited volumes of *The Papers of William Alexander Graham* as well as numerous articles, many of which have appeared in the *North Carolina Historical Review*. He is currently finishing a biography of William Alexander Graham.

INDEX